PENGUIN BOOKS

# YUKTAHAAR

Munmun Ganeriwal is an award-winning nutritionist and celebrated lifestyle consultant based in Mumbai. Over the last 19 years, she has worked as a nutrition and exercise consultant with a diverse set of clients from all walks of life and across the globe. Her clientele includes Taapsee Pannu, Rakul Preet Singh, Nayanthara and many more.

Munmun is the only gut microbiome specialist in the world who combines traditional Indian foods, ancient Indian yogic practices and Ayurveda principles with gut microbiota study to understand and fight obesity and other diseases. She has a master's degree in nutrition science, is an internationally certified fitness instructor and is a yoga teacher following the Sivananda lineage of yogic traditions. Munmun has also been studying Advaita Vedanta—propounded by Sri Adi Shankaracharya—for a few years now.

For more details, see www.munmunganeriwal.com.

T0243727

# YUKTAHAAR

## THE BELLY AND BRAIN DIET

## MUNMUN GANERIWAL

*foreword by* TAAPSEE PANNU

PENGUIN BOOKS

An imprint of Penguin Random House

PENGUIN BOOKS

USA | Canada | UK | Ireland | Australia
New Zealand | India | South Africa | China

Penguin Books is part of the Penguin Random House group of companies
whose addresses can be found at global.penguinrandomhouse.com

Published by Penguin Random House India Pvt. Ltd
4th Floor, Capital Tower 1, MG Road,
Gurugram 122 002, Haryana, India

First published in Penguin Books by Penguin Random House India 2021

ISBN 9780143454380

Typeset in Bembo Std by Manipal Technologies Limited, Manipal

www.penguin.co.in

ईश्वरः परमः कृष्णः सच्चिदानन्दः विग्रहः,
अनादिरादि गोविन्दः सर्व कारण कारणम् |

*īśvaraḥ paramaḥ kṛṣṇaḥ sac-cid-ānanda-vigrahaḥ*
*anādir ādir govindaḥ sarva-kāraṇa-kāraṇam*

—Brahma Samhita (5.1)

*For my late father, Shri Ravindra Ganeriwal (Rasiwasia),*
*who passed on to me his courage to pursue dreams*

# Contents

# Foreword

Lights. Camera. Action. After having spent 10 precious years in the challenging film industry, I can say with conviction, 'What shows, sells.' Showbiz, as they say, is all about being a perfect 10 with no mercy. And the fact that food triggers your body goes beyond the literal meaning for me. Born and brought up in what I call the food capital of India, Delhi, I couldn't escape from being obsessed with food. So much so that my driving force behind going to various places to hang out was food more than meetings. From my mood to my calendar, a lot depended upon what I wanted to eat and at what time.

Now here comes the twist in the tale. Once I crossed 30, I realized that apart from good skin and hair, I had unfortunately also inherited a weak metabolism from my mother. Until then, I had been living under the delusion that my active life, aggressive workouts and some strong genes on my father's side would help me digest everything I ate.

Then Munmun entered my life. I was introduced to her through a small homemade gift pack that her PR representative sent to my house. I found it fascinating that in this day and age, when everyone is busy creating new diet products and fancy diet regimes as antidotes to various health issues, here was someone recommending natural, easily available, regular foods for all sorts of issues related to health. It made me contact her, and since then, I've been hooked.

When Munmun told me about this book, I couldn't have been happier for her. At the same time, I'm also happy for all the people who are confused by so many diet and exercise recommendations floating around. This book will bust many myths and set the record straight once and for all. It will also help you realize that if you want to lose weight or rid yourself of any disease, extreme forms of diets or torturing your body with insane workouts is never the solution. For all of you who want a long-term solution—one that is sustainable and that stays constant in spite of changing trends, that simplifies your life and leaves you happy and content—this book will be your bible. I assure you that you will be hooked to this new, yet old, way of living, just like I've been!

Munmun's expertise lies in blending the new microbiome science with ancient knowledge. The eating habits she introduced me to helped accelerate my metabolism when I thought it was almost close to dead. Her emphasis on traditional foods and yogic way of living, along with a thorough knowledge of how these can be adapted to suit the needs of urban life, has helped me bring alive a variety of characters on screen, from Rashmi's fight for her self-respect to Amrita's journey of self-discovery.

So, I can't wait for you to start reading this insightful piece of work. I have already adopted its truths in my life. Now, I can confidently say that as long as I stay true to my body with what I eat and how I live, I can continue to play a college girl on screen (yes, irrespective of my ticking biological clock!). And no, I am not going to brag about its result on my body. That information is available in the public domain, or on public theatre screens for all of you to see. I shall only tell you about the feelings it gives you: the motivation to kick-start each day happily, the energy to sustain an 18-hour work day and the freshness and glow you need to maintain to sell dreams to this world. I wish you all the luck! Happy reading!

Taapsee Pannu
Actor
Mumbai, 2021

# Personal Note

According to *Pandava Gita*, Duryodhana was once asked how, in spite of belonging to a great lineage and being taught by enlightened gurus, he did such horrendous things. To this, Duryodhana replied, 'I know what dharma (righteousness) is, yet I cannot get myself to follow it! I know what adharma is, yet I cannot retire from it!'

Like Duryodhana, we too know right from wrong. We know that gorging on chocolates and cakes is unhealthy, we know we should sleep early, and we also know we should exercise to stay fit and healthy. Yet, like Duryodhana, we are unable to bridge the gap between 'knowing' and 'doing'. My wish for you is that you practise The Belly and Brain Diet (TBBD) not just for 10 weeks but for life. My wish for you is that you bridge the gap between 'knowing' and 'doing'.

*Oh yes! Why not? Easier said than done!* I know this is real life with real stress, and I am aware that a zillion things may happen that can derail you every time you resolve to work on your health. Ranging from a heartbreak or illness or overtime at work to losing your job or someone in the family or simply travelling frequently, life comes with its ups and downs. Amidst all of this, it becomes difficult to stick to your food and fitness routine. So, what do you do? What if I say that the answer can be found in the *Bhagavad Gita*? Do you remember, at some point of time during the great battle of Mahabharata, Arjuna was also in the same boat as Duryodhana? He too was confused and delusional. What, then, led to the downfall of one and victory of the other? Unlike Duryodhana, Arjuna sought an answer from the right source, Lord Krishna. That is when Krishna expounded the *Gita* to him, on the battlefield of Kurukshetra. The *Gita* gave Arjuna an insight into profoundly important aspects of life and death, one of them being *resilience*.

Resilience means the ability to rebound, to be able to grow through what we go through. It is not a fixed trait we are born with; it is rather a skill we can practise and master, a quality that is built with time and effort. Resilience is what differentiates successful people from others. Resilient people acknowledge the situation, are prepared for ever-changing circumstances, and bounce back amid stress and chaos. You can look at stress as a challenge to overcome and address it in positive ways, or you can view it as a paralysing force, feel overwhelmed by it and resort to oversleeping, eating sugar (emotional eating), etc. The difference is in the outlook. So how do you build resilience?

Lord Krishna says that we should work on our body and mind, as these are the only instruments available to us (*Bhagavad Gita 6.5* and *6.6*). You cannot race on a Formula 1 circuit with a rattletrap, can you? Transforming your short-term fitness goals (read: flat tummy, beach bod, etc.) into life-changing results that are truly meaningful and sustainable requires work. A knife, if you know how to weild it, can help you cook a meal; the same knife can injure you if you haven't learnt to use it properly. It is up to you how well you manage your body and mind to make them work *for* you instead of *against* you.

My own journey in life from being a nobody to being counted as one of the top health experts in the country is not due to any inheritance, connections or back-ups; it is only because of *pure resilience*. Six years ago, when I walked out of my marriage, instead of going to my parents' house, I travelled straight to Mumbai along with my daughter, who was then just six years old. Mumbai, (in)famously called the most difficult Indian city to live in, was then a new place for me, and I knew absolutely no one. Naturally, I had to face many adversities, one of them being my fellow contemporaries trying hard to bring me down. But I wasn't there to merely survive, I wanted to thrive. So I did. And so can you!

Using the four tools of food, exercise, sleep and neural retraining on an everyday basis, you can refine and strengthen your body and mind, so that they support you when the inevitable stressors come your way. You might get affected, but they won't take a heavy toll on your physical and mental health. You may fall off the wagon, but not for good. You will bounce back soon. These tools have helped me and my many clients become more resilient. Lord Krishna has, time and again, at different places in the *Gita*, talked about the importance of eating right, sleeping right, and practising *yog* and *dhyana* (meditation). Today, modern research supports his teachings. The teachings of the *Gita* are not about preparing the road for yourself; it is about preparing yourself for the road. And that is ultimately what resilience is all about. Om Tat Sat.

Munmun Ganeriwal
Mumbai, 2021

# 1

# The Gut Microbiome

Allow me to introduce you to Madhav Mehta, a 21-year-old Gujarati boy studying in Narsee Monjee College at Juhu, Mumbai. When we first met, he was overweight and was following a self-imposed diet. His first meal was at noon, after he returned home from college that was from 7 a.m. to 10.30 a.m. 'The world seems to be indulging in intermittent fasting and bidding adieu to breakfast these days. So how is that a big deal anyway?' he thought. He was following all the other 'rules' that a guy aspiring to look lean ought to follow: The masala chips that he loved were swapped with protein chips, dinner was reduced to a bowl of salad, and for lunch, he had somehow learned to develop a fondness for quinoa and kale. This was not all. To burn off all those exotic foods, he kicked and boxed during his evening mixed martial art (MMA) classes, and once he felt 'warmed up enough', he lifted weights at the gym. In the morning before college, he made sure to jog in the park to get his quota of cardio. 'Food math you see. Weight lost equals calories in minus calories out,' he quipped.

Just like his self-conceived combat plan, on the surface, Madhav also appeared to be holding it together. However, that was not the case. He was diagnosed with high-functioning anxiety. He faced difficulty in breathing, although not during exercise; he felt foggy and had trouble concentrating on an everyday basis; he suffered panic attacks during situations he perceived as stressful, like around exam time; and he also felt chronically bloated, gassy and constipated.

More knowledge about health is available now than ever before, and yet, like Madhav, most of us are dealing with symptoms we never had. On the one hand, we can boast of living in the most advanced era in human history with more medical breakthroughs than ever before, but on the other hand, there is an exponential rise in obesity, metabolic diseases like diabetes, and cancer. Just as we match our shoes with our clothes, we now have a buffet of diets and fitness regimes to pick from and match with every occasion in life. Between gluten-free, dairy-free, fat-free and even food-free regimes, there is an array of restrictive diets focused on excluding foods rather than including. Not only that, diet apps and Facebook fitness groups ensure these are at our fingertips, quite literally! And yet, our health seems to be plummeting. Millions of people are dealing with mood slumps, skin problems, hormonal swings and lethargy every single day. Why do we find ourselves struggling with sugar cravings, chronic fatigue, migraine, inflamed joints, low immunity and insomnia on an everyday basis? So many of us are struggling with ailments and diseases that were rare until just a few decades ago. For instance, obesity today enjoys the status of a global epidemic. Did it come about just because people are lazy, stupid and lack willpower? Or is there something else at work?

The fact is that the story of weight loss, chronic illness, and mental health are much more nuanced than what the health and weight-loss industry would have you believe.

## An Ecosystem Approach for the Many Dimensions of Health

'Look deep into nature, and then you will understand everything better,' said Albert Einstein. There can be no teacher as good as nature herself. If we can see beyond what meets the eye, we will find around us all the answers that we have been seeking. I'll take a cue from the man who revolutionized our understanding of time, space, gravity and the universe; let me take you to the village of Karakuwa in Japan.

The Kesennuma Sanriku fishing grounds in Karakuwa is one of the three most productive seafood regions in the world. The oysters harvested there are known to be larger and more impressive than almost anywhere else. This rare feat isn't a mere coincidence. To accomplish it, the farmers of Karakuwa employ unique cultivation methods, not on the sea but on the mountains surrounding the sea! They understand that the forests, the mountains and the seas are deeply interconnected. Hence, instead of feeding the oysters, the sea farmers of Kesennuma nurture the forests and mountains that feed the rivers flowing into the bay. To help the marine life thrive, they run tree-planting campaigns in the surrounding mountains and forests. For decades, this is how they have devoted themselves to raising oysters—by honouring the forest–river–tree interrelationship.

Similarly, to find a solution to our problems, we need to learn to honour our body as a whole, complex ecosystem. If we want to address the health crisis of our modern times, we cannot afford to overlook the greater ecosystem of physical, mental and emotional influences. Though seemingly unrelated, all the three domains—physical, mental and emotional—that constitute what I call 'deep health' are deeply entwined and interdependent. When you find yourself struggling in one, you will invariably see yourself struggling in the others, leading to weight gain, mood disorders or unrelenting illnesses. An ecosystem approach takes into account the multidimensional thriving of a whole person, and this in turn helps resolve the complexity of weight gain and chronic illness, and increasing stress, anxiety and depression.

But instead of calling for integrated multilateral solutions, we make rigid boundaries that separate our body, brain and mind, and these in turn affect our ability to lose fat and/or improve our overall health. This is why Madhav's weight did not budge, even though he diligently followed the conventional weight-loss method of eating less and moving more. It did not occur to him that his anxiety might have been rooted in his body, not just in his mind or in his brain. He was expending a lot of effort calculating the calories and macros he consumed, when on the contrary, he should have been delving into the root cause of his ailments and addressing them from a broader, holistic perspective. This is what Functional Medicine is all about: improving the basic physiology and the metabolic and biochemical processes that go askew in a state of disease or ill health.

At the heart of functional medicine lies the gut microbiome: your own microbial ecosystem that dwells inside you, or in your colon (large intestine) to be precise. This is a new line of research in modern medicine that is investigating the influence of our gut microbes on our health and well-being. The role of the gut microbiome and its neural network in human health—physical, mental and emotional—has been one of the most significant discoveries of the recent decade. It has changed our understanding of obesity, mental health and disease. We can no longer simply evaluate the human body without considering how it interacts with the environment and with the trillions of bacteria residing on and in our bodies. Our microbiome is extremely complex, and science is only now beginning to understand its potential influence on all aspects of our health—both body and brain. Since dysfunctions in the microbiome are the most significant causes of obesity and diseases of the modern world, looking after your microbiome is akin to working on your core problems.

However, while scientists are fascinated by this new world that is gradually revealing itself, the public is completely unaware of it. In the public consciousness, depression is still treated exclusively as a mental health issue, and disorders like irritable bowel syndrome (IBS) are regarded as solely digestive health problems. But in reality, depression may be the result of an unhappy gut, and IBS symptoms may actually have links with your brain. The consensus in scientific circles is clear: Our tiny gut dwellers are crucial to us as they dictate our metabolism, immune system, brain health and of course, our body weight.

The reason why none of the diets in the past have seemed to work, and why we are seeing a surge in obesity and diseases, is because we have only focused on the host, that is, you. We have turned obesity into an issue of self-control and willpower, when in reality, microbes in your body regulate the hormones that signal satiation in the brain, and an imbalance in these microbes could be making you overeat. We can continue to have a fling with low carb diets, vegan diets, low-fat diets and everything in between, but a long-lasting solution will never be found if we don't shift our focus from 'us' to 'them'—to the human-gut microbiome connection.

## Gut Microbiome: Your Inner Ecosystem

'Oh boy! Nothing could be easier than this!' I got up from my seat, faced my team and joined my 10 fingers in the shape of a heart.

I hardly had to wait for them to answer. In a matter of a few seconds, all of them replied in a chorus, '*Arre, arre, Dil! Aamir aur Madhuri ki movie!*'

In just one hour of dumb charades, I realized that Bollywood really holds our 'hearts' in high regard. The number of movie titles with the word 'dil' is insane, to say the least! But our guts are left to make do with names like *paapi pet*. And Bollywood isn't only to blame. All of us admire the heart and the brain and consider them central to our life. Mothers love it when someone tells them the secret to boosting their children's memory and learning ability. We are always supremely concerned if someone complains of chest pain. But anything related to the gut is most often met with embarrassment. In most people's eyes, the gut is only there to make sure we can pee and poo and toss things out of the body. Apart from that, people think, it just hangs around to break wind now and then. Through this book, I hope I can change this perception, because when it comes to your deep health, your gut, and the bacteria it shelters, is the prime actor in the game. And yet, it might be the one we know the least about.

Our intestinal tracts are far more important than people think. The trillions of bacteria housed in our digestive tract affect many conditions that go beyond our digestive system. For instance, recent advances have begun to unpick how the balance and diversity of these microbes play a significant role in obesity and diabetes. *Nearly all chronic issues are rooted in an imbalanced microbiome.* Disruptions in the balance of our belly-based microscopic community not only increase the risk of chronic diseases but also impact our mood, behaviour, happiness, and a general sense of well-being. As you delve further into this book, you will see that these bacteria influence our emotions, and hence, they decide whether someone is happy and optimistic, or sad and pessimistic.

It is true that physiology drives psychology. Clients I have worked with in all these years will vouch for it. Take Nisha Rawat from Jaipur, for instance. She is a housewife living in a joint family, and she had given up all hope of pursuing her cherished dream of becoming an entrepreneur. Of course, the reasons she signed up with me were quite different: hormonal imbalance and several failed attempts at losing weight. It took us a year to reboot her metabolism from the gut, and in the end, she successfully lost all the excess weight and got rid of all her hormonal issues. But the icing on the cake was that sometime in the middle of the programme, she gained confidence and started her own handicraft business, which she had wanted to do for the last 20 years! When you carefully rebalance your microbiome, wonderful things happen. These may be subtle and not measurable by blood tests, but they do significantly improve your quality of life. *How does this happen?*

Through this book, I shall attempt to unfold the fascinating new revelation that we each have a hidden second brain that is being called the *gut brain*, and this may be the key link between all aspects of our health. In a world obsessed with using antibiotics to kill germs at the very first sign of an apparent illness, this may sound contradictory. For the longest time, we have been taught that we should live in sterile environments and maximize our hygiene. Adding to it, the recent pandemic has left us germophobic, even more. TV commercials also don't let up any chance to drive the point home. The latest commercial I came across was of anti-bacterial wall paints—It said, '*Vo jo bacteria ko kill kar de!*' But it's time we learn that just like '*daag acche hai*', in the same way bacteria *bhi acche hai.* We require both good and bad microbes around us, because that's how our immune cells get trained. Our immune system develops in combat!

*What about the current COVID-19 guideline that tells to disinfect almost everything?* Well, COVID-19 isn't a normal situation. Until the pandemic is over, we need to temporarily step up our cleaning game. Once things return to normal, you should not disinfect too much, because it will kill off your natural flora and lead to more harm than good. For now, know that our gut microbes can help us lose weight, be happy and live long, and therefore, we *must* adopt a greater appreciation for them.

**Ignorance Is Bliss, but Not Always**

Physical health: obesity, heart disease, diabetes, high blood pressure, high cholesterol, hormonal issues, autoimmune diseases, liver diseases, cancer, allergies, infections, skin problems, asthma, digestive issues

Mental health: chronic stress, anxiety, depression, mood disorders, insomnia, bipolar disorder

Emotional health: joy, happiness, sadness, stability, clarity, resilience, anger, optimism, confidence

The gut microbiome is at the centre of 'deep health'. It helps open the doors to every aspect of health. If you don't nurture your biome, everything else will fail.

The World Health Organization (WHO) has named depression 'the leading cause of disability' in the world. We know that cases of mental health are escalating on a global scale. For the last 30-odd years, all we have had to therapeutically deal with this is medication and counselling. But that's clearly not good enough, or else depression wouldn't have become the crisis it is today.

Psychiatrists, psychologists and psychotherapists are different professionals, and each has an important role to play in the treatment of mental health disorders. Unfortunately, functional microbiome medicine hasn't been mainstreamed as an equally significant actor, especially in India, even when scientific evidence of the gut–microbiome–brain relationship is compelling. A team of researchers from the Shanghai Mental Health Center reviewed 21 studies that evaluated 1,503 people, and the researchers suggested that in addition to using psychiatric drugs for treatment, regulating intestinal flora could help alleviate anxiety symptoms. This review is just one among many conducted till date in the field of mental health. Hence, it is clearly not an either-or situation. To form the best solution, all professionals should ideally work together in a multi-disciplinary way, because mood imbalances like depression and anxiety are complex, nuanced conditions. Just like obesity, many variables are at play here, both at the individual and at the social and environmental levels.

Naturally, such findings also give a lot of hope. People fighting mental health issues are often engulfed in hopelessness, and to them, hope is a great thing. To know that depression may have originated in the body, and not in the brain or mind, can be a relief. Because the body you can touch, you can see, you can feel, but when it comes to the subtleties of the mind, we do not quite understand the why, the where and the what.

Our ignorance of our microbiome should not lead us to downplay the profound effects it can have on our mental health. In mild to moderate cases, microbiome restoration— through the principles underlined in this book—works great as a stand–alone treatment. For moderate and severe cases, microbiome restoration still proves to be very useful when used as a *non-negotiable adjunct* to medication and counselling.

## The Ancient Code of Deep Health

*Samadosha samagnischa samadhatumala kriyaha*
*prasanna atmenindriya manaha swasthya ityabhidheeyate*

—Sushruta Samhita

The *Sushruta Samhita*, the ancient Sanskrit text on medicine, defines health in the above verse, which when translated means that an individual is healthy when his physical–physiological–psychological life forces are in equilibrium. When one's body's metabolism, digestion and excretion function properly, when he is happy and exuberant, only then can such a person be said to be in a state of good health.

Similarly, if we take a look at all the other ancient wisdom surrounding health from around the world, we will find that they dovetail nicely with the concept of the gut microbiome and deep health. In the yogic tradition, chakras are said to be the main energy centres of our bodies. Out of the seven primary chakras that we are known to have, the base or the root chakra is called the *Muladhara* (*Mula-adhaar*, literally meaning fundamental). It is said to be the foundation, closely connecting the whole body in one way or the other, thereby having an effect on the system as a whole. Your colon (intestine), which is home to the microbes living inside you, happens to be at the Muladhara. Hippocrates, the ancient Greek physician who is regarded as the father of Western medicine, has also been quoted saying, 'You are only as healthy as your digestion,' and 'all disease begins in the gut.' One of the oldest words in the vocabulary of modern science is 'eupeptic', which means having good digestion as well as a happy frame of mind.

These, among many other things, probably led a group of Pune-based scientists to initiate the first-ever study in India correlating Ayurveda and gut bacteria. In September 2019, scientists at the National Centre for Cell Science (NCCS) established that according to the Ayurveda principle of *prakriti*—comprising *vata, pitta* and *kapha*—gut microbes are an important factor that determines the behaviour, nature and physical well-being of a person.

Your belly is ground zero for microbiome imbalance. I hope by now you are convinced that to lose weight and gain health, we need to make the right call to action to rebuild and rehabilitate our gut microbiome that has gone awry due to our modern diet and lifestyle.

## The Belly and Brain Diet (TBBD): Your Call to Action

*Oh! I get what you're saying. I know the drill—eat more yoghurt and fermented foods, include probiotics in your diet, right?*

It will not surprise me if you have started thinking along these lines. Our knowledge of our body and health is at the mercy of fast-moving newsfeeds and social media, and those are, unfortunately, mostly dominated by anti-science or junk science. Supporting and nurturing your biome is a lot more than that. Your inner ecosystem is as diverse and complex as the Amazon rainforest. Just as you cannot throw a few seeds into the rainforest and expect them to thrive, in the same way, merely eating a few cups of yoghurt will not help restore the ecosystem inside you. What is required is an integrated, whole-systems approach that will remap the gut ecology by encouraging a sustainable environment in which these organisms can flourish. This in turn will lead to better metabolism, immunity, health, moods, brain function, and yes, weight loss. That's what The Belly and Brain Diet (TBBD) and this book is all about; *it is the only programme in the world that combines traditional Indian foods, ancient Indian yogic practices and Ayurveda principles with gut microbiota study to understand and fight obesity and other diseases.*

The Belly and Brain Diet is the outcome of my studies and research to understand the interactions between our lifestyle and gut microbiota during the onset and progression of chronic diseases. It is also the result of my experience working with my clients across a span of 19 years. The TBBD is a three-phased programme spread across 10 weeks, and focuses on improving the balance and diversity of our microbial community.

Of all the factors that influence how the microbiome takes shape, food is the most powerful, because what you eat feeds not only you but also the microorganisms living inside you. In the chapters ahead, you will find interventions I have formulated that integrate traditional Indian foods and supplements into the modern-day diet to modulate the relationship between gut microbiota and humans. You will learn about foods that should be avoided and favourable foods that foster the growth of lean, metabolism-promoting bacteria.

Along with diet, many other factors interact with each other and exert their cumulative effect on the microbiome. In this book, you will find the tools to make these factors work in your favour, and help you overcome your struggle with long-lasting weight loss. In the process, you will not only reduce your cravings and feel vibrant, but you may also see most of your chronic health complaints disappear. That's why I say that *TBBD is not just a diet. It is a holistic programme that encourages a gut-balancing lifestyle, mainly consisting of food, exercise, sleep hygiene, and neural retraining.*

# 2

# Welcome to the World of Microbes

It was April 2019 and the Maharashtra Lok Sabha elections were around the corner. One fine morning, on my way back from the gym, I stopped at the traffic signal close to my place. My elbow was on the ledge of the rolled-down window and my fingers were closed into a fist, resting on my lips (that's my customary car pose); I was waiting for the lights to turn green. And then I heard someone rapping lyrics (*Gully Boy* had just released a month back, so no surprises there!). I turned and saw a boy sitting on a bike, looking up and ahead, somewhere towards my left. He seemed to be reading and simultaneously rapping what he saw and read. My eyes followed his gaze and there it was—a billboard advertising a news channel company, flying high on pre-election duties. Written in bold was, *'Jhoot kaa shor nahin, yeh hai sach kaa jor!'* And I immediately said to myself, *'Kya baat hai!'* Of course, I was struck by the fact that we can find unique talent like the boy's so easily on the streets of our country. But I was also thinking how relevant the advertisement's line was—when applied to both 'trending elections' as well as the 'trending diet' scene. It is a fact that the voices that are far away from the truth are often the loudest. They play on repeat mode until people start accepting their words as facts. But as Mahatma Gandhi had rightly said, 'An error does not become truth by reason of multiplied propagation, nor does truth become error because nobody sees it.'

A new diet trend is like a new ruling party. Both come in amidst the *shor-sharabba* of claims and promises, but sooner than later, both fail to live up to their tall claims. From low-fat diets (carbs are no problem!) to low-carb diets (fats are great!), you may have done it all, only to end up thinking *why praan jaye, par wajan naa jaye.* Then there are the low-calorie prophets who have subscribed to the calories-in–calories-out (CICO) model of obesity. The rhetoric of calories eaten versus calories burned is actually used to imply that it's all your fault—if you could only control your eating and exercise enough, you would not be fat. On the flip side, this also suggests that the worldwide epidemic of obesity has come about simply because of a simultaneous lack of willpower and character among people on a global scale! Really?

Mark Twain had said, 'It's easier to fool people than to convince them that they have been fooled.' So, I'm taking up this rather difficult task to prove to you that the calories-in–versus–calories-out philosophy is a pack of lies fed to us by the weight-loss industry that profits by fat-shaming and shifting the blame.

## Why Everything You Know about Calories Is Wrong

Maths and I don't get along. So, when I dropped out of engineering, I felt relieved that we would never cross paths again. But it seems God had other plans for me. As soon as I 'formally' entered the world of diet and nutrition, I was introduced to a mathematical equation called the energy balance equation or the CICO model:

Body weight gained or lost = Calories in - Calories out

Assuming that 1 gm of fat contains 9 calories, the CICO aficionados posit that if we reduce our food intake by 500 calories and expend 200 more in the gym, you will lose around 500 gm of body fat in a week ($700/9 \times 7$ days). On the surface, it looks like a simple formula. But it isn't. Unfortunately, your body isn't a cash machine, it's a dynamic ecosystem. And like all complex ecosystems, it also has mechanisms in place to maintain a relatively stable equilibrium, which in scientific lingo is called 'Homeostasis'. *Huh?* Let me explain.

The 'calories out' component is not composed only of exercise, but of two things: your basal metabolic rate or BMR (think of it simply as your metabolism) and exercise. The BMR is the energy or calories used by your body systems—your reproductive system, circulatory system, etc.—to keep you alive. An average BMR is taken to be 2,000 calories per day, far higher than the 200 to 250 calories you use, say, during an hour's walk. The problem is that the CICO equation assumes that every time you eat fewer calories, the BMR remains stable. But studies have shown that a reduction in the intake of calories is simultaneously met by a decrease in BMR. This isn't difficult to understand. I meet such cases almost on a daily basis. For instance, I remember a girl who started eating lesser deliberately; she lost weight initially but then her weight plateaued; her periods went out of whack (body turned off the reproductive system) and she constantly felt cold (thermoregulatory system turned low). The CICO equation does not consider this drop of BMR, and that's the problem.

Every time there's a calorie deficit, your many body systems adjust their functioning, and they do so because your body wants you to survive, not die. In fact, your body does everything possible to ensure that there isn't a calorie deficit in the first place. So, when you eat lesser, you end up with lower energy and feel tired, and so you do lesser; when you do more, your appetite gets a boost and you end up eating more! All diets based on restrictive eating are, therefore, not realistic; they work only in the short term. In the long run, you ought to regain all the weight that you lose, and in most cases, a couple of kilos more. This yo-yoing—where your weight goes through more ups and downs than the elevator of a business hotel—further causes biological complications that make it even harder for you to lose weight in your subsequent attempts. This goes on until you feel convinced that it's all your fault, and you call it quits forever!

## A Calorie Is a Calorie, Only until It Enters a Human Body

Not only is the theory of calories flawed, but it is also outdated. Modern science has proved beyond doubt that the calories we eat differ wildly from the calories we actually extract! *Depending on the composition of their gut bacteria, different individuals yield different numbers of calories from a diet that is exactly the same, both in terms of food and quantity.*

Instead of fixing our diet and seeding the gut with good fat-burning bacteria, we blindly follow diet trends that end up disturbing the balance and diversity of our gut flora even further. Yo-yo dieting messes with our gut bacteria significantly; the more your weight fluctuates, the bigger the mess is. Since the microbes play a significant role in our long-term physical and mental health, this partly answers our question as to why we have more diseases today—both of the body and brain—than ever before. A study conducted by immunologist Eran Elinav and his team at the Weizmann Institute of Science in Israel was one of the first to show that yo-yo dieters tend to see a rebound in their post-dieting weight, because their gut bacteria retains a 'memory' of their past weight. Many subsequent studies have emphasized that we must target the microbiome by completely rebooting, restoring and renewing it in order to prevent the yo-yoing and have long-lasting, sustainable weight loss.

At this point, I hope you realize that it's the microbes—which have been largely ignored—and not the CICO theory that require your attention. Since the gut microbes play such key roles, it's worth spending some time knowing its whereabouts. Right? *Let's go!*

## Gut Microbiome: The Hidden Organ

'Hey, you guys were fab, ya! It was such an informative session, not like those gossipy, size-zero kinds. You were so bang on about the association of immunity and inflammation. I wish I had found you years before. Just that, these microbes in our gut that you mentioned, did you seriously mean that? I mean, how can these tiny little things that are not even visible to our naked eye influence our health so much?'

Supriya from Houston was talking about the live conversation that I had with Taapsee Pannu on the actor's Instagram page. After listening to the conversation, Supriya had immediately signed up with me in the hopes of getting relief from many of the issues she had been dealing with for a few years—obesity, Hashimoto's thyroiditis, fibromyalgia, depression, anxiety, insomnia and brain fog. After years of being under the guidance of her doctors, this self-proclaimed Google queen was aware that much of her agony was related to chronic inflammation and hyperimmune response. In fact, weight gain too is now known to be linked to chronic, low-grade inflammation (I told you that there's much more to the story of weight loss than counting carbs or calories!). But nobody had told her before about the gut microflora, and that's why she sounded fascinated but confused. Most conventional medicine doctors have little to no training in the microbiome, so her query didn't surprise me at all. In the cycle of inflammation, obesity and disease, the gut microbiome happens to be the overlooked performer.

Anyway, in reply to Supriya's question, I said, 'If we laid the bacteria in our body end to end, they would circle the earth two-and-a-half times. Through the process of human evolution, if our bodies chose to retain these bacteria, and that too in such large numbers, then they must surely be significant, right?'

Case in point: the human appendix. Once thought of as a useless organ, scientists have now discovered that the few-inches small appendix is not really useless! It is an important component of our immune system and acts as a storehouse of good, beneficial microbes, protecting us during a bout of illness. Similarly, the gut microbes too could not be present just for kicks. Many scientists now argue that our gut microbiota is an organ in its own right, and is as vital as the heart and brain. We can survive without the appendix, but without the bugs lurking inside our gut, we wouldn't survive long. Our immunity would be crippled to such an extent that a random rendezvous with any germ in the outside world could very well kill us.

*The term 'microbiota' literally means little life (micro means little, biota means life), and is the community of microorganisms living in a specific environment.* Although there is a subtle difference, both the terms 'microbiota' and 'microbiome' are used interchangeably these days. Vast ecosystems of microbes are located throughout our body: in the mouth, urinary tract, skin, vagina and of course, the gut. So, the oral microbiota refers to all microbial communities residing in the mouth cavity, the vaginal microbiota is found in the vagina of a woman and so on. But it is our gut, particularly our large intestine or colon (our stomachs and small intestines are sparsely colonized and with good reason, as we will learn in the chapter ahead) that is home to 90 to 95 per cent of all the microbes living inside us. In fact, *the gut microbiota is one of the most densely populated microbial habitats known on earth!* For the longest time, it was believed that the 100 trillion bacterial cells in our gut outnumber all the other cells in our body put together by a factor of about 10:1. This means that for every human cell in our body, there are about 10 resident microbes. Predictably, you will find many articles with the typical did-you-know (or DYK) headline created to hook readers: 'Did you know you are more bacteria than you are human?'. But then, in 2016, biologist Ron Milo and his team from the Weizmann Institute of Science revised the microbes–to–man ratio as 1.3:1. Though this current estimate is nowhere close to the former 10:1, it still means that more than half of our body isn't human after all!

It doesn't stop here. From the genetic standpoint as well, our intestinal microbiome beats us hands down. The human genome as we know it is the complete set of genetic information (called genes) of a human being. Going by the Human Genome Project, humans are estimated to have between 20,000 and 25,000 genes. Likewise, our intestinal bugs also have their genes. In fact, *when we say 'microbiome', it means the community of microorganisms living in a specific environment AND their genetic material.* The genes in our microbiome, however, are estimated to be between two and 20 million, making us 99 per cent microbial and only one per cent human (genetically speaking)! So much for the *'yeh diabetes mujhe mere papa se mila hai'* argument!

What is intriguing is that each person's microbiome is as unique as his or her fingerprints. *No two people have the exact same microbiome!* Each gut harbours more than 1,000 species of bacteria. A lot of factors—the dominant being diet—decides the relative proportions of these species across individuals, making each microbiome highly personalized and specialized to each of us. By studying a person's microbial signature alone, it is possible to accurately predict a lot of things about that person, whether he is obese or lean, if he is under any medication, whether he lives in Asia or Europe and much more. Called *microbiome sequencing* by scientists, this is being used in the field of medical research. And it may even soon be utilized in forensics and crime-solving, much like the system of cataloguing fingerprints we use today!

*OK, now that you are done giving a Sherlock Holmes twist to a self-help diet book, can you please explain what these trillions of microbes, in thousands of species, and with millions of genes actually do?* Right away!

## What Do These Microbes Do?

These internal lodgers that share our body space consist of both helpful and potentially harmful microbes. While we are aware that diarrhoea and upset stomach are caused by the bad bugs, these are actually in the minority. Called *pathogens* or *pathogenic bacteria*, they are fewer in number compared to most of the others, which consist of harmless freeloaders *called commensals* and beneficial bacteria *called symbiotic or symbionts*. In a healthy gut, all of them coexist in harmony with you, the host. This state is called 'normobiosis'. Similar to the relationship between a man and a woman in a happy marriage, this is a mutually beneficial relationship between the microbes and us, so to speak. We give them a place to live in our bodies and feed them with the food we eat. They, in turn, help us deal with stuff that would otherwise be far too complicated for us.

Each species of microbes specializes in a task or set of tasks. For instance, one helps prevent the formation of kidney stones, while others help squeeze out calories from food. A diverse gut with many different microbes is like a diverse workforce that brings a variety of skills to the table. Applying the same rules of the corporate world, a 'healthy' gut microbial community should, therefore, be diverse, balanced and stable in order to enhance its productivity and perform its many different functions properly. What we also know of corporate offices around the world is that they consist of employees with specialized skill sets and work experiences, and these employees differ from one corporate house to the next. There is no common core in terms of its unique, performing members, and yet, each corporate ecosystem performs a whole suite of common functions such as finance, human resources, procurement, IT, legal and facilities management. So, the common core is represented not at the level of the employees, but at the functional level. Similarly, though the species in a microbial community may differ wildly from one gut to another, as an ecosystem, a healthy gut microbial community is found to perform an extensive common core of metabolic activities. These activities are:

1. Regulate fat metabolism and storage
2. Influence appetite and your ability to gain or lose weight
3. Calibrate your metabolism
4. Develop, educate and train the immune system
5. Produce vitamins, hormones and essential amino acids (bacteria are tiny factories)
6. Modulate bone mass density and influence athleticism
7. Help digest food, unlock its nutrients, extract energy and produce important by-products
8. Protect against cell death and cancer
9. Defend against harmful pathogens and disease-causing viruses

10. Control blood sugar, blood lipids and blood cholesterol levels
11. Break down toxins and medications
12. Produce key brain chemicals like serotonin (the happy hormone)
13. Influence liver, kidney, skin, nerves and vaginal tract function
14. Help absorb minerals like calcium, magnesium and iron
15. Regulate and support brain development and brain health

As you can see, the gut microbes are involved in just about every process in our body. This explains why depletion of healthy gut flora is linked to disease and weight gain, while keeping them in good health is known to offer a multitude of benefits. *But why do they go off-balance?*

## Why Does the Microbiome Go Out of Balance?

Ecologists know that when we disturb the environment in a major way, the relationships between interconnected species shift, and the structure of the ecosystem changes dramatically. Slowly, the ecosystem becomes unstable and then eventually it transforms and breaks down the environment.

So, it should come as no surprise that after we have spent years significantly disturbing the environment we live in, the otherwise stable ecosystem of flora and fauna coexisting within it (and with us) has altered profoundly. These changes in the ecology have resulted in unexpected and drastic consequences for the environment that we now know as climate change, global warming, pollution, extinction crisis, etc. The reason I write this is because COVID-19 has been the grimmest reminder of the extent to which we have brought about a major perturbation in the ecosystem we are a part of. We occupied the water, land and air, thinking of them solely as ours, but in the process, we lost the sense of how clean air smells, how clean water tastes and how exuberant nature is. We forgot the meaning of coexistence until Mother Nature spoke back to us. It took as much as shutting down everything to get the blue skies filled with chirping birds, hear news of vibrant flamingos in the skies and dancing dolphins in the water, watch viral videos of endangered animals and wildlife out on the streets—a beautiful (or should I say revengeful?) picture of Mother Nature reclaiming her space. I hope we understand that this joy of nature that went viral on social media has come at a huge and unacceptable cost to millions of people around the world. So, the least we can do is learn from our mistakes.

Much like the earth's ecology, your internal ecosystem, if diverse, stable and balanced is beneficial to your health in more ways than one. But if we disturb the environment, i.e., the human body, then the ecosystem of these otherwise stable microbial communities coexisting within the body gets profoundly altered. *This is a situation that scientists call 'dysbiosis'*, literally meaning 'life in distress'. Such changes in the microbiome can result in unexpected and drastic consequences for human health.

The microbiome is an important component within us, and it relies completely on us for its nutrition. Even in genetically identical twins, it has been found that microbiome composition can vary by up to 20 per cent due to differences in their diet and lifestyle. So, the host's genetics actually play a very minor role; diet and lifestyle are by far the most dominant factors that shape our microbiome composition. What we eat will determine what the microbes are and what they do. Of course, multiple other factors also interact with each other and exert their effect on the microbiome. But diet is considered to be one of the environmental factors with the most significant influence on how the microbiome takes shape. Depending on whether you adequately nourish your key microbes or not, your microbiome may either be beneficial to your health or put you at a greater risk of diseases. You may have heard of the saying 'you are what you eat,' but it would be more accurate to say, 'you are what your microbes eat!' Today's modern food culture—industrialized food production, changing diet trends, junk snacking, unconscious consumerism, etc.—is starving our microbes out of existence. Stanford microbiologist and author Justin Sonnenburg calls this idea 'starving the microbial self'. This diet-driven extinction spasm of the microbial species within us has fuelled, at least in part, the recent rise in obesity, chronic illnesses and mental health diseases.

Along with diet, other factors like living with high stress, not getting enough sleep and many others can create an environment inside our body that encourages the growth of harmful microbes, reduces microbial diversity and increases predisposition to diseases. I have compiled an extensive list of disruptors that may negatively influence the shape of microbial population inside our bodies and lead to dysbiosis. Details on a few of these will follow in the chapters ahead.

## Causes of Dysbiosis

Diet-related disruptors:

1.  History of crash diets and yo-yo dieting
2.  Following diet trends like low-carb, low-fat, high-protein, etc.
3.  Intake of processed, industrialized foods (irrespective of whether they are gluten-free, fat-free, sugar-free or keto)
4.  Overconsumption of non-vegetarian foods
5.  Frequent alcohol consumption
6.  Irregular meal timings
7.  Frequent late-night dinners

Lifestyle disruptors:

1.  Physical inactivity
2.  Sleep deprivation
3.  Chronic stress or anxiety
4.  Frequent long-distance trans-meridian (east-west or west-east) travel
5.  Indoor urban living with no connect with natural surroundings
6.  Obsession with hygiene
7.  Smoking
8.  Overexposure to environmental pollutants, pesticides, chemicals in cosmetics and fragrances, industrial chemicals and plastics (collectively termed 'xenobiotics')

Other disruptors:

1.  Indiscriminate use of antibiotics and other pharmaceuticals
2.  Immigration to a Western country
3.  C-section birth
4.  Formula feeding during infancy or lack of breastfeeding

Then how do you restore an out-of-balance gut microbiome? You follow the three-phase diet and lifestyle change system that I have created, called *The Belly and Brain Diet*.

## The Three Phases of TBBD

Diet and lifestyle interventions that target the microbiome are paving the way towards more effective modes of losing weight permanently and improving our physical and mental health. By now, you can probably appreciate that restocking your gut flora isn't as simple as going on a grocery store tour and picking up bottles of kimchi and yoghurt from the fermented foods aisle. In fact, including fermented foods in your diet at the wrong time can disrupt the balance of your gut microbiome further. A multistep strategy is required to fine-tune the gut microbiome, reduce dysbiosis, and re-establish a robust inner ecology. That's why TBBD is divided into three distinct phases:

Phase 1—Reboot and Remove: Weeding the Lawn

Imagine a large lawn overgrown with weeds, insects, fungi, etc. If you want to regrow a healthy, vibrant, green garden on this piece of dry, untended land, would you start planting new seeds straightaway? No, right? The first thing you would do is kill off the weeds, fungi, etc. and prepare the soil. Similarly, before you try to repopulate your gut with healthy bacteria, you need to weed out your inner garden and till the soil of your gut. This is what the first phase, which lasts only two weeks, is designed to do. It aims to remove unhealthy, noxious bacteria, and because these pathogens feed on inflammatory molecules, the first phase also aims to cool down systemic inflammation. It preps the gut for the next phase; without this prep, the foods you introduce in phase 2 will not be able to serve their purpose of strengthening and diversifying your inner ecosystem.

## Phase 2—Repair and Repopulate: Reseeding the Lawn

Now that you have rebooted your gut microbiome and weeded out your inner garden, it's time to reseed your gut with beneficial, friendly bacteria, and fertilize it with the right foods that will help the good bugs to thrive. Instead of foods that feed your 'chubby' bacteria, you will focus on special foods that turn on the fat-burning machinery and promote a lean metabolism. In the process, you will also find many of your chronic symptoms disappearing or reducing in severity. This phase consists of the major chunk of TBBD, and is designed to last six weeks.

## Phase 3—Reintroduce and Renew: Your Lifetime Tune-Up

At the end of eight weeks, your gut microbiome should be completely restored to the right balance of friendly and unfriendly bacteria in your gut. At this point, it's imperative to have a long-term, flexible and sustainable eating plan so that you can maintain the gut microbiome balance permanently. The last phase is two weeks and beyond. It may be considered as the maintenance phase with no recommended length. Foods that you avoided in the previous phases for repair and rebalancing are reintroduced in phase 3. So, once you transition to this phase, your diet will allow you to eat all kinds of food, while still helping you maintain your weight loss— and good health—for the long haul. As you can see, unlike the vast majority of diets in the market, TBBD isn't some gimmicky crash diet that fails in the long term and leads to your weight yo-yoing.

To make TBBD easy to implement in your everyday life, I have created regional, season-wise meal plans for each phase. You will also find a multitude of flavourful, anti-inflammatory, fat-burning, microbiome-diversifying and blood sugar-balancing recipes that I specifically developed keeping in mind the goals of each phase.

Since I believe eating, not deprivation, is the route to lifelong good health, I always ensure that my clients celebrate life with 'treat' meals once every week. I refuse to call it a 'cheat' meal—it's high time we cultivate a healthy and compassionate relationship with food. I have created a few appetizing suggestions for treat meals that carry my seal of approval, and that you have the freedom to indulge in weekly! Not only that, you will also find a food chart consisting of foods to eliminate, eat fewer of and favour for each phase. Using this chart, you can create your own meals and recipes in case you want a change from the meals I have suggested in the plan. Ultimately, you will have plenty of choices and hardly any chance to get bored while you are on this programme!

## Is This Programme for Me?

What happens in Vegas stays in Vegas, but unfortunately, your gut isn't Las Vegas. What happens in there doesn't stay in there. An altered gut microbiome has not been observed in people with digestive symptoms only. In Chapter 1, we have already seen a host of chronic diseases of various body systems that can be initiated by dysbiosis. An abnormal microbiota may not be the cause of all these conditions, but it has been shown to be an important factor. The Belly and Brain Diet can help get the gut microbiota back in shape. It is crucial to correct dysbiosis—or prevent it in the first place—because an imbalanced microbiome is a common denominator in a myriad of symptoms. So, for instance, if you are dealing with stubborn weight that doesn't seem to budge despite your being active, if you struggle to lose weight or keep it off, then it is highly likely that your gut microflora is out of balance.

A few signs of an unbalanced inner ecosystem are:

- Weight gain or being overweight
- Hormonal imbalance
- Fatigue, low energy, feeling of dullness
- Digestive distress like gas, bloating, acidity and indigestion
- Trouble falling asleep
- Acne and other skin disorders
- Chronic illness and disease
- Headaches
- Fibromyalgia

- Brain fog
- Sore joints
- Relentless allergies
- Feeling of heaviness, lethargy and congestion in the morning
- Food sensitivities or intolerance
- Food cravings
- Mood issues
- Breath that stinks

When you support your inner ecosystem, you optimize your entire biology. By restoring your gut health through the programme outlined in this book, you will burn fat and succeed in keeping it off for the long term. At the same time, it will help cool down inflammation in your body, eliminate cravings, rebalance your hormones, rev up your overall metabolism, reverse damage done by yo-yo dieting and reduce insulin resistance. During personal consultation with my clients, I further fine-tune the diet and lifestyle recommendations to their specific requirements. But for the purpose of this book, I have tried to keep everything acceptable for the population in general, so that anyone reading this book and following the programme can reap the maximum benefit from it.

In the next chapter, I will show you some of the ways in which diet exerts a big influence in shaping the gut microbial community. These will give you a basic understanding of why I have suggested that you avoid certain foods and eat more of some others in different phases. They will also help you appreciate how much influence these microscopic organisms have on your deep health.

# 3

# You Are Not What You Eat; You Are What Your Microbes Eat

Everything we consume—from the basic dal–chawal to the exotic berries—has an effect on our gut microbes, which, in turn, influences our behaviour, body weight and health outcomes. But how exactly do diet and the microbiome interact with each other in a way that either makes us lose weight or put on a couple of kilos? Let's look at five different ways in which diet and the microbes' interaction sets the stage for weight gain, illness and depression. They will help you understand why making wrong and hasty decisions about food can have far-reaching consequences.

## Pathway No. 1: The Duality of Inflammation

There is a duality in the nature of everything in our world. Krishna called it 'Dvand' (*Bhagavad Gita, 5.3*), which is a Sanskrit word that means 'pair of opposites'. So, if there's joy, then there is pain. If there are things that you like, then there are also things that you dislike. Summer is only relevant because of the existence of winter. The trick, however, is to stay undisturbed and maintain your balance in this world of duality.

Inflammation is no exception to this rule. Although inflammation carries a negative reputation today, we still need to know that it isn't intrinsically good or bad. Instead, it's about balance—acute versus chronic and controlled versus uncontrolled. When you get a paper cut, the area turns red, swells and warms up. When you are fighting off a cold, your body temperature elevates and you get a fever. These are signs of immune and (acute) inflammatory processes that the body launches to defend itself against potential harm.

The problem occurs if inflammation gets out of control. Unlike acute inflammation that is confined to a spot, inflammatory molecules then travel along with the bloodstream to all body parts, causing damage that shows up as an extensive list of symptoms throughout the body. This is called systemic chronic inflammation (SCI), and is recognized by leading scientific research as the cornerstone of most, if not all, the chronic diseases (of both body and brain) we are dealing with today. According to modern medicine, the belly fat that you so detest is also closely linked with low grade, system-wide inflammation.

So, what's the link between your gut and inflammation?

You may think that your gut only digests your food and extracts the goodies from it, but it actually does much more. It forms a protective lining—called the intestinal barrier—separating the contents of your gut from the internal organs. You can think of this as the physical border of a country. This protective lining consists of a single, thin layer of cells called the epithelium. These cells carry out some important duties. The epithelial cells are held together by proteins called 'tight junctions'. Directly underneath this single layer of cells reside 70–80 per cent of the immune cells present throughout our body. Think of them as the border patrol. They discriminate between the good guys, the good guys without a passport, and the bad guys that may have crossed the border.

The friendly bacteria of your gut microbiome play a critical role in maintaining normal barrier function. Hence, as long as you eat right, and maintain a state of normobiosis, the gut epithelial cells (the physical border) control what enters the rest of the body (the country). However, when you get influenced by so-called 'diet influencers' on social media and start rattling off things like *'Eeeee, no ghee!'* and *'carb, baap re baap!'* and so on, you set the stage for dysbiosis, and this barrier becomes compromised. As a result, more inflammatory molecules are released compared to anti-inflammatory ones. This loosens the tight junctions that seal the cells of the gut lining together, creating breaches or microscopic holes in the lining. The border is now open, giving an all-access pass to bad bacteria, large undigested food particles and toxic waste to enter your bloodstream and the rest of your body. This intestinal permeability is labelled as a 'leaky gut'. Thanks to this leaky gut, quite unsurprisingly, the symptoms can show up anywhere, from the gut to the heart, from the skin to the brain. Mayhem ensues, and it's not pretty. The free flow of undesirable elements across the border puts an undue amount of stress on the border patrol, which is your immune system, leading to chronic immune activation and SCI.

Since a dysfunctional intestinal barrier is rarely talked about, you may not have heard about it in your day to day life. Yet, in scientific circles, it is believed that such dysfunction underpins the very process of uncontrolled weight gain and other health conditions that millions of people are struggling with. As long as you don't cool down the inflammatory response, your metabolism will continue to be slower, your ability to burn fat will be weaker and you will take longer to feel full. Therefore, the intestinal barrier is one of the important dimensions that I work on—through the principles listed in this book—with my clients.

## Pathway No. 2: How Can Microbes Make You Fat?

Eating is a fascinating process and digestion even more so. Here's a quick rundown on how it works.

Some of the food that you eat starts to get broken down by the salivary enzymes in your mouth. The food then moves down to your food pipe and drops into your stomach. The stomach has an extremely acidic environment, and for good reason. The hydrochloric acid in the stomach activates digestive enzymes and sterilizes the food that you consume. The enzymes in the stomach then break the food down into microscopic fragments. This partially digested food, called 'chyme', then leaves the stomach and passes into the small intestine. If you can recall the illustration of the digestive system from your school textbooks, you will remember the small intestine as the one that meanders sometimes to the right, sometimes to the left. It is 20 feet long, and it is where the chyme mixes with additional digestive juices. The mesh-like, permeable walls help absorb nutrients from the mix into the bloodstream. The leftovers enter the large intestine, i.e., your colon. If you remember, this is the upside-down U-shaped bulging structure that surrounds the small intestine on the outside like a roly-poly photo frame, so to speak. Approximately five feet long, this is where the vast majority of your microbial community lives. The colon is their place to shine. What are undigested food remains for you is a feast for them. And everything the bugs don't eat comes out finally in your poop.

This is when things get even more interesting. If millions of Mumbaikars, all unique in their own way, can be broadly divided into two main groups—*Worli link ke iss paar aur uss paar wale*—then bacteria *kis khet ki mooli hai*. Biologists have found that the majority of our gut's inhabitants belong to one of two main taxonomic groups or phyla: *Bacteroidetes* and *Firmicutes*. It has been observed that the gut microbiota of obese individuals have an increased level of Firmicutes and a reduced level of Bacteroidetes. The overall consensus amongst research bacteriologists is that Firmicutes are fat-forming bugs. I like to call them the 'chubby' bacteria. Our microbes dismantle the foods that we eat but cannot digest, and in the process, they produce end products or 'metabolites' that diffuse into our blood stream. Because Firmicutes over-digest the food you eat and produce more energy-dense metabolites, more calories make their way into the circulation, and if they go unused, they get stored as fat. This makes some people put on 'extra' weight, even though they don't eat more than someone whose microbial landscape has a preponderance of bacteria from the phylum Bacteroidetes.

I hope this shows why the calories you harvest from what you eat are largely determined by the type of microbial tribe you develop and harbour. Unfortunately, there is no way for you to accurately calculate the number of calories your gut bugs are harvesting for you. So much for all the calorie calculators and the calories-in–calories-out diet approach!

The foods that we eat feed different types of bacteria. Whatever you choose to dump—for instance, a banana or a chocolate cake—onto your colonic community of microbes, those that specialize in fermenting that food will bloom. If we consume the foods that the 'lean bacteria' relish and starve the 'obese bacteria', we can eventually change the bacterial population in our gut.

By now, if you are wondering what these foods are and what you can do to get a fat-burning floral fingerprint, then fret not. *The 10-week TBBD will help you reverse the Firmicutes–to–Bacteroidetes* ratio.

## Pathway No. 3: The Relatively Unexplored Condition of SIBO

What Is SIBO?

SIBO is small intestinal bacterial overgrowth. Until a few years ago, it was thought of as a rare condition. Doctors were trained to understand that it happens very rarely, and results mostly from structural disorders due to surgeries. Now, in an era of booming microbiome research, awareness is increasing, and SIBO is under the scanner again with respect to the health and well-being of the general population.

Under normal circumstances, very few gut bacteria reside in the small intestine, which, if you remember, is where most of your nutrients are absorbed. It is only natural, therefore, for your small bowel to go all out to stop the bacterial species interfering in its work. It limits the growth of gut bugs by creating a more challenging environment for microbial colonizers. The suppressive action of stomach acid and digestive enzymes and the presence of a high level of bile acid keep your upper digestive tract relatively sterile. The large intestine, on the other hand, is characterized by slow flow rates and neutral to mildly acidic pH. Because of this favourable environment, the highest concentration of bacteria is found in your large intestine, closer to the end of your digestive tract. But if the equilibrium is disturbed and large numbers of overconfident bacteria crawl up into your small intestine or aren't cleared from it properly, then we have a case of SIBO or small intestinal bacterial overgrowth.

## Why Does SIBO Occur?

The two key ways in which your small intestine keeps a check on bacterial overabundance are stomach acid and intestinal movement. Anything that affects these will naturally promote bacterial overgrowth.

Gastric acid is a major player that keeps the territory hostile, so that organisms ingested with food or those trying to come up from the colon are kept at bay. So, if you keep taking antacids for a few months or longer, then you've really taken away a major defensive unit. This is precisely the same reason why obsessing over alkaline water or following alkaline diets is harmful in the long run.

Just like you have a housekeeping system to clear the leftovers after a party, in the same way, after your meal, the residual undigested food, fibre, debris and bacteria are swept through the digestive tube and out of the body by the contractions of your gut. The technical name for this cleansing wave is migrating motor complex (MMC). When you hear your stomach growl, it's actually your MMC at work. If the MMC becomes inhibited, the gastric contents and organisms will sit around in your gut instead of being flushed out of the body. This creates a perfect environment for any number of bugs to get a foothold and make a home, thus resulting in SIBO.

## How Will SIBO Affect You?

Studies have shown that bacterial overgrowth in the small intestine forces your body to pack on extra kilos. The connection between SIBO and obesity is well established, further proving that the story of weight loss is multi-dimensional and not as straightforward as the diet industry will have you believe. A study conducted in 2011 revealed that SIBO prevalence is higher in obese individuals than in those who are lean. Additionally, it has also been confirmed that SIBO weakens the integrity of the intestinal lining, leading to the leaky gut that I explained earlier. All of this shows how SIBO and weight gain are interconnected.

Does this imply that you have SIBO if you are overweight? Not really. But if your body fat has gotten stubborn and refuses to budge despite your trying many diets, or if you show symptoms that are typical of SIBO, then you may well be harbouring bugs in the wrong part of your system.

## Symptoms of SIBO

In SIBO cases, the excessive bacteria in the small intestine start fermenting the foods you eat before the nutrients are absorbed, leading to symptoms that include:

- Digestive complaints: gas, bloating and flatulence, especially after meals; constipation; diarrhoea; abdominal pain or discomfort; food sensitivity and intolerance; early satiation; nausea; abdominal distension; belching; IBS
- Non-digestive complaints: nutrient and vitamin deficiencies (particularly B12, iron, D3, calcium), anaemia, chronic fatigue syndrome, fibromyalgia, rosacea, restless leg syndrome, edema, joint pain, muscle spasm, feeling of disorientation (brain fog)

## What Can You Do about SIBO?

I hope that by now, you appreciate why consuming probiotics or 'friendly bacteria' as the first go-to solution to revamp the gut microbiome isn't helpful. Because the problem in SIBO isn't a lack of good bacteria, but that the otherwise healthy bacteria are found to overgrow in the wrong place, i.e., in the small intestine! Most cases of SIBO will show no improvement, or even get worse with probiotics. Of course, I am not implying that probiotics are bad. But you should have them only when the problem of bacterial overgrowth is first fixed and the bad bugs have been killed. Fortunately, diet has been found to play a profound role in starving out the overpopulation of bacteria and microbes in the small bowel. The first phase of TBBD is designed to exactly do this. Also, how efficiently your MMC functions and clears the bugs from your small bowel is *determined by your gut clock—the internal clock of your gut—the alarm of which is affected by when you eat. Not only what you eat but when you eat is also important!* You will learn about the right timing of consuming your food in the chapter ahead.

## Pathway No. 4: The Fascinating World of Epigenetics

How often do you blame your genes for that unsightly flab on your chin? Or the love handles you are flaunting on your waist? Quite a few times, I am sure. In fact, we are programmed to believe that most diseases or illnesses are genetic and there's nothing we can do about them. But what if I told you that we are not locked into the genes we have? Before I elaborate further, let me introduce you to the concept of genotype and phenotype.

Suppose that you have come up with a plan. You have provided all the necessary information and instructions for the plan. But to put it into action, the plan has to be read and implemented, right? Similarly, your genes are nothing but plans. Unless they are 'expressed', they represent only possibilities. Of course, there are some genes that will find expression no matter what you do: for instance, those that decide the colour of your eyes, the shape of your face or whether your lifespan is that of a human or a deer! Other genes just offer up their abilities, and it is up to us whether to put them to use or not. There are genes you get from your parents and grandparents; you can carry these genes around for a lifetime without them ever being expressed, as in the case of genes for obesity and diseases.

These set of 'hard-coded' genes in your DNA that you inherit from your parents is called the 'genotype'. However, your genotype is only a plan about who you will become: large-breasted or small, star student of the class or backbencher, etc. Environmental influences like your diet, exercise, stress levels and more interact with the genotype, and their outcome is your physical and observable characteristics, which is called 'phenotype'. This means that what you eat, how much you move, how you think have the ability to reprogramme the expression of the genotype, and this contributes to your observable traits, i.e., the phenotype. The colour of flamingos is a classic example that I love to cite to illustrate my point.

Flamingos are known for their bright pink colour. However, their natural colour is white, not pink. The pigments in the organisms they feed on cause them to turn vibrantly pink! Likewise, although we have no control over our genotype, all of us have the ability to 'turn off and on' our genes and influence their expression, which can alter health outcomes. So, it is both nature and nurture! And what I would like you to do is focus more on nurture, rather than on nature. Focus on what you can do to lead your body in the direction of health and healing. I can assure you that you are not stuck with the genes you have. You have the power to do something about them! We all have.

This recent discovery of the ability of environmental influences to alter gene expression without involving changes to the underlying DNA sequence—a change in phenotype without a change in genotype—has opened up a whole new world called 'epigenetics'. One of the key influencers of epigenetic modification is the food that you eat. Your diet impacts your genetic expression, and the flora in your gut is one of the primary means by which this occurs! Your gut microbiome 'talks' to your genes. The genes that you got from your parents cannot be changed, and so we can't do an awful lot with it, but the microbes can be changed through dietary patterns. While your inherited genes are more or less fixed, it is possible to reshape, even cultivate, the trillions of gut bacteria that control your genetic expression. I find this intriguing, because through your microbes living inside your body, you actually have a say on whether or not the diabetes genes inherited from your *daadi* or *naani* will express and give you diabetes. You cannot talk to your genes, but your microbes can not only talk to them, but also manipulate their expression in your favour.

The key takeaway is pretty straightforward: Your gut microbiome is a powerful means for improving your health. It exerts an influence as great as—and possibly even greater than—the genes you inherit. Hence, to lose weight, treat and prevent diseases and bolster overall well-being, you need to reshape and rebalance the gut microbiome. The good news is that it is far easier to change the gut than your genes.

### What Inspired the Discovery of DNA?

You may have heard of Dr Francis Crick, the molecular biologist who won the Nobel Prize for the discovery of

DNA. Dr Crick credited the book called *What is Life?* as the inspiration behind his key insight that paved the way for his revolutionary discovery of the genetic code. But did you know that the book, in turn, happens to be purely inspired by the ancient wisdom of the *Upanishads*? I haven't had the chance to read the book yet, but as someone who is studying the *Vedas* and the *Upanishads*, I am not a bit surprised.

Of the many fundamental things that the *Upanishads* teach about life and its complexities, one is the law of karma. The events in your life that are predetermined and therefore inevitable are called your *'prarabdha karma'*. Think of it as destiny. There are different kinds of prarabdha karma: *prabal*, *madhyam* and *durbal prarabdha*. The family you are born into, the type of nose—long, short, stout, etc.—you have, the complexion of your skin that you are born with are categorically classified as your prabal prarabdha, because you have no control over these. But for most of the situations in life, we do have free will, a choice to act, that is called *'prayatna'* in Vedic textbooks. Your destiny only presents itself as a situation. The choice to act in the given situation using your free will and intellect remains with you.

Whether you surrender to the situation or whether you gather the courage to break free and live with your head held high is your free will. As you act, so shall you live. The difference between someone surrendering to a disease and others not only surviving it but emerging stronger and more evolved lies in how they chose to deal with it. In this sense, you are the architect of your own life, not the one sitting above. Adi Shankaracharya has time and again glorified human life, calling it a rare privilege. Unlike all other animals and beings programmed to behave on their instincts, we humans have the faculty of our mind, *buddhi*, which distinguishes us from them and gives us the freedom to choose and act wisely. The ultimate path to peace, purpose and fulfilment in life is through 'wisdom in action'. This is one of the profound aspects of the Indian scriptural thought.

Therefore, not only the science of the microbiome but the *Vedanta* too rejects the belief of fatalism. To take charge of your life, including your physical and mental health, is your fundamental responsibility. The responsibility of who you are and what you can become must be borne by you. Only when you take ownership will you be able to do the best you can for yourself. And whatever best you can do, must happen.

## Pathway No. 5: The Belly–Brain Axis

The brain may seem to be geographically disconnected from the stomach, but the truth of the matter is that your belly and your brain are in constant communication through a sophisticated signalling system. This dynamic two-way link between them is called the *gut–brain axis* (GBA). The scientific evidence uncovering the association between gut health and brain health is strong and gathering momentum. As it turns out, the gut microbiota play an important role. Mood disorders, chronic stress, depression and anxiety have all been tied to dysbiosis. And it has been shown that improving the gut microbiome helps brain function.

There are predominantly three mechanisms by which gut microbes and the brain communicate.

1.  ENS and the vagus nerve: If our brains possess 100 billion neurons, then our guts are also made up of 100 million nerves. This highly sophisticated, intrinsic neural network can take in information, process it and store it; it can even change and adapt, just like the brain. The gut's network of nerves is called the enteric nervous system (ENS). Because it is as large and complex as the 'first brain' housed in your head, American researcher and author Dr Michael Gershon referred to it as the 'second brain' in his book. The interesting thing is that both our brains are interconnected, like Siamese twins. You have no inkling of it, but your gut is constantly and intimately communicating with your brain. If one gets upset, the other does, too.

    The vagus nerve is a long nerve that serves as the fastest connection linking the gut and the brain, sending signals in both directions. Your gut uses this vagus nerve almost like a walkie-talkie to tell your brain how you are feeling. Whether your brain should trigger vomiting after an overdose of alcohol at last night's party, whether you should be feeling like a wreck after a break-up or instead dance to the new break-up song with your friends—these are just a few of the important messages that your second brain passes on to the first one. The most direct route of communication within the GBA is found to be among the gut microbiota, the ENS and the vagus nerve. Bacteria in your gut affect the brain by changing the actions of ENS neurons and the vagus nerve. They can talk to your brain via the vagus nerve for implications with depression, anxiety and brain fog.

2. Neurotransmitters: That gut feeling you can vouch for, the feeling of happiness that you get after a workout or the joy experienced while having a meal in the company of a loved one are because of certain chemicals called neurotransmitters. Recent research has shown that most of these neurotransmitters are produced not in our brain but in our gut. Not only does the gut talk with the brain via the vagus nerve, but it also releases these chemicals, which are then taken to the brain by blood. The most striking of these chemicals are our feel-good neurotransmitter, serotonin, and our reward neurotransmitter, dopamine. It has been observed that 90 per cent of our serotonin and 50 per cent of our dopamine are produced in our gut. Hence, an imbalance in the neurotransmitters in our brain usually means we have an imbalance of neurotransmitters in our gut. An abundance or dearth of neurotransmitters in our brain is linked to depression or anxiety, and an abundance or dearth of neurotransmitters in our gut creates cramping, slow digestion, constipation or diarrhea.

You will often, although not always, see such symptoms married to each other. For instance, Madhav, whom I introduced in Chapter 1, had high-functioning anxiety coexisting with constipation. From one of her interviews, I also recall Deepika Padukone talking about experiencing a sick, empty pit-like feeling in her stomach for days on end before she was diagnosed with depression in 2014.

What is intriguing is that bacteria from our gut microbiota regulate the synthesis of serotonin. And because we can fix our biome with the help of dietary changes, it also means that we can fix the production of these neurotransmitters in our body by paying attention to what we eat. That is really cool!

3. Inflammation: By now, I am sure you are well aware of the diet–gut microbiota–inflammation link. As we found out earlier, a leaky gut triggers the production of inflammatory molecules. There is growing evidence that these inflammatory proteins circulate in the bloodstream, and can send signals across the blood–brain barrier (BBB) to cause damage or alter the activity of brain regions that control mood. They can also cause a change in the emotion-processing networks of nerve cells in the brain. All of this can result in an episode of clinical depression or feelings of negativity and fatigue.

One of my clients had rheumatoid arthritis (RA). Along with the swollen painful joints that are typical of RA, she also had low energy and pessimistic, depressive thoughts. She believed she was depressed because she knew she had a chronic inflammatory disease. This is again something that conventional medical wisdom pushes us to believe: 'It's all in the mind.' However, more recent studies have begun to produce evidence that inflammation is not merely linked with depression, but it can directly *cause* depression. According to data from the National Health and Nutrition Examination Survey, a remarkable 47 per cent of people with clinical depression also have 'heightened' inflammation. Inflamed bodies can lead to depressed minds. It didn't occur to my client that she might be depressed not because she knew she was inflamed, but because she actually *was* inflamed.

Depression and inflammation fuel one another. When they co-occur, treating them side by side can enhance recovery and reduce the risk of recurrence far more than treatment with conventional antidepressant drugs alone.

As you can see, almost all aspects of brain health are dependent on the microbes in our gut, but it doesn't end there. The bacteria in our gut may actually play a role in our behaviour too.

### My Visit to a Tiger Zoo in Thailand

My daughter Devika loves to holiday at the beach. So, when it's time for a family vacay, we invariably choose a beach holiday. A few years back, when we were in Pattaya, we visited a tiger zoo in the outskirts of the city. One of the highlights of the place was pigs and tigers in the same enclosure, living in perfect harmony. Out of curiosity, my daughter asked the guide how the zoo had achieved this rare feat. We were told that as soon as a tiger cub is born, it is taken away from its mother and instead brought to live with the pig. The pig mothers it with its milk, alongside its own piglets. As a result, the tiger cub grows up behaving like a piglet, timid and docile.

Two things then started running through my mind. The first was a feeling of guilt at visiting a place that not only keeps animals caged but also forcibly removes them from their mothers. So much for the animal tourism business! My daughter and I exchanged looks, and we knew that we would never visit any such establishment again. But the second thought that started racing through my mind was one of curiosity: Was the altered bacteria in the cubs' gut responsible for the dramatic change in their behaviour? I already knew that a change in the environment can alter the composition of gut bacteria, but could it also influence behaviour? As soon as I got home, I dove into research, and found that yes, it does!

Stephen Collins of McMaster University, Canada, and his research collaborators used two specific strains of mice—BALB/c and NIH Swiss—and exchanged their microbial gut contents. One week later, the NIH Swiss mice that are normally outgoing and exploratory became hesitant and anxious, whereas the normally timid BALB/c mice were now very friendly and gregarious. This is just one of the many studies that confirm that our brain can receive information from the gut and this, in turn, can influence our behaviour, feelings, emotions, intentions, thoughts, happiness and well-being. American neurobiologist and author Bud Craig have spent over 30 years studying the insular cortex—part of the brain that receives information from the gut and generates feelings. It became clearer to me why most of my clients start to show more positive behavioural attributes. Rebalancing the gut microbiome has more perks than you would believe. One of them is that it may also help you to better your 'self'.

Despite all the complexities of how the human body functions, TBBD is a wonderfully simple approach that you can take to lose body fat and enhance your general well-being. Its ecosystems approach, which involves not only a gut-friendly diet, but also a gut-balancing lifestyle comprising more movement, nervous system retraining and cultivating sleep hygiene, will help rebalance your gut microbiome and optimize all the five pathways discussed in this chapter. From the next chapter onwards, you will learn how exactly we shall do this.

4

# The Three Rs of TBBD

What is the perfect microbiota? Well, no one knows that yet. But what we do know is the scientific community's recommendations of a healthy eating pattern that will eventually result in a healthy microbiota. The three-phased approach of TBBD, as you will see in the chapters ahead, involves certain dos and don'ts in each phase. A few foods are to be avoided and a few are recommended more than others specifically for each phase. But there are certain guidelines of a healthy eating pattern that you need to follow in general during all three phases. Not doing so can upset the microbes and undo the effort we put in as we progress from one phase to the other.

I have divided these guidelines into the Three Rs.

1. Right quality: What to eat?
2. Right quantity: How much to eat?
3. Right timing: When to eat?

You see, you are not only what your microbes eat; you are what, how and when your microbes eat! The *Bhagavad Gita* also talks about '*yuktahaar*', where '*yukt*' means right quality, amount and timing, and '*ahaar*' is food (*Bhagavad Gita, 6.17*). In a world of extreme diets, yuktahaar is the common-sense approach of moderation and sums up my programme in a nutshell.

## The First R: Right Quality

'Munmun, my cousins and friends think that there's some superfood you have told me about, like some hidden secret that I have! Honestly, I don't know how to answer them. I try telling them about things that I have learned from you, but to no avail!' Taapsee sounded both amused and concerned as she spoke to me. I could very well relate to what she felt.

My social media pages are bombarded with such queries all the time. Many people are looking to add expensive functional foods, superfoods or dietary supplements in their daily meals, thinking they are a sure-shot way to weight loss and good health. However, researchers strongly recommend addressing the foundation first and foremost: Make better selections of food for daily meals.

For many obvious reasons, fixing what we eat isn't about making choices based on the caloric value of foods. Calories are not equal; they differ in nutritional quality according to their source. For example, all kinds of dietary fats carry the same calories per gram, but they can influence health in different ways. Trans-fats are known to increase the risk of heart diseases, whereas monounsaturated fats have the opposite effect. Instead of focusing on counting calories or macros (grams of carbs, proteins and fats), one should focus on the quality of ingredients and dietary sources. *When it comes to food, quality is the king.* TBBD encourages eating good-quality whole foods, and excludes foods that are known to reduce the health of your gut and microbiome. The foods that, at least initially, should be completely avoided are ultra-processed foods.

## Ultra-Processed Foods

Somebody has said, *'Jo dikhta hai, woh bikta hai,'* and who better than us, the present generation of people, to validate this statement. From selfies on Instagram to profiles on Tinder, almost everything is packaged into more attractive and desirable forms. Everything is hunky-dory until you stop scratching the surface and get to know things better. When you walk down the aisle of a supermarket, you see food packaged in bright colours. Phrases like 'take a break' and 'you are worth it' are carefully planted to tap into your need for self-care. And of course, buzzwords like 'organic', 'vegan' and 'gluten-free' are optimally exploited to create the illusion of health. Food-marketing tricks make cheap, nutrient-poor, inferior-quality foods seem good for you.

While the processes and ingredients used in the manufacture of ultra-processed foods make them convenient and attractive, at the same time, the very same processes and ingredients make them nutritionally unbalanced. Many studies undertaken in around 100 countries have shown that consumption of ultra-processed foods is associated with several non-communicable diseases such as obesity, type 2 diabetes, hypertension, cancer, depression, gastrointestinal disorders and anxiety. But why are these foods linked to weight gain and diseases? Can our microbiome explain?

Highly processed foods are formulated in ways that disturb the gut microbiome on many different fronts. Modern, Western diets high in ultra-processed foods are a major driver of microbial dysbiosis. They create a gut environment favouring microbes that kill off many friendly species, disrupt gut barrier function and promote low-grade inflammation. These alterations, in turn, heighten the risk of obesity and other lifestyle diseases.

Before you embark on the 10-week gut microbiome rebalancing journey with me, I want you to take an inventory of your kitchen and eliminate these items that you will no longer be consuming. To do so, it is imperative that you know what they are and how you can identify them.

Classifying Food Based on Processing

Food processing is not the issue, as it is a useful step that helps transform our agricultural produce to consumable items. The term 'processing' is very general and unhelpful, and it is quite meaningless to judge foods simply because they are 'processed'. To address this concern, Carlos Monteiro, a professor of nutrition and public health at the University of São Paulo in Brazil, proposed the NOVA food classification system in 2009.

In the NOVA classification system, all foods are grouped according to the nature, extent and purposes of the industrial processes they undergo after they are separated from nature, and before they are made into meals and consumed. Instead of providing recommendations on caloric intake or macronutrient consumption, which we have seen are flawed concepts, these new food and meal-based dietary guidelines recommend being mindful of the quality of foods one consumes. Its golden rule is to always prefer natural, unprocessed foods that can be consumed by themselves—like fruits and nuts, minimally-processed foods and freshly-made meals—to highly (ultra) processed, industrialized foods.

## Identifying Ultra-Processed Foods

Ultra-processed foods are created in factories. They are pumped full of inexpensive commodity ingredients that are exclusively for industrial use, such as protein isolates, modified starches, dextrose, etc. To convert the industrially manufactured foods into something edible, to prolong its shelf life and to make it look appetizing, multiple difficult-to-pronounce chemicals, preservatives, colourings, enzymes, binders, bulkers, flavourings, additives, emulsifiers, trans-fats and artificial sweeteners are usually added. All of these chemicals can upset our gut communities. The industry has got around this by hiding controversial ingredients under names and varieties that sound less deadly. So artificial colours are masked under E numbers, like E110 or E104, modified starch is called E1422 and so on.

For all practical purposes, a product is identified as ultra-processed if its list of ingredients contains at least one item characteristic of the ultra-processed food group. These substances are never or rarely used in kitchens, such as high fructose corn syrup, hydrogenated oils, hydrolysed proteins, etc. They usually appear in the beginning or in the middle of the ingredients list. The presence of classes of additives in the list of ingredients also identifies a product as ultra-processed. They are at the end of lists of ingredients and expressed as a class, such as flavourings or natural flavours or artificial flavours.

So, going by the NOVA classification, instant noodles, ice creams, chips, biscuits, cookies, ketchup, cakes, sauces, colas, sugary drinks, candies, crisps, crackers, jams, jellies, instant soups and ready-to-eat, ready-to-drink or ready-to-heat, 'fast' or 'convenient' packaged products and the like are all ultra-processed foods, and it is not difficult to understand why.

I also want to talk about foods that are assumed to be healthy but are processed junk in disguise. Many products you may not have thought about are actually ultra-processed. For instance, you'd think that multigrain bread is healthy. But the front of food packaging can be very misleading and cannot be trusted. Instead, you need to look at the back of the label. I found multigrain bread from one of India's oldest food companies packed with over a dozen or two undesirable ingredients. So, the multigrain bread that you toast up for a healthy breakfast comes under the NOVA category of ultra-processed foods. Mass-produced, pre-packaged bread is filled with junk, irrespective of whether it is whole wheat, whole grain or multigrain. A traditional loaf needs only four ingredients: flour, water, yeast and salt. Bread that is truly healthy is the one that is close to the original recipe. It is no wonder then that according to the Supreme Court in Ireland, Subway bread is not legally bread! In October 2020, the court ruled that because of the high level of sugar it contains, Subway's bread is legally closer to cake than bread! It cannot be denied that Subway's slogan '*Eat fresh*' fools us into believing that the food is healthy.

On the other hand, a samosa is often looked down upon as unhealthy and fattening because it is made from maida. As a matter of fact, when made at home, mixed with fat-burning spices like jeera, etc. and fried in good-quality filtered oil, the samosa is devoid of any ingredients characteristic of the ultra-processed food group. There isn't any compelling reason to think of it as harmful. Not that I am advocating that one should eat samosas all day or every day. With regard to grains, a bowl of khichri, for example, sits at the top of the hierarchy, as it is packed with more nutrients than a samosa. But is a samosa healthier than the pack of mass-produced bread picked up from a swanky speciality store? Hell yes!

## Junk in Disguise

Let's discuss a few more apparently clean foods and try to interpret what their label says.

1.  Nut milk alternatives: Cartons of almond milk, cashew milk lined up on the shelves of your neighbourhood supermarket scream 'health'. But to thicken, emulsify and preserve the milk, an additive called Carrageenan (E407) is used. There is evidence that Carrageenan is associated

with leaky gut, is highly inflammatory and toxic to the digestive tract. It has been found to cause cancer in lab rats.

2. Sugar-free delights: Ever asked yourself how the 'sugar-free' or 'no added sugar' desserts, frostings and sweets taste so sweet? They contain sugar alcohols (e.g., sorbitol, mannitol, xylitol). Though sugar alcohols are processed and commercially produced from sugars itself (such as from glucose in corn starch), marketers don't need to declare them as sugar and can safely label the foods as 'zero sugar' products.

3. Gluten-free innocence: Gluten, the name of a wheat protein that no one outside the scientific community knew of 20 years ago; but today, everyone seems to know its name! I will address whether you should go gluten-free or not in later chapters, but for now, you should know that many of the gluten-free products are filled with highly refined modified starches (tapioca or corn or potato flour), artificial sugars, inflammatory vegetable oils, food dyes, food stabilizers and gums. Just because something is labelled 'gluten-free' does not mean it is a healthy choice; it is still ultra-processed junk food.

4. Low-fat miracles: Food products labelled 'low fat' are in reality high in sugar. They contain trans-fats and end up having a very similar calorie count to the original product. Here's how: To maintain the taste and texture of the food that has been stripped of fats, manufacturers need to add or increase sugar in them. If you read the ingredients carefully, you will find that many low-fat products have as much sugar as a candy bar.

| NOVA Ultra-processed foods | Minimally processed homemade substitutes |
|---|---|
| Breakfast cereals, instant oats, muesli, cornflakes | Millet flakes, millet puffs, puffed rice (muri), rice flakes (chivda/poha) |
| Packaged chips | Potato, banana wafers |
| Ketchup, sauces and dips | Chutney |
| Energy bars, protein bars | Laddus |
| Processed meat like sausages, salami, canned meat, bacon | Fresh meat and fish |
| Mass-produced bread | Homemade bread, rotis, artisanal bread |
| Candies | Murabba |
| Mass-produced chocolates, ice creams, cakes | Mithai |
| Bhujia, namkeen, etc. | Homemade variety of the same |
| Colas and soft drinks | Sherbets |
| Biscuits, cookies, rusks | *Chikkis* |
| Fruit jams and jellies | Homemade fruit compote and fruit salsa |
| Refined cooking oil | Cold pressed/*kachhi ghaani* oils |

It should now be clear to you that what matters most about food is not calories or nutrients, but whether it has been cooked by a human being or a corporation. The quality of your food depends on who is cooking your food. The fact that there are often ingredients in the industrialized foods that don't 'have to' appear on the label adds to the challenge of sorting the good from the bad. *The thumb rule is to avoid foods that come in slick packaging with nutrition labels and long shelf lives.*

Modern diets consist of these edible food-like products or 'ingestibles', as I like to call them, whereas long-established traditional dietary patterns are based on *real* foods that are minimally-processed and freshly-prepared. The benefits of the latter have been proven as well; let me illustrate with an example. Villagers in Burkina Faso, a country in west Africa, have continued to retain their traditional practices of eating. They subsist on a diet of mostly millet, sorghum, beans and rice. In 2010, a group of Italian microbiologists compared the microbes the young villagers harboured with those of children who were being brought up on Western diets in Florence, Italy. The study revealed that compared to the Florentines, the otherwise poor villagers seemed wealthier in a way that science is only now beginning to appreciate. Despite their relative material poverty, these villagers had higher microbial diversity, whereas a lot of these bacteria were found to be lost in the Western human microbiota.

The good news is that the losses aren't permanent and can be reversed by correcting what we eat. *Eliminating ultra-processed foods and feeding your microbes with foods that your family has traditionally been eating over generations is an important first step towards this goal.*

## The Conflict between Healthy Food and Tasty Food

A common misconception about someone studying ancient Indian scriptures that focus on self-realization as the goal is that they need to abandon all ambitions for money and luxuries in life. The luxury car that you want to buy, the European holiday that you're dying to go on, in short, all the things that we seek for pleasure, comfort and enjoyment are categorically called *preyas* in the *Vedas*, literally meaning 'that which is pleasant to the senses'. And the pursuit of self-realization is called *shreyas*, translated as 'that which is the ultimate good'. No one is prohibited to choose preyas, as long as it does not hinder his pursuit of shreyas. So, while *brahmacharya*—recommended in the *Yoga Sutras*—is often misunderstood as celibacy, traditional scriptural texts do not suggest complete abstinence from sex. What it teaches is to practise monogamy over philandering—choosing pleasure but not overriding that which is ultimately good or right for us.

Similarly, when it comes to food, we must strive to establish the right balance between the shreyas—foods that are healthy and hence good for us—and the preyas—tasty foods that give us sensory pleasure but may or may not be good for us. Eating foods that you don't like isn't something you would do for very long. Your new way of eating has to be enjoyable and include the foods you like. The attitude new dieters have of *'kuch bhi kha kar wajan kam karna hai'* only leads to failure in the long term. On the other side are those who make short-term choices based on the need for a sensory fix. They keep their drawers filled with processed junk and insist that healthy food cannot be tasty: *'Do-char din ki zindagi, khao piyo mauj karo.'* Resorting to both the extremes is unhelpful. *Instead, we must learn to cultivate a balance; choose foods that are both good for us and that we actually like and enjoy eating as well.* And that's the whole point of TBBD. The meal plans and recipes that I am going to provide in the book will train your body to love a way of eating you never thought possible before. When you begin to incorporate these flavoursome, delectable meals and recipes that are also good for your health, it will help you create a balance between the shreyas and the preyas.

## The Second R: Right Quantity

'Is "mindful eating" the best way to watch how much we eat? You see, anything with a prefix "mindful" to it is the new cool these days!' *(Laughs)*

I had just finished my talk at the Federation of Indian Chambers of Commerce and Industry (FICCI) FLO in Mumbai and the floor has been opened to audience questions. 'As with any question on nutrition, it depends,' I replied.

Counting calories (or grams) is certainly outdated, unscientific and far from being the whole picture. And let's face it: For most people, it is tedious to measure everything before they put it into their mouths, because of which they often do not continue it for long. This makes the weight loss, if any, unsustainable and sets them up for weight gain, disease and failure.

I am all for eating mindfully. At the same time, mindful eating may not initially work for everyone. *Huh?* Let me explain.

'Mindful eating' or 'intuitive eating' is a self-regulating method that is based on tuning in to your body's hunger and fullness cues. But how are you supposed to listen to your fullness if you don't even have sensations of fullness? The release of hormones that makes it possible to have the appropriate hunger and satiation cues are highly influenced by gut microbes. So if your gut microbiota is out of whack, your fullness will be too!

## Gut Bacteria Affects Your Appetite

Ultimately, it is your feelings of hunger and satiation that control the amount of food that you eat; your new high-end fitness app just doesn't cut the mustard. And your appetite is in turn regulated by several hormones. Multiple studies have shown that disturbances in the gut microbiome interfere with the action of these hormones, hampering the body's ability to feel satiated; this subsequently leads to overeating. On the contrary, when you eat foods that your gut microbes love, they send out 'happy' messages, cranking up the body's production of satiation-signal transmitters in the right amounts; this makes you feel satisfied and helps you lose weight. Now you know why you almost always end up binge-eating the (un)happy meal at an American fast food restaurant chain, but not on a meal of, say, *bhakri and saag*.

Highly processed diets cause people to eat more because it antagonizes the microbiota, which encourage overeating. Not only this, when you have been eating unhealthy foods for some time, the resultant bacterial mixture in the gut also asks the brain to supply more of the same foods. Your microbiome helps to generate cravings for more unhealthy foods to keep the bacterial mixture in the gut as it is. So, when you crave chips and colas after being on a diet for three days, perhaps it's your microbes telling you to go for it. Eventually, you find yourself caught in a vicious circle: You try to eat healthy to feed your microbes well, but behind the scenes, the microbes are guiding your uncontrolled cravings for junk and unhealthy foods, making it difficult for you to course-correct. Intuitive eating or mindful eating would be of little help in this situation.

Listening to your hunger and fullness is certainly a great self-regulating method to manage your food intake and identify the right amount of food for your body. It's a skill that takes practice, and I will explain how you can master it.

However, I am sure you will agree that you can self-terminate a meal only when there is a sense of feeling full. After all, you can listen to 'something' only when there is a 'something' to listen to, right? That's why, out of the three phases of TBBD, the first is designed to completely reboot your gut ecosystem and remove microbes that trigger undeniable cravings. A few of you may find it restrictive (although phase 1 is only for two weeks, remember), but it goes a long way towards making intuitive eating far easier for the long haul. Unlike others who try eating mindfully but fail to succeed at it, when you follow TBBD, you will be able to listen or tune in to your stomach with ease, simply because your gut will tell you when you have had enough to eat.

## The SPAR Technique

Did you know that the practice of mindfulness that has caught on like wildfire in recent times originated from ancient Indian culture? For instance, the *Vedas* consider the partaking of food to be a *'yagya'* or spiritual sacrifice. According to the *Chandogya Upanishad*, when we eat, we 'offer' food into our digestive fire, *'Agni',* and in turn receive a great blessing of abundance and good health as *'prasad'*. Strikingly different from the modern world that views food as a commodity, the ancient Vedic culture revered food as an oblation to the sacred fire of our bellies. When food is consumed with this spiritual attitude, one can focus on the act of eating instead of indulging in other tasks while eating, and can, therefore, enjoy good health.

Based on both our ancient wisdom and modern-day science, 'SPAR' is a basic technique that I have developed to train my clients to be more mindful. I would like you to employ it every day as soon as you embark on your 10-week TBBD journey. It will help you build fundamental eating skills that you can then use forever.

S—Strive for a Quiet, Stress-Free Eating Environment

Mindfulness is simply being in a state of attentive, moment-to-moment awareness. When it comes to mindful eating, a great starting point is creating an environment conducive to it. Here's how.

a)  Sit down to eat: Educating an adult to sit down for his meals is almost like training him to flush the toilet after use. Yes, it's really that basic. But it seems that in our fast-paced lifestyles, it's the simple things that are oddly far too overlooked. So, let me say it again, 'You have to sit down to eat.' This means you can't eat while walking or standing, and the worst I have come across is lying down and eating. Eat in a clean place that is free from clutter. Avoid taking meals at your work desk, on the bed, on the couch and in your car (you got that right, you shouldn't drive while eating).

b) Stop multitasking: We are living in an age where multitasking is equated with efficiency and is looked upon as a virtue. In reality, people do not multitask, they only switch tasks. This, by the way, not only makes you inefficient but is also one of the most stressful things to do. When it comes to mealtimes, stress of any kind compromises the entire digestive process. This means you will not only extract lesser nutrition from your food, but the food itself will take longer to digest, thereby putting the gut under unnecessary strain. So, at least while you are eating, I want you to try mono-tasking. When you eat, just eat. Turn off your phones, put away your reading material, switch off your TV and media. Passive entertainment while you eat results in overeating. Think of the huge bucket of popcorn that you finish while watching a movie. Now imagine yourself eating it in your living room while doing nothing else. Will you be able to finish it? I rest my case.

c) Keep your mind relaxed: A calm and peaceful atmosphere is imperative while we eat. Digestion occurs most effectively when your parasympathetic nervous system is dominant in your body (you will learn about this system in Chapter 8). This simply means that someone who is pleasantly relaxed during the act of eating is a more efficient digester than someone who is engaged in heated discussions or is upset while eating.

P—Pay Attention as You Eat

Mindful eating is a consciousness-based approach to health that requires you to bring your full attention to the event of eating. This is facilitated by taking small bites of food and chewing it well. Taking time to finish your meal—around 15 to 20 minutes— and chewing it thoroughly will help you savour the food and focus on its flavours and textures. It also allows the food to be mixed well with the enzyme-filled saliva that partially breaks down food in your mouth. Go slow, take breaks throughout the meal. Simply sit and breathe. Avoid gulping down your food.

A—Assess Your Level of Fullness

When we eat, we are more inclined to finish what is on the plate rather than finishing because our stomachs have had enough to eat. That is why it is worth pausing throughout your meal to assess your state of satiation. The idea is to feel satisfied, but not stuffed. You should stop eating when you know that you can eat more, but you would be okay if you stopped. Avoid going beyond the level of comfort after which you start feeling heavy and lethargic, or at which you feel you cannot eat anymore. Remember, you can eat the healthiest food in the world, but if you overeat, the same food that was supposed to nourish you can create toxicity in your body.

R—Retire Briefly after Each Meal

Avoid rushing into things the moment you finish eating. The emails, phone calls or household chores may need your attention, but they can wait. I strongly advise you to take a short, gentle walk—about 10 to 20 minutes—even if its inside your home or office space after each meal. For a post-lunch afternoon nap, lie down on your left side, or if you are at work, recline in your chair for 10 to 15 minutes, but only after you have taken the stroll.

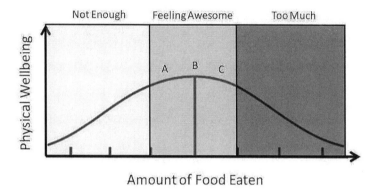

Illustration 1: Moderation—The Name of the Game

## The Third R: Right Timing

For decades, we have been told that the quantity and the type of food we consume determine our weight and susceptibility to diseases. But both Ayurveda and modern science suggest that in addition to what and how much we eat, *when* we eat also matters. The timing of your meals is an important factor that decides whether you have a healthy, fat-burning microbiome or an unhealthy, fat-forming one. That's because your body receives food differently depending on a variety of factors, including, you guessed it, the time of day.

Circadian Clock: What Is It and Why Is It Important?

Ask a new (and sleepless) parent about how baffling and
disorganized a newborn's sleep schedule is. A newborn sleeps
in short bouts, never for long, and at seemingly random times
throughout the day and night. Not only this, new parents
usually feed their child up to a dozen times a day, at completely
random times. Ever wondered why? That's because very
young babies have not fully developed their *circadian clock*—or
biological clock—yet. It is only after a few months that their
bodies actually pick up a clock and sanity comes back to the
parents' life.

Not too different from the clock on your cell phone,
your circadian clock is a real, built-into-your-body 24-hour
clock. Think of the many musicians in an orchestra. They
take cues from the conductor, which allows them to keep
time, helps them play in a synchronized way, and not resort
to their individual styles. Likewise, the synchrony between
the master clock in your brain and the individual clocks in
each cell is directly influenced by environmental cues, the
main cue being sunlight. Your natural circadian rhythm is the
innate timekeeping that regulates the timing of almost every
physiological process in your body; for example, it helps you
know when to wake up, when to eat, when to sleep and
when to release certain biochemicals that can impact your
metabolism, mood and immune system. And this circadian
rhythm is governed by the rising and setting of the sun.

Almost all animals have evolved to respond to the solar
day's cues by eating and staying active during daylight, and
fasting and sleeping during darkness. But human beings are

the only ones who can consciously choose to ignore them. We stay up late at night and eat whenever we want. This weakens our clock and disrupts the circadian rhythm. When these disruptions continue for weeks at a time, our health gets affected. A disrupted body clock has been called the mother of all maladies, and is associated with obesity, heart disease, sleep disorders, diabetes, reproductive disorders, inflammation, cancer and increased risk of depression and anxiety.

## Time Your Diet to Your Circadian Clock

Aligning your food intake with your circadian rhythm has potential health benefits not only against dysbiosis, obesity and inflammation, but also for sleep, muscle endurance, etc. So how do you do it? You can harness the power of your body's circadian rhythm by following these four simple rules that line up with both Ayurvedic principles and Western science.

### Eat with the Sun

If, like me, you have lived away from home, either during college or at any other point in your life, you will surely agree that it is the most enriching experience in one's life. However, students often gain weight during their first year of living away from their parents' home. In the United States, they call this phenomenon the 'freshman 15', referring to the 15 pounds young adults typically accumulate during their freshman year. Circadian biologist and author Satchidananda Panda from Salk Institute in San Diego suspects circadian disruption in the students to be the primary reason behind the weight gain.

Once they leave home, young students typically do not sleep until late at night, and it results in late-night eating. This extends the overall window of time in which they consume food—their 'eating' window. Additionally, they still need to get up for classes the next morning, and this—assuming they eat breakfast—further reduces the length of their night-time fast or fasting window. It's not just these students; most of us have late dinners, often till 10 p.m. The majority of people eat over the course of 15 or more hours each day, and this makes them prone to inflammation, weight gain and diseases. This was shown in a landmark study conducted by Dr Panda in 2012. He along with his colleagues gave one set of mice free access—at any time of day or night—to fatty, sugary foods, while another group was allowed to consume the same food, and the same number of calories, within a 12-hour window during their 'daytime'. They found that despite eating the same foods, the mice that were placed on a time-restricted eating schedule were protected from diseases, unlike the other group that became obese and diabetic within a few weeks. The fact that the diseased mice, when put on scheduled feeding, reversed their diseases without the use of medicines or change in diet, speaks volumes about the importance of right timings in keeping you lean, fit and healthy.

*Wake up early and feed yourself soon after you wake up.* It all starts with the sun. Our circadian rhythm expects us to eat during the day when the sun is shining. The first light of morning resets the master clock in our brain, and similarly, the first meal of the morning resets all other organ clocks. By having a hot, herbal drink (recipes given in Chapter 10) soon after you wake up, you reinforce the message that it is morning to the clocks in our liver and digestive system. This will keep your circadian clock running in synchrony.

*Eat within a window of maximum 12 hours.* Once you have taken your first morning drink, the body can efficiently process food for the next 12 hours at best. For example, if you wake up and have your first meal by 7 a.m., then you must take your last meal latest by 7 p.m.

*Keep a 12-hour fast after your last meal.* The circadian rhythm diet isn't about restricted eating. It's about getting back to a more natural cycle where you don't eat at night, but instead, eat when the sun is up. This is when your body wants you to eat, and this is how ancestors lived. Ancient Chinese medics firmly held that one should eat in harmony with the sun, because they believed that the flow of energy around the body is in parallel with the sun's movements. The Jains in India have been known to finish eating the last meal before sunset. Prior to the invention of the electric light, humans were forced to sleep early and finish all their food during daytime. And science has found reasons showing that they were doing it right!

Remember the 'housekeeper' of your digestive tract, the migrating motor complex or MMC from Chapter 3? When you eat an early dinner, the cleansing wave weeds bugs out of your small bowel. However, the MMC is diminished and not active at night. As a result, eating too late in the evening causes a build-up of bacteria and organisms in your small intestine, simply because the housekeeper is fast asleep. This sets the stage for SIBO, dysbiosis and weight gain. Food eaten late at night, even if it's healthy, turns out to be junk for the body. So, eat an early dinner, and thereafter, keep 12 hours of fast between that last meal of your day and the first of the next day. (You can, however, have herbal tea or milk after dinner if you feel hungry during the fasting window.) For example, if you take your last meal by 7 p.m., then you should fast until 7 a.m. the next morning. Since you will be sleeping for most of it, it's really not that difficult.

## Make Lunch the Biggest Meal of Your Day

'Arre, but isn't this a famous proverb, "Eat breakfast like a king, lunch like a prince, and dinner like a pauper?"'

Taapsee and I had just begun working together. Our topic of discussion was her lunch that was missing from her daily routine. Missing because she was going by the popular saying and believed in eating a king-size breakfast. Consequently, she was never hungry until late afternoon, i.e., 3–4 p.m. When we started out, one of the first things I told her to correct was making lunch the most important meal of the day, not breakfast.

I know a lot of people go by this proverb, but a heavy breakfast typically leads to skimping on lunch and then gorging at dinner to make up for all the calories not consumed during the day. Interestingly, many studies have shown that 75 per cent of what we eat in a day should be consumed before 3 p.m. Late lunches and big dinners are damaging to both weight loss efforts and health, even if the total calories consumed in a day are the same. Our modern lifestyles are often at the mercy of our work schedules, and so we consume more food in the first three hours of the evening after work, between 6 and 9 p.m., than we eat in the first eight hours of the day.

Our organ clocks favour different biochemical reactions at different times of the day. This allows our internal organs to switch tasks and recuperate. Our liver, for example, is very good at metabolizing food early in the day, but it cannot process a big meal in the evening and night. When you eat contrary to this rhythm, our digestive systems have less time to recuperate, simply because you cannot repair a highway when the traffic is still moving. Moreover, human studies have shown that people who eat the most calories at lunch tend to lose more weight than people who eat most of their calories for breakfast or late in the day. *That's because your biggest meal of the day should be when the sun is at its peak, and that happens to be midday.* This also means that it's worth making a social shift and steering your feasts and get-togethers towards lunch instead of an evening party.

I recommend that you follow the schedule given below on a day-to-day basis. Eating this way will make you feel more satisfied, more energetic and less hungry throughout the day. It will help reduce fat mass, lower glucose levels and improve insulin sensitivity.

Breakfast: latest by 9 a.m. – Light, small meal
Lunch: between 11 a.m. and 1 p.m. – Main, big meal
Dinner: latest by 7 p.m. – Light, small meal

Eat but Don't Graze

One of the reasons why my clients love me is because my diets are eating-centric. Unlike most others, I don't ask you to deprive yourself of food. Having said that, eating isn't the same as grazing. Your MMC requires a few hours of fasting so that it can complete its housekeeping duties properly. If you eat even a small snack within that fasting window, the MMC stops doing its job. Fasting for at least two to three hours between meals is crucial, as it lets the MMC finish its cycle and prepare your body to handle the digestive process of the next meal. *A good guideline, although not a hard-and-fast rule, is to eat three meals (breakfast, lunch, dinner) and one mid-meal in between.* Such a pattern will also prevent your appetite and blood sugar from moving wildly up and down like a roller coaster. Many a time, I have seen that people who intend to lose weight plan their meals and eat every two hours even when they're not hungry. While it is good to plan your meals ahead, ensure you don't end up eating for the sake of it. *Eat only when you feel hungry.* By the end of the 10 weeks of TBBD, you will see that you no longer have sugar cravings or the urge to graze continuously. You will eat, but not graze.

Maintain Regular Meal Timings

Your body loves consistency. If that wasn't the case, then jetlag wouldn't have existed. Travelling across time zones causes us to fall out of sync with our usual routine. Consequently, we feel awkward and uncomfortable. The grogginess we feel is because there's a conflict between what our internal time says and what the external time is. Similarly, when we eat at irregular times on a daily basis, when we randomly change our meal timings from day to day, our gut clocks and circadian clocks get confused and we feel tired. *This timing conflict is what circadian scientists term 'metabolic jetlag'.* In the long term, metabolic jetlag increases our risk of obesity and various diseases.

The advantage of all these circadian clocks is that they help us anticipate and prepare for regular events in our environment, such as the arrival of food. Suppose you eat breakfast at 9 a.m. every day. An hour before, your pancreas, liver and gut will start making digestive juices in anticipation of the breakfast ahead. But because it's the weekend, let's say you decide to eat late, at a different time. The food you eat will not encounter the same kind of digestive juices that were present earlier, simply because you missed the bus. Your digestive organs think that they're in a different time zone and try to adapt to the new time. But then, along comes Monday, and there's a shift in timing again, causing the food to arrive when the body isn't ready.

This timing conflict or metabolic jetlag isn't a problem if it's just an occasional change in routine, but if it's a regular occurrence, it may have longer-term consequences for your health. If you show up for work 30 minutes late occasionally, it may not matter, but if it becomes a frequent habit, it will land you in trouble, right? Unfortunately, most of the time, we take our work more seriously than our meals and our health, ignoring the fundamental fact that only if we keep ourselves healthy will we be armed to work better and for more years.

Keeping a regular routine of eating is the most powerful way to nurture and sustain a robust circadian clock in our brain and body. *Take your meals at roughly the same time daily, including weekends and holidays.* Having a consistent, regular schedule for eating also helps keep cravings at bay and avoid overeating.

# PHASE 1

## Reboot and Remove

## Weeks 1–2

5

# Weeding the Lawn

As microbiome science gains popularity, more and more people are looking to include foods in their diet that will help in microbiome rewilding. 'Eat a diverse diet, eat lots of fermented foods, maybe take probiotics, enzymes or "gut healing" supplements'—all these may be great advice, but they are not helpful when the microbiome is already out of balance. In fact, these foods may just add fuel to the fire and cause further problems. The strategy for maintaining a healthy gut is very different from what it takes to repair dysfunction.

So, before we step into phase 2 of TBBD, during which we repopulate and reseed the gut with beneficial, friendly bacteria found in fermented foods, we will first weed out the digestive tract in phase 1 and remove the pathogenic bugs that cause weight gain and inflammatory symptoms in the body. This will help prepare the gut for phase 2. Simply following a restricted diet—gluten-free, dairy-free, keto, etc.—will do *nothing* to actually wipe out the bad microbes and the consequent inflammation. It instead requires a stepwise action plan, starting with rebooting the ecosystem in your gut.

## Rebooting Your Gut Ecosystem—Day 0

Remember Kritika, Taapsee Pannu's character in *Mission Mangal*? She was told that a switch-off–switch-on tactic always works, and that's exactly how she saved the satellite when it lost communication with her team. Space science isn't my cup of tea, but when it comes to food science, let me assure you that switch-off–switch-on does work! Rebooting your body will help jump-start your weight loss, boost metabolism and lower inflammation. There are two methods you can choose from, and if neither method really tickle your fancy, then feel free to bunk them and straight away head to 'Getting Started: Weeks 1–2'.

## Method 1: Optional 24-hour Yogic Cleanse

One fine afternoon, my office received a call from someone who introduced himself as Nayanthara's manager. Almost simultaneously, I received a text from Taapsee that read, 'Hey, Nayanthara is trying to get in touch with you.' I realized Nayanthara was one of those people who did not need an introduction, but unfortunately, I was clueless about who she is. My office dashed over to her Wikipedia page, which said that she was referred to as 'the *lady superstar* of south Indian cinema'. It also said she was 'the only South Indian female actor to have made it to the *Forbes India* "Celebrity 100", 2018 list'. 'Woohoo!' I exclaimed, and replied to Taapsee's text, 'Yes, will connect with her soon!'

Every time I travel to the southern part of our country for attending yoga courses, I am overwhelmed at how it feels like another world altogether. For example, if you are eating at a local restaurant in Delhi, Mumbai, Kolkata or any city up north, calling to your server requires only choosing between names like 'boss' or 'bhaiya'. But south India is different. You have to arm yourself with special language skills to find your way there. And this time, realizing how anonymous the south Indian film industry was to me compared to our Hindi film industry, I was left surprised even more.

When I spoke to Nayanthara, I found her extremely humble in spite of her superstar status. She was also very clear on what she wanted. She wanted to lose weight for a particular role in a film. Her shoots were to start soon and she wanted to knock off at least a few kilos before that, at the same time making sure it was done in a sensible and sustainable manner. Since her body had gone through so many diets in the past, I knew she would need a complete reboot to begin with. So I asked her to start with 'kunjar kriyā'. Huh, what's that?

The *Hatha Yoga Pradipīkā*, one among the most influential surviving texts on yoga, prescribes a set of six cleansing techniques called '*shatkriyas*' or '*shatkarmas*' that are known to have astonishing pro-health effects on the body. One of the shatkriyas that I recommended to Nayanthara—and that I recommend to you as well—is the kunjar kriyā. It helps detoxify and remove waste matter and toxins accumulated in your digestive tract.

Nayanthara started with the kriyā and then followed the two-week diet in phase 1 of TBBD. At the end of two weeks, she was a couple of kilos lighter in her body and several tonnes lighter in her mind. 'I can't believe this! Losing weight looked impossible even a few weeks back. Thanks for making this happen, Munmun,' she said. Till date, I plan her meals around the core principles of TBBD. Thanks to her discipline and commitment, not only has she lost a huge amount of weight, but she has also been able to sustain that weight loss for over a year.

Technique

Kunjar kriyā is performed by drinking lukewarm salt water up to the point where you feel like throwing up. The salt dissolves any mucus that may have accumulated in the stomach and dilutes the excess acid. The water that you throw up rids you of all this waste, but it does not have the unpleasant nausea and bad smell associated with vomiting. The water is usually clean, comes out quickly and easily, and leaves you feeling light, fresh and clean inside. Here's how you do it.

1.  Prepare saline, tepid water. Add roughly one teaspoon of salt—Himalayan pink salt is recommended—per litre. The water should be as salty as your tear drops.
2.  Drink four to eight glasses of this water in large gulps, in quick succession, up to the point where you feel you cannot drink any more.
3.  Either bend forward from a standing position or squat. You may just throw up automatically. If not, press your stomach with one hand and put two fingers of your other hand down your throat. This will create the urge to vomit, and the water will be thrown back out in a series

of quick gushes. Continue till you feel you cannot throw up anymore.

Important Dos and Don'ts

1.  The kriyā should be done first thing in the morning on a completely empty stomach. The best time to do it is early morning, between 6 and 6.30 a.m.

2.  I advise you do it over a weekend when you are not overstressed with work and daily routines. Also, you may need to stay close to your bathroom for the first few hours of the morning.

3.  During the 10-week programme, you will do this kriyā only once—the day before you begin the 10-week diet. If you would like to continue it henceforth, you can do it as frequently as once every one or two weeks. Please note that it is never done daily.

4.  Avoid having a late and heavy dinner the night before. Eat an early and light dinner. A few options are daliya porridge, rice kanji, khichri, etc. Avoid non-vegetarian feasts, fried foods, etc. the previous night.

5.  Avoid all high-intensity exercises during the day of the kriyā. Light stretches, low-intensity yoga or cardio is fine. Deep breathing and meditation can also be practised.

6.  Contra-indications or Limitations: Do not practise the kriyā if you have eating disorders like bulimia nervosa or anorexia nervosa, etc., pregnancy, high blood pressure, heart disease, diabetes with eye problems, gastric or duodenal ulcers, hernia or if you are in post-surgery recuperation or during fever and respiratory infections.

7. On the day of the cleanse, it is extremely beneficial, although not mandatory, to fast for the rest of the day. If you wish to eat, then after the kriyā, wait for at least 30 minutes before you eat the first meal. Traditionally, khichri with lots of cow ghee is eaten as the first meal after the cleanse. *Consume light, easily digestible, vegetarian food with no or minimum salt and spices throughout the day.* Here's a sample meal plan that you may follow.

**Table 1: Sample Meal Plan (Kunjar Kriya Day)**

| Meals | Meal plan |
|---|---|
| Meal One—Breakfast | Khichri/Rice kanji/Ven pongal/ Daliya porridge |
| Meal Two—Lunch | Rice, dal, sabzi/Roti, sabzi |
| Meal Three—Late afternoon | Vegetable soup/Fruit/Buttermilk/ Coconut water |
| Meal Four—Dinner | Khichri/Rice kanji/Ven pongal/ Daliya porridge |
| Meal Five—Bedtime (if hungry) | Milk |

## Method 2: Optional 24-hour Fast

Here's an alternative. Instead of the yogic cleanse, you can choose to fast for a day. You may also choose to do the cleanse first and then fast for the rest of the day. But why a fast?

You now know that an overweight or obese state is characterized by chronic inflammation. Short-term (24-hour) fasting induces an anti-inflammatory effect on the body. It boosts metabolism, enhances detoxification and accelerates weight loss. Because food is not ingested during a fasting state, your digestive system gets adequate rest and the body gets enough time to cleanse and eliminate accumulated toxins and wastes. Fasting for a short period like this can power up the body's internal antioxidant network and also strengthen your immunity. No wonder that for centuries, fasting has been an integral part of various cultures and faiths, and is often endorsed as a means to reboot the body physically, mentally, emotionally and spiritually.

Technique

The duration of the fast I recommend is 24 hours. Here are three fasting protocols that you can choose from, depending on what you find most comfortable.

1. Restrict solid foods. Consume only liquids every few hours in the form of warm water, herbal teas, vegetable broths or lentil soups, vegetable juices, coconut water, diluted fruit juices, homemade sherbets like nimbu sherbet, etc.
2. Avoid all foods, both solids and liquids, and drink water only.
3. Avoid both food and water.

Important Dos and Don'ts

1. If you are currently under any medication, speak with your doctor before beginning a fasting protocol.
2. Avoid all high-intensity exercises. Light stretches, low-intensity yoga or cardio is fine. Deep breathing and meditation can also be practised.

3.  Fasting isn't the same as starvation. In fasting, one wilfully gives up food for the betterment of physical and mental health. If you find yourself only thinking of food, having strong cravings and waiting for the fast to be over, then it is better not to fast, as it won't benefit you.

4.  During the 10-week programme, you will fast only once—the day before you begin the 10-week diet of TBBD. If you would like to continue it henceforth, you can do it as frequently as once every week to once every month. Please be aware that fasting every other day or most days of the week can have damaging side effects.

5.  Take up fasting on a day—maybe over a weekend—when you are not overstressed with work and daily routines. It should not be done during a stressful time or when you have too many obligations to fulfil.

Intermittent Fasting: Ancient Practice or Modern Trend?

The most interesting phone conversations you will ever witness are those between my office and the inquiry calls we receive. *What's trending in the market?* My team and I would never know unless we hear them earnestly asking for it: 'Do you give keto diet plans?' 'What about alkaline diet?'

Sanjay from Gurgaon, a chartered accountant by profession, called up and said, 'I am looking to lose weight. I want an intermittent fasting plan.' My team had just begun to respond, 'Hi Sanjay, we don't really give out intermittent fasting plans. The reason being—' 'Oh come on, sorry to interrupt but I have been following Munmun on Instagram and she has just spoken about the benefits of one-day fasts at every season change. Pretty much the same thing, isn't it? (*Laughs*) Look, I have been reading a lot about the benefits of intermittent fasting and I am pretty convinced about it. If she can give me a plan accordingly, I will immediately sign up.'

Intermittent fasting is the diet of the moment. It is the latest health trend in the weight loss industry. Experts often try to validate it by referring to fasting as an ancient way of body cleansing that has been practised for thousands of years. Its roots, some say, can be traced to the days of the sages, and it is the reason for their longevity. In India, fasting has been a part of most religious customs, with some people fasting once a week and some on full moon days. Basically, if something is good, more of it will be better, right? At least that's the funda the health industry works on. That's why the ancient way of thoughtful fasting has been meticulously pushed aside to give way to obsessive fasting.

As a result, today, there are many different methods you can choose from—from extreme versions that require going several days without food to the 5:2 pattern (eating for five days and fasting for two days in a week) to alternate day fasting (ADF), where one is supposed to fast every alternate day, to the two-meals-a-day fasting plan. But just like eating more and more protein cannot endlessly improve muscle growth, fasting longer and more often does not endlessly improve your health and weight loss outcomes. If a 24-hour fast is good for you, it doesn't imply that a 48-hour fast will necessarily be better. At some point, more is simply pointless and can, in fact, have opposite and deleterious effects.

'Huh, so what's the real deal? Fasting or no fasting?' Let me explain.

To call intermittent fasting ancient wisdom is like calling the virtual battleground game PUBG a real cross-border war. Though they may look similar on the surface, they differ in intention (why) and preparation (how).

Why?

While intermittent fasting is an offshoot of the modern weight-loss industry promising quick detox and body transformations, the actual intention behind the age-old wisdom of fasting was spiritual upliftment. The reason why fasts have traditionally been observed on select auspicious occasions or periods— Ekadashi, Navratri, Lent, Ramzan, etc.—is because people have been found to be most receptive to spiritual growth during these periods.

Yogic textbooks talk about *brahmacharya* (control of sensual desires) and *tapas* (austerity) as important prerequisites (called *yama* and *niyama*) for a person's spiritual progress. Fasting acts as a means to practise that self-control over your sense organs, particularly of taste, and to not seek stimulation through them. It teaches you tapas by helping you realize that it is not only possible but completely OK to rid yourself of attachments you otherwise hold essential. Hence, you forego sleep during Shivratri, and wilfully renounce food during fasts. Fasting is thus a practice of self-discipline that aims to bring about self-refinement. It was not meant for detox of the body per se, but rather the detox of the fluctuations of the mind and senses. Once that happens, it helps develop *ojas* (vigour) and your physical health and body benefits from it too, including weight loss!

But when you spend all your fasting time thinking about food, or try to keep yourself stimulated by constantly having tea or coffee (irrespective of whether it is green tea or bullet coffee), you lose the very essence of fasting. *When fasting is enforced upon you, either by yourself or by your health expert, and you are desperate to go back to food, then it is called suppression, not renunciation.* We tend to believe that food is the only thing that feeds us, but it isn't. Your thoughts, feelings and emotions also feed your body and mind. So if you are on a fast, but you are stressed, angry and frustrated because of a hungry belly and anxious to start your eating window, then you are still feeding toxins to your body. Fasting, therefore, should be observed with a conscious intent otherwise it would be like a marriage that lacks love, trust and respect. The couple can live together, have children together, but live a very unhappy life simply because the essence of marriage, the basic fabric or intent, is absent.

How?

Fasting must always be practised under the right circumstances and in the right state of mind. In the days of yore, if one took up a fast, he would stop routine activities and instead spend his day chanting, praying and meditating. The idea was to turn the mind inwards, not to the world outside. Instead of his attention jumping through several external objects, it was made to stick to one place (one-pointedness of attention, called chitta ekagrata). Consequently, the mind stayed tranquil.

Scientifically speaking, when you devote yourself to such calming practices, your body and mind turn into an efficient machine. This is attributed to the increase of parasympathetic activity (you will read about this in Chapter 8). Through concentration and breathing techniques, you can lower your metabolism rate. You will breathe deeper but take fewer breaths in a minute. Once the breath rate goes down, the number of thoughts running around in your brain also reduces drastically. As a result, you expend lesser energy throughout the day. Your brain is the most metabolically active tissue in your body; it requires 16 times more energy than your muscles (that's why exercising your brain in a game of Sudoku may be more rewarding for weight loss than flexing your biceps in a gym!). When your body's requirements decrease, you need a much lesser food intake, and so fasting can be practised with ease. On the other hand, it is a known fact that breathing and meditation practices are done better on a lighter stomach than a full one. In short, the prayers, chanting, worship and meditation help you to function on a lesser intake of fuel (food), and eating lesser in turn enables you to perform these practices better. A symbiotic relationship is there if you look at it carefully.

On the contrary, when you arbitrarily take up an intermittent fast, your mind is not given the time and place to de-stress. Imagine returning from work and being stuck in traffic. Your cortisol levels increase and you start craving something sweet or salty. In such a frame of mind, your intermittent fasting plan can only be a disaster, to say the least. When you approach fasting correctly, your body will feel relaxed and light, your mind will have increased clarity and you are bound to feel more energetic. The reason why a lot of people end up instead with acidity, indigestion, lack of energy, headaches and drowsiness during fasts is because they do not spend much time preparing the mind and body for the fasting process. The right food in the right proportion with the right attitude always matters, but it matters the most during states of fasting for you to actually benefit from it.

My Conclusion

Fasting is a fantastic tool that can help you get better and healthier. But do not overdo it and get obsessive about it. Undertake it on days when you can withdraw at least partially from your daily routine of work, household chores, traffics, deadlines, etc., and instead spend some time doing any spiritual practices that can help calm your mind. Since our modern lifestyle does not allow us to do this very often, the age-old way of fasting once a week, once every fortnight, once each month or on certain auspicious periods is the best way to time the frequency of your fasts. And most importantly, do not fast if you do not feel like it or if you think you are not ready for it!

## Getting Started: Weeks 1–2

Cleanse the Intestines

A diverse gut microbiota is synonymous to good health. An incredibly beautiful and healthy ecosystem is one that has many different strains and many different communities of both helpful and noxious bacteria. The name of the game isn't removing all the bad bugs completely. Of course you want to have plenty of the good bugs in your gut, but some of the bad guys are also needed, because your immune system must train and learn from those pathogenic bacteria. Those who take competitive exams know that to give a good answer in an actual interview, it is only wise that they learn the skill first in a mock interview. The harmful bacteria should, of course, not take over the whole gut and outnumber the good ones. That's when they cause diseases. A pathogen count of 2 to 5 per cent is termed absolutely normal and according to microbiologists, this is where we get the best balance.

The natural antimicrobial foods and supplements that we will use in phase 1 will help kill the harmful, inflammation-causing bacteria but not completely wipe them off. On the other hand, bad bacteria use a lot of inflammatory molecules to survive in the gut. The inflammatory by-products are their feed. If we consume more of anti-inflammatory foods and herbs, the microbes will not have enough inflammation to thrive on and will perish. Hence, by using antimicrobial and anti-inflammatory foods together, we will weed out the harmful bacteria, and only then can we introduce beneficial, fat-burning bugs in phase 2. The bugs will then have the most pristine environment to thrive.

## The Lymphatic System—Your Body's Overlooked Detox Hero

We all know about our circulatory system, but few people know that there are twice as many lymph vessels as there are blood vessels in our body. These lymph vessels carry a clear fluid called lymph and comprise the lymphatic system, which is known to be our body's immune and detox system hero. As the lymph moves around the body, it collects cellular waste, debris, disease-causing pathogens, toxic matter as well as cancer cells. The lymph itself is filled with immune cells that help protect against foreign invaders.

The lymphatic system is your body's garbage collector. So, when the lymph does not flow well, you can end up with an accumulation of waste and toxins that can antagonize a healthy metabolism and weight. Weight gain and belly fat, puffiness in the eyes or face, swelling in the fingers (tight rings) or ankles, bloating, water retention, soreness or stiffness upon waking, tenderness in breasts, cellulite, sinus infections, constipation and fatigue are a few signs that tell you that the lymphatic fluid may not be moving around effectively in your body.

### Here's How You Can Encourage Lymph Drainage

As we start phase 1, your lymphatic system should keep up with the demands of removing toxic waste from your body. Here are some easy activities that you can incorporate into your day to help 'move' and drain the lymph, because unlike blood, which is pumped around by your heart, the lymphatic system has no built-in pump.

1. Movement: It is well known that exercise and movement stimulate lymphatic flow. Movement and muscle

contraction exert pressure on the lymphatic vessels and push the health-promoting and immune-enhancing lymphatic fluid around. So, one of the best things that anyone can do is to be more active.

2. Deep breathing: The role of breath in powering up the lymphatic system has been identified recently. Now scientists know that deep breathing can improve lymph flow. In Chapter 8, I have provided deep breathing techniques that you can incorporate into your daily life.

3. Massage: Since lymph vessels sit right beneath the surface of the skin, a few minutes of massage every day can enhance lymphatic flow, aid in detoxification and promote relaxation. A self-massage with warm, cold-pressed oils (almond and sesame oil in winters, coconut oil in summers) helps optimize lymph flow. Warm the oil by immersing its container in hot water. After the massage, let the oil stay on your skin for 15 to 30 minutes, and follow it up with a warm shower or bath. An alternative to oil massage is dry skin-brushing. Brushes made with natural bristles are available especially for this practice. Simply brush your skin gently before bathing. This will help remove dead skin cells as well as increase lymphatic flow.

4. Stay hydrated: Drinking lots of water each day helps to continually flush toxins. There's also evidence that increased water consumption can spur weight loss. A good way to assess your intake is to check your urine colour. Make sure it is clear and colourless.

## Supplements for Phase 1

To correct dysbiosis and give a hard push to get the 'bad life' out of you, I highly recommend the use of a few herbal supplements in addition to the diet. In my practice, I've had pretty good success combining an anti-inflammatory diet with the antimicrobial agents mentioned below to help fight against pathogenic bugs and improve intestinal microbial composition.

Unlike pharmaceutical antibiotics, herbs offer a more sustainable and safe way of removing unhealthy bacteria over a long period of time. Conventional antibiotics tend to wipe out lots of beneficial bacteria, and not kill all the bad. This gives the bad bugs an opportunity to over-colonize once the competition is wiped out. In fact, antibiotics themselves are often a main contributor to the gut microbiome dysbiosis in the first place. Herbal products of higher, medicinal plants, on the other hand, selectively kill pathogenic and overgrown bacteria, while providing food that boosts beneficial bacteria and promotes bacterial diversity. This makes these products more effective and less detrimental to commensal flora than a pharmaceutical antibiotic.

The continuous emergence of multidrug-resistant (MDR) bacteria due to the indiscriminate use of modern antibiotic drugs in recent years has become a global public health problem. Fortunately, there are a few herbal preparations that no pathogen has learned to resist, despite thousands of years of their continual use in humans. Medicinal plants are safe and cheap, and they affect a wide range of microorganisms without having the side effects that are often associated with conventional antibiotics. Hence, in addition to diet, I recommend the use of these supplements. In phase 1, TBBD supplements include Ayurvedic herbs that enhance *agni* (digestive fire; think of it as metabolism) and eliminate *ama* (toxic residue created due to poor metabolism). These supplements are described in the following pages.

Triphala

I am not sure if you have heard of this ancient digestive gem that is native to our country, but you may be surprised to know that it is fast becoming a top herbal remedy in the Western world. I can assure you that in the next few years, triphala will achieve the same buzz as *ashwagandha* or turmeric. The remarkable growth rate of its sales in the US is proof of what I say. What makes this herbal formulation one of the most valuable in the world? Let's find out!

Literally meaning 'three fruits', triphala is made of three fruits, namely amla, bibhitaki and haritaki. The potent, synergistic combination of these three fruits makes triphala a great detoxifier and colon cleanser. Elimination of waste is more important than you think. Most of my clients who had chronic conditions of various kinds had been constipated for years prior to the development of their condition. Simply getting them to produce consistent bowel movements led to a significant improvement in their general well-being.

Preclinical studies have shown that daily consumption of triphala creates a favourable environment for beneficial bacteria and an unfavourable environment for harmful, pathogenic bacteria. Triphala and its constituents possess significant antibacterial effects against diverse pathogenic bacteria, including the ones that are MDR, making it a great supplement to add to your TBBD diet. It is a time-tested recipe that relieves inflammation and therefore helps almost all systems in the body. So much so that there's actually a popular folk saying in India that goes, 'Just as a mother cares for her children, triphala too takes care of the body's internal organs in the same way.'

From helping to optimize the metabolism to being a powerful antioxidant that protects against free radicals, this miracle herb is known as a panacea against various disease conditions. It helps reduce serum cholesterol, lower blood pressure, improve liver function and immunity, enhance mental faculties, scrape the insides for old accumulations and mucus build-ups that can aid the growth of bacteria and pathogens—the list of its benefits is really endless. Since triphala works as a mild laxative (not habit-forming), you must not use it on days when you have loose stools or diarrhoea.

Trikatu

Another natural herb that has been a mainstay in India for centuries and is fast becoming available in the West is Trikatu, which is a Sanskrit word meaning 'three spices'. Trikatu is made from long pepper, black pepper and ginger. It's been shown to have anti-inflammatory effects. It helps boost the beneficial bacteria count, and at the same time, exhibits potent antibacterial, antiviral and antifungal properties against harmful pathogens. The synergistic action of the three pungents promotes healthy detoxification and fat metabolism. Its gentle heating action promotes digestion, rapid absorption of nutrients and efficient removal of excess mucus and waste from the body.

Trikatu is a classic herb used to reset the coordinated function of the triad—the stomach, liver-gall bladder and pancreas. It boosts the natural production of hydrochloric acid (HCl) in the stomach. And we now know from Chapter 3 that optimal HCl levels are necessary to prevent and treat SIBO, which in turn is associated with weight gain. The herb also supports the production and stimulation of bile and activates the digestive enzymes.

Hence, trikatu is helpful for all aspects of digestive health. It supports immunity, reduces LDL (bad) cholesterol and enhances the health of the heart, skin and joints. Because it is hot in potency, trikatu is taken in very small doses, and is contraindicated in a few situations, which are given below.

**Contraindications:** Hyperacidity, heartburn, mouth ulcer, gastric ulcer, ulcerative colitis, hypertension, acne, migraine, burning or heat sensation in any part of the body, pregnancy, lactation, redness in eyes, bleeding haemorrhoids and frequent, heavy and prolonged menstrual periods

Chitrak (*Plumbago zeylanica*)

Chitrak is Sanskrit for fire. And fire it is, hot and fiery! Chitrak is so heating and potent that merely touching the leaves or other parts of the herb can cause a burning sensation. Because of its hot and fiery nature, it needs to be approached with respect! A little of it goes a long way. This herb is so powerful that, even in small doses, it can rev up your digestive fire and bolster your body's metabolism.

The reason why you could eat anything but still get away with it 10 to 15 years back but not now is because your body's metabolism slows down with age. It is because of this sluggish metabolism that you end up making sweeping statements like,

'*Mera weight toh bas, hawa aur paani se hi badh jaata hai!*' Chitrak helps in this case, having stood the test of time as a herb that increases the strength of your digestion. The stronger your digestion, the easier it is for your body to process food, metabolize fat and assimilate nutrients. Chitrak's anti-inflammatory, antibacterial and antiviral properties help in correcting dysbiosis, thus making it highly beneficial for weight loss.

It isn't surprising, therefore, that triphala, trikatu and chitrak are among the medicinal herbs recommended in the guidelines for COVID-19 released by the Indian government's Ministry of AYUSH.

**Contraindications:** Hyperacidity, heartburn, mouth ulcer, gastric ulcer, ulcerative colitis, hypertension, acne, migraine, burning or heat sensation in any body part, pregnancy, lactation, redness in eyes, bleeding haemorrhoids, frequent, heavy and prolonged menstrual periods

Daruharidra or Daruhald (*Berberis aristata*)

Daruharidra or tree turmeric is a revered herb found in the Indian Himalayas. Just like curcumin is the main active ingredient in turmeric, the bark, root, stem and rhizome of tree turmeric carry a naturally therapeutic, alkaloid extract called berberine. This is a yellow herbal extract that has been historically used in both India and China. It possesses antibacterial properties and has been reported to have a wide antibacterial spectrum.

Findings suggest that berberine is effective against insulin resistance, obesity, diabetes and other metabolic disorders. It has also been widely reported to have an impact on the structural modulation of gut microbiota in both animal and human studies.

In recent years, berberine has attracted a lot of attention for its usefulness as a natural supplement that helps significantly decrease cholesterol levels, support normal blood sugar level, improve the cardiovascular and gastrointestinal system, support the immune system as well as produce better cognitive health. Berberine's anti-inflammatory properties reduce lung inflammation caused by smoking and help alleviate joint aches and pains associated with rheumatism, arthritis and osteoporosis.

**Table 2: Dosage and Application**

| | Triphala | Trikatu | Daruhald | Chitrak |
|---|---|---|---|---|
| Dosage | 1 teaspoon mixed in around 100 ml warm water. | 2 to 3 pinches of trikatu and a pinch of rock salt mixed in 100 ml warm water. This is a test dose.<br><br>If you feel comfortable with this dose, then after 3 days, increase trikatu to a quarter teaspoon and consume along with a pinch of rock salt as suggested above. | Mix daruhald and chitrak in 2:1 ratio. Add 1 teaspoon of this mixture in 200 ml water. Boil on low flame for three to five minutes. Strain and sip the tea. This is a test dose.<br><br>If you feel comfortable with this dose, then after 3 days, modify the ratio to 1:1 and consume as suggested above. | |
| Timings | At bedtime. If you are constipated, then instead of bedtime, take it first thing in the morning on an empty stomach. | After breakfast and after dinner. | 30 minutes before breakfast and before dinner. | |

*Notes*

1.  All the supplements have an outstanding safety profile and are not known to produce any side effects or interfere with any Western drugs or medicines. However, if you have a medical condition or are on any prescription medication, it is recommended that you speak to your doctor *before* taking these supplements.

2.  Of the four supplements, trikatu and chitrak are especially hot and strong. Hence, for these two herbs, it is recommended that you first administer a test dose. If upon taking the test dose, you experience no heat or burning sensation in the body, then you can gradually increase the dosage as explained in the table. Otherwise, you can continue to consume the test dose itself.

3.  If you cannot take trikatu or chitrak because of any contraindications that I mentioned, then take 1 teaspoon of triphala twice in a day, once first thing in the morning on an empty stomach and again at bedtime. Also, you can skip the chitrak and make daruhald tea using 1 teaspoon of daruhald and consume as advised in the table.

4.  If you find the daruhald–chitrak tea unpalatable, then you may add some honey to the tea to improve its taste. Make sure the honey is raw, unfiltered and unrefined.

5.  All the four supplements are highly accessible today both online and through retail outlets. However, for them to have maximum benefit, you need to ensure that you consume high-quality herbs. A list of brands that I recommend can be found on my website www. munmunganeriwal.com.

6.  These supplements are available in both powder *(churna)* form as well as tablets. For maximum benefit, I recommend you use them as powder. They may taste bitter but will yield the best results.

## Cleanse the Oral Cavity

Your mouth isn't just for eating, talking and kissing. It harbours the second most diverse biome of the body, and like the gut, it also affects your weight, inflammation and disease status. That's because bad bacteria in your mouth can migrate to other parts of the body. Quite interestingly, dysbiosis in the mouth can be reversed with good dental hygiene and improved oral care.

## TBBD Dental Care

Modern dental care is based on disinfecting, sanitizing and cleaning the mouth. Instead of supporting a healthy, diverse flora within the oral cavity, alcohol-based mouthwashes disrupt its delicate balance. Pretty much like antibiotics, these kill almost 99 per cent of all good and bad bacteria and thereby set the stage for bacterial overgrowth. Rather than killing all the bacteria, they should be 'managed' to encourage the growth of beneficial bugs. Good bacteria produce hydrogen peroxide, which has antibacterial activities that keep harmful bacteria under control. Hence, I do not recommend conventional mouthwashes as part of a daily dental routine. They are to be used only occasionally to get rid of infections, if any, but on a regular basis I want you to avoid mouthwashes and instead try natural alternatives that will help support the microbiota of the mouth.

Oil Pulling

Oil pulling is an ancient dental technique that is known to draw out toxins in your body. This method pulls the pathogens from the oral tissue, and at the same time, helps support the good bacteria. It not only improves oral flora but also enhances your overall health.

You can choose any one of the following techniques.

1.  Take one tablespoon of cold-pressed sesame oil. Add five drops of clove oil. Swish the oil around your mouth, moving it around all sides and through the teeth. Continue for two to three minutes (gradually over a few days, work the time up to 15 to 20 minutes). Spit out the oil and rinse with warm water; be sure not to swallow any of it. Do this twice a day.

    **Contraindications:** Any kind of mouth ulcers or burning sensation in the mouth

2.  Take one tablespoon of cold-pressed coconut oil. Swish the oil around your mouth, moving it around all sides and through the teeth. Continue for two to three minutes (gradually over a few days, work the time up to 15 to 20 minutes). Spit out the oil and rise with warm water; be sure not to swallow any of it. Do this twice a day.

    **Contraindications:** None

*Note:* For best results, oil pulling should be done on an empty stomach before you brush, first thing in the morning and at bedtime.

## Brushing

After you finish oil pulling, brush your teeth. Ditch the industrially manufactured toothpastes and choose natural alternatives. I personally love the neem twig (*datun*) to clean my teeth and gums. This used to be our traditional toothbrush, and it is eco-friendly too! The small branches of the neem tree are used to make the sticks, which are chewed until they start shedding bristles.

Neem has immense detoxifying properties. Even when used in small amounts, it exhibits anti-cancerous, anti-diabetic, antibacterial and antiviral properties. If you can get hold of some neem datuns, go for it. Alternatively, you can mix half a teaspoon of turmeric powder, one teaspoon of fine pink Himalayan salt (grind the salt in a food processor for a fine texture, if required) and sufficient mustard oil to make a paste. Instead of using toothpaste, rub the teeth and gums with this paste twice daily.

## Flossing

Flossing is often ignored but is just as important. It helps dislodge food particles that would otherwise collect bacteria and contribute to inflammation and infection of the gums. Brush and floss after waking up and immediately before bed.

## Microbiome–Drug Interactions

More often than not, when I speak with my clients for the first time, they tell me things like, 'I am hypertensive but

I'm taking medicines for it. So, it's fine, nothing to worry.' While I am not anti-medication, I believe taking medicines and thinking you are healthy is like taking a loan and thinking you are rich! Everything that you eat, including drugs and medication, comes in contact with your intestines and drives the composition of the microbiome. The majority of people who take medicines are not aware of the risks and the potential harms, and that is where the problem lies.

Several recent studies have revealed that commonly used pharmaceuticals alter the gut microbiota signatures and are deleterious to human health. Statins (prescribed in high cholesterol), for example, have been associated with profound remodelling of the gut microbiota and an increased risk of new-onset diabetes. Non-steroidal anti-inflammatory drugs or NSAIDs are a type of painkiller that is often used in menstrual cramps, dental pain, backaches and arthritis pain. The most common NSAIDs are ibuprofen, aspirin and naproxen sodium. Studies have shown that two-thirds of regular NSAID users have a leaky gut.

Overuse of medicines decimates the microbiome and wipes out beneficial strains of bacteria. The biggest offenders are:

Antibiotics

The first antibiotic, penicillin, was discovered in 1928. Since then, there's been a race to produce other antibiotics. In our fear of microbes, we waged war on them, spent a century trying to kill them, and it has led to bacterial extinction. We have turned our intestinal rainforests into barren wastelands.

Antibiotics are indiscriminate killers; they don't bother to differentiate friend from foe. While some can be more precise than others, all of them eliminate good bacteria along with the bad. A short five-day course of a common antibiotic can kill up to a third of the gut microbiome!

Going by recent evidence, every antibiotic course you take produces unfavourable alterations in the composition of your gut biome, and this may be permanent. Increasing overuse of antibiotics is one of the factors responsible for the boom in obesity rates we see today (sorry to burst your bubble but weight gain isn't all about calories and carbs). There is also a strong correlation between antibiotic use and mood disorders like anxiety, panic attack and depression. Antibiotics can trigger allergic reactions as well, and cause or contribute to inflammatory bowel disease. Not difficult to understand why. Antibiotic drugs destroy the gut flora, and as a result, you develop a leaky gut and get overly inflamed. And we have already seen the different pathways in Chapter 3 through which inflammation can set the stage for weight gain, depression, allergic reactions and other chronic diseases.

So, should you avoid antibiotics? The answer is both yes and no. Since they can slay infectious bacteria, sometimes antibiotics are absolutely required to clear an infection. The problem is when we do not use them judiciously.

Antibiotics Are Not for Common Cold,
Flu or Viral Infections

If I asked you the number of times you took antibiotics to feel better from an episode of cold and cough, I am sure you would not be able to count them. But allow me to reveal a truth: Antibiotic drugs cannot resolve a viral infection. Bronchitis, viral pneumonia, common cold, cough and flu are viral in origin and self-limiting in nature. Using antibiotics for them is useless, because viral infections can't be treated by antibiotic drugs at all. Not only that, mild stomach upset and diarrhoea too are viral in nature and therefore won't benefit from antibiotics.

Antibiotics are *only* appropriate for bacterial infections. Antibiotics do nothing to actually resolve the viral infection; on the contrary, it disrupts your gut flora and increases your predisposition to obesity and certain diseases. That you feel better when you take antibiotics for cold, fever, etc. is merely due to the 'placebo' effect—that is when you believe the drug will work, it actually does!

## Antacids

Antacids are prescribed for heartburn, acid reflux and acid-related disorders. Non-prescription antacids for self-treating are easily available over the counter. It is no wonder then that in my work life, I have met many people who have been consuming them for years without being aware of their consequences. So this discussion holds immense value.

## We Need Stomach Acid

Stomach acid, also known as hydrochloric acid (HCl), is made in the stomach to perform various critical functions like breaking down food for easier digestion, absorbing nutrients and minerals, activating the intrinsic factor that is required to absorb B12 and much more. Most importantly, an acidic stomach acts as the first line of defence against foreign organisms—from viruses to bacteria—that get into our gastrointestinal (GI) tract through our food.

This acid is so strong that most pathogens cannot survive the environment of the stomach. When we suppress stomach acid (through alkaline diets or antacids), we leave ourselves more susceptible to SIBO (and do remember that SIBO is associated with weight gain), gut dysbiosis, anaemia, nutritional deficiencies like B12 and Vitamin C, autoimmune conditions, digestive discomfort like indigestion, gas, bloating and serious gut infections.

Pills Don't Fix Your Problem

Hence, we need to get over the false concept we have been fed about keeping our body alkaline at all times. If you suffer from heartburn or acidity, then you should know that acid blocking medicines are good at only suppressing symptoms in the short term. It's like taking the batteries out of a beeping smoke detector and thinking that all is well.

The problem of acid reflux and heartburn cannot be permanently solved by suppressing gastric acid with antacids or alkalizers. Over time, these medicines decrease stomach acid so much that the food you eat enters the stomach but doesn't get fully broken down or digested. The food then begins to ferment and causes gas and acid production and bloating. The gas and acids now start backing up into your food pipe, and this is perceived as acid reflux. The antacid that you take only helps for the time being by neutralizing these gases and reflux, but in the long term, having an optimal amount of stomach acid will improve digestion, which will increase the emptying of food from the stomach into the intestine rather than have it travel back up. Contrary to mainstream belief, there's an alternative opinion in research circles that a lot of the origin of acid-related issues are in reality caused by low stomach acid levels, not high!

In my practice, I have worked with many clients who have had a long history of gastroesophageal reflux disease (GERD) and acidity. Instead of taking a band-aid approach of using medicines, alkalizers or an alkaline diet, I get to the root of the problem to help them achieve long-term relief. In fact, when I met Taapsee, acid reflux was one of her main concerns. In spite of restricting gluten, dairy and trying everything that could alkalize her body, she could not get rid of her acidity. By following the simple principles of TBBD, in a few weeks, we were able to resolve her severe and long-standing problem of acid reflux. Her detailed action plan is given in Chapter 9.

The Three-Fs Approach to Eating

Instead of a one-dimensional approach of 'eat this, not that', TBBD offers guidelines that aren't as black and white, but serve as a good benchmark for how to plan meals during each phase. I have categorized these principles into *Three Fs—Forget, Few, Favour*. Do note that the foods included in the Three Fs change from phase to phase.

**Forget:** These are foods I expect you to completely omit. There are some foods that you will avoid in phase 1, but not in phase 2, while all of them will be reintroduced in phase 3.

**Few:** These are foods that you don't have to eliminate entirely, but their intake must be restricted. Again, the foods that you limit will differ in each phase.

**Favour:** These are the healthy, whole foods that are aligned with the goals of each phase. These foods will help your friendly flora flourish and are those that you should favour the most in a given phase.

The sample meal plans in the book are built on the principles of the Three Fs for each phase, so you can follow the meal plans exactly as designed. If you want to build your own menu, then make use of the Three Fs' list and you will be on track! Now, let's get to know about the foods that I want you to forget, eat few of and favour in phase 1.

Foods to Forget in Phase 1

To prepare the soil of your gut, the first and most important step is to cut off the food supply of fat-forming bad bugs. By taking away inflammatory foods that feed the bad bacteria, you provide less fuel to an out-of-balance microbiome, and this will eventually help you get leaner and healthier. Once you have restored balance to the microbiome, we will work all these foods back in during phase 3. The foods to forget in phase 1 are as follows.

Gluten

Meher Rahman, wife of south Indian actor Rahman, had just signed up with me. During the first consultation session, when I was trying to understand her current diet and areas of concern, she said, 'I feel I am allergic to wheat.'

'Why do you say that?' I asked her.

'Actually, I feel I am allergic to almost everything. Whenever I eat bread, rice, chapatis, millets, even chana or dal for that matter, I get excessively bloated. I have reached a point where I fear food and don't know what to eat. Anything I eat gives me lots of belching and flatulence. I was earlier on keto, because I wanted to lose some weight. *Weight toh aise hi rah gaya, Munmun, aur ulta,* my digestive problems increased further. Now I have started eating carbs but have continued to restrict gluten.'

'Why?'

'Because *sab yahi bolte hai ki gluten bandh kar do.*'

'So what are you eating? No rotis, no chapatis?'

'No, no, I am having low-gluten rotis, made from khapli wheat atta, you must be knowing it na? So many famous nutritionists are promoting it. But still, there's no relief from my symptoms, weight loss *bhi nahi ho raha hai.*'

I am sure many of you can relate to Meher's problem. The idea that gluten can be responsible for myriad health issues has grown so out of control that every next person looking to lose weight is banning gluten foods, i.e., wheat, barley and rye. As a result, gluten-free dessert options and snacks like gluten-free cookies, cakes, muffins, crackers, breads, pizzas, cereals and so on are increasingly taking up a good portion of the real estate in supermarkets. In the quest to live a gluten-free life, we often forget that these gluten-free products that the new market has created are as ultra-processed and as much junk (maybe even potentially worse) as their gluten-packed counterparts are. Hence, they do not deserve a place in your diet.

OK, but what about gluten free rotis? I mean, what's the deal? Is gluten good or is it bad?

During our school days, if you remember, there was something called 'writing with reference to context' in our English classes. We had to write the explanation of a quote or a literary piece with relation to its context in the work, not as is. Similarly, when it comes to health, context is everything. Diet arguments today are based on a 'this is good food, this is bad food' statement, and are therefore pointless. The context is missing from these health discussions. Almost everything is both healthy and not healthy, it depends on the context and isn't as simple as 'this is good' and 'this is bad'.

Gluten Isn't the Problem, Bad Microbes Are

*Gluten—and gluten-filled foods like wheat, barley and rye—does not cause dysbiosis, but it can help sustain dysbiosis if you already have one.* When your microbiome is altered, then gluten can exacerbate these problems. It does so by feeding the bad, inflammatory bugs in your gut. Gluten per se isn't bad, but when it is consumed by someone who shows signs and symptoms of microbial imbalance—not limited to digestive symptoms, but all the symptoms as covered in previous chapters—then it can be challenging to reverse the situation. When the problematic microbes in your gut eat gluten foods, they can release more inflammatory molecules that they can further feed on and *wreak havoc on your metabolism, waistline and overall health.*

So why was Meher not feeling better and losing weight even after eliminating gluten from her meals? Because simply eliminating foods to avoid symptoms of an underlying issue is like ignoring your spouse and sleeping in a separate room because you're having marital problems. Those problems won't just magically disappear. This is where most of the anti-gluten people go wrong. If you are struggling with a chronic health issue, or obesity that doesn't seem to budge, then remove gluten for some time. But in the meanwhile, actively work on rebalancing the microbiome: Clean it up, repair the gut lining and nourish your good bugs. The microbiome, in the meanwhile, should be strategically built back up rather than just torn down with concepts like 'This is good food, and this is bad food'. This is what we will do in phase 1 and phase 2.

Simply avoiding gluten and doing nothing isn't adding any value to your health. By the time you step into phase 3 of TBBD, your body will have been healed, microbiome restored and inflammation cooled down, and at that time gluten food sources will be reintroduced. In such a healthy and balanced microbiome, the helpful microbes are present in abundance. They produce enzymes that easily and efficiently break down the gliadin proteins in gluten. Eating gluten foods then poses no threat to your health, and any fear around eating gluten would be simply unfounded (celiac diagnosis is a different story). This is how Meher and many clients I have worked with have resolved their long-standing issues. I advised Meher to stay off gluten (khapli wheat too!) initially. After a few weeks of being in the programme, during which we worked on repairing her gut from a foundation level, wheat was reintroduced. Not only did she lose weight, but the bloating, belching and flatulence had disappeared. 'I have not relished eating food like this in a long, long time. Had lost all hopes! Thanks yaa, Munmun,' she said.

To conclude, eliminate gluten foods, including low gluten food options, completely in phase 1. Make sure you are not replacing your gluten-filled options with processed gluten-free alternatives. The modified starches and designer molecules they are packed with will induce metabolic and hormonal responses that will have detrimental consequences in terms of satiation and weight gain. Instead, focus on whole, unadulterated, naturally-occurring gluten-free foods.

Lactose

Lactose is a sugar found in milk, dairy protein powders and fresh, wet cheeses like ricotta, cream cheese and Indian paneer. There are many NOVA ultra-processed foods with hidden sources of lactose, like ice creams, custards, energy bars, milk chocolates, baked goods, frozen meals, biscuits, canned soups, processed meats, salad dressings, etc. These are the foods you have to stay away from in phase 1. When dairy that is not ultra-processed is consumed, it isn't really bad. After all, milk products are known to be a great source of calcium and enriched with Vitamin D—two critical cofactors in building a strong skeletal structure and enhancing the lean muscle mass of the body. But again, we need to start thinking more about context if we want to truly heal, instead of getting into this dogma of 'this is good, this is bad'.

For lactose to be easily absorbed into the bloodstream and turned into energy—the fuel for our bodies—it needs to be hydrolysed or broken down into simpler sugar forms called glucose and galactose. This work is executed by an enzyme called lactase. The thing with lactase is that it is available plentifully in newborn babies, but from around two years of age, as you get older, your body starts making less of it. As a result, undigested sugars pass into the colon and are metabolized by colonic bacteria. Noxious bacteria then feed on it, and in a large proportion of the population, this can cause inflammation, resulting in digestive issues such as bloating, gas, constipation and diarrhoea, as well as other symptoms including acne.

Reactions to dairy are highly individualized, but if you have an altered microbiome, then there is evidence that lactose can promote an inflammatory response when consumed. That's why we will remove lactose food sources from the diet in phase 1 and phase 2. However, you don't need to stay away from it forever, just long enough for your body to reset itself. Later, when we get to phase 3, we will reintegrate it into your diet plan. For the next eight weeks—two weeks of phase 1 and six weeks of phase 2—instead of milk, you can consume dairy alternatives like almond milk, coconut milk, cashew milk, etc.

In the past decade, we've seen a renaissance of non-dairy milks. So, it's important to clarify that I am not trying to imply that they are nutritionally superior to dairy milk. Until we don't heal our gut ecosystem, they can work as great alternatives if you really want to have some. Needless to say, ensure that you make your own milk substitutes at home, since most of the nut milks found in supermarkets are

NOVA ultra-processed. Most versions of non-dairy milks, including some organic versions, are loaded with sugar, gums and thickeners and contain additives designed to make nut and water look and taste like cow's milk. If making at home isn't possible and if you must buy, then look at the ingredients of various brands and choose an unsweetened version that carries no emulsifying or thickening agent or anything else that sounds like it was made in a lab. For instance, as I explained earlier, carrageenan—a thickener derived from seaweeds and used to improve the texture of non-dairy milks—has been found to have zero nutritional value and is associated with ulcers, leaky gut, inflammation and even autoimmune diseases.

## What about Curd and Yoghurt?

Home-made dahi and yoghurts with live and active bacteria cultures have the least amount of lactose in it, and most of the time, none. That's because during bacterial fermentation, lactose in the milk is broken down and converted to lactic acid. This lactic acid is responsible for the thickening of yogurt as well as for its tartness. The more acidic a curd is, the lesser the amount of lactose in it. Having said that, *the only dairy you are going to have in phase 1 is ghee, which is lactose free too!*

If curd and yoghurt are lactose free, then why cannot I consume them in phase 1?

Curd, yoghurt and all such fermented foods as well as probiotics are full of live, beneficial microbes. It will be counterintuitive and counteractive to consume them in phase 1, where the chief objective is to kill microbes using antimicrobial foods and supplements. What most people don't know is that it is not just enough to consume live bacteria in the form of foods or supplements; they must also adhere to the gut lining to have beneficial effects. It takes about six to eight weeks of constant consumption for them to reach a certain abundance, after which their favourable properties can be felt. This is why phase 2 is six weeks long. But during that time, if we bombard the gut with natural antibiotics, the good bacteria won't establish themselves for you to feel the beneficial properties. That is why we will include curd, yoghurt, fermented foods and probiotics in the diet only in phase 2.

Secondly, unlike bad microbes, the beneficial microbes do not thrive on inflammation. The chances of their establishing themselves in your gut increase when the environment is conducive and free of inflammation. They may not adhere to your gut lining at all if we consume them without first clearing the inflammation. Hence, in phase 1, the gut is first prepared to provide a foundation for the friendly microbes. Only then are curd, yoghurt, fermented foods and probiotics introduced in the phase 2 diet.

Food Intolerance vs Food Allergy

What's the difference between a food allergy and food sensitivity or intolerance? A lot of the time I hear people talk about being allergic, sensitive or intolerant to a certain food without realizing that being allergic to a food is not the same as being sensitive or intolerant to it.

Cause

A food allergy is an immune-mediated reaction to the food, which means that when you have a food allergy, your immune system causes the reaction. The seat of your immunity, as you know now, is your gut. A leaky gut could trigger a food allergy or exacerbate it and worsen the conditions. Here's how. Due to damaged tight junctions in a leaky gut, partially-digested food particles—protein chains from peanuts, for instance—can slip through your intestinal lining and make their way into your bloodstream. Your body will spot this material as foreign and will respond by launching an immune attack, thus causing an allergic response every time you eat peanuts.

The difference between an allergy and sensitivity lies in the response of the body. Unlike a food allergy, where your immune system causes the reaction, in food sensitivity or intolerance, the reaction is triggered by the digestive system. Food sensitivities and intolerances do not involve the immune system but are caused by an inability to process or digest a food. For example, lactose intolerance is when your body can't properly break down lactose. Food intolerances and sensitivities are a big, warning sign of a disturbed microbiome that can include an overgrowth of pathogens, low levels of beneficial microbes, intestinal inflammation, etc.

In recent times, it has become clear that food reactions, irrespective of whether they are an allergy or intolerance towards a food, are related to changes in the gut microbiota. The good news is that feeding the gut microbes well can help protect you from food reactions.

Symptoms

Food allergies lead to immediate symptoms that may include hives, itchiness, swollen lips, swelling, shortness of breath, anaphylaxis, wheezing, dizziness, etc. The responses in an allergy can be very dangerous.

But unlike a food allergy that can be fatal, intolerance or sensitivity is not life-threatening. Rather than an immediate reaction, the effects of such sensitivity are generally more like a cascade of events in the body and are more damaging in the long term. Symptoms can occur in a wide variety of forms and can develop immediately after eating, or the peak effects can occur one to two days after consumption. Symptoms of food intolerance include gas, bloating, diarrhoea, constipation, nausea, cramping, joint pain, arthritis, chronic fatigue, eczema, brain fog, headaches, migraine, depression and anxiety.

Diagnostic Tests and Action Plan

A true food allergy can be diagnosed with an immunoglobulin E or IgE test. IgEs are allergic antibodies that your immune system produces to fight the food proteins it inappropriately perceives as an invader. If the test results reveal any food that you are allergic to, then eliminate that food allergen from your diet. Simultaneously, feed your microbes well with foods they prefer, as this will help repair the gut barrier that has started leaking and will prevent worsening of the condition.

Testing for food sensitivities isn't this straightforward though. There are a lot of gimmicky tests out there, among which *the IgG food sensitivity test is most commonly used by many practitioners*. In my work, I meet many clients who have run such tests and carry a long list of several foods that they've been told they are sensitive to. This makes their diets highly restrictive and difficult to follow, and creates unreasonable stress that aggravates digestive issues further. What makes it worse is that even after removing all the offending foods as per the list, most of them still experienced symptoms and found little to no relief. Hence, instead of running food sensitivity tests and placing multiple foods in the no-eating category, you will benefit more from exploring and fixing the underlying issues using the elimination and reintroduction method. Eliminate foods that you have identified past reactions to, work on your gut microbiome ecosystem in the meanwhile, and then after the period of avoidance, methodically reintroduce the eliminated foods one by one. This is by far the best way to identify and deal with food sensitivities.

Food sensitivities usually don't last forever. Once you address the core problem, you should be able to reintroduce foods that were previously problematic. There is no need to stay on a highly restricted diet for life. When Taapsee and I started working together, she told me that she was intolerant to gluten and dairy. She had been following a self-devised diet for many years that was completely gluten and dairy-free. After working together for a few months and rebalancing her gut, I could safely introduce gluten and lactose foods back into her plan. Today, she eats everything under the sun, right from wheat to barley to curd to buttermilk and looks like a million bucks effortlessly! In fact, during prepping her for an athlete's role in *Rashmi Rocket*, I had given her protein shakes (whey and casein) that were both dairy-based. Her body responded to it beautifully and we have all seen that on screen, haven't we?

## Red Meat

Red meat—beef, lamb and mutton, pork, veal—provides micronutrients that feed the bad bacteria and help sustain the imbalance in the microbial communities in your digestive tract. A cross-sectional study published in the *European Journal of Nutrition* studied 2,198 men and women and suggested that consumption of red meat is associated with inflammation.

Large-scale and unregulated use of antibiotics in industrially raised meats poses a major health risk. Some experts opine that there are more antibiotics being used in the beef, poultry and pork industries than in humans. The large quantities of antibiotics used promote the animals' growth and enhance their production but disrupt their gut microbiome. When you consume meat with such high levels of antibiotics, they alter your own gut microbiome and contribute to obesity.

First of all, conventionally raised, antibiotic-laden red meat and processed meat products like canned meats, deli meats, salami, ham, bacon, sliced luncheon meats, hot dogs, etc. commonly found in the marketplace are not only associated with weight gain but also to various chronic diseases, including heart diseases, diabetes and certain cancers. The second thing is that it doesn't matter if your meat is processed or unprocessed, or how the red meat was raised or produced (read organic, grass-fed, antibiotic-free, etc.) The truth is that there are compounds naturally found in red meat that increase their inflammatory profile. That is why, based on all the available evidence, I elect to eliminate red meat in both phase 1 and phase 2 of TBBD. If you really like to indulge in your Rogan Josh or Laal Maas curry, then fret not, because in phase 3, I will tell you ways of incorporating some red meat back into your diet. But for now, you'll avoid them.


Alcohol

Every time I ask my clients to stay off alcohol, I am quickly met with a barrage of responses.

'Breezer *toh chalega, na?*'

'Beer is not *daaru*, trust me!'

'You are into *health-shealth isilye aapko pata nahi hai,* but wine is not alcohol!'

Studies suggest that alcohol consumption alters the intestinal microbiome. It can induce dysbiosis and leaky gut, resulting in systemic inflammation. Following exposure to alcohol, the harmful microbes that are pro-inflammatory in nature tend to increase and the team of your good, helpful bugs shrinks. Alcohol can feed the bad bugs in your intestine (ever wondered why rotten fruit tastes alcoholic?) and mess with your microbiome. In fact, feeling hung over after having alcohol is essentially a sign of acute damage done to your gut's friendly inhabitants.

*For these reasons, I insist that you stay away from alcohol.* In fact, you must eliminate alcoholic drinks of all kinds completely in phase 1, which is only two weeks long! And before you start thinking about how dry (pun intended) and boring your life is going to be, let me tell you that if you must drink, then there is some relaxation allowed in phase 2, the details of which you will find out about in Chapter 6.

Foods to Eat Few of in Phase 1

'So, you make eggs at home?'

*'Arre nahi yaar, ghar par toh ande banana allowed hi nahi hai.* My staff gets me boiled eggs from outside every evening. *Ab health ke liye kuch toh karna hi padega na.'* Meet Puja Agarwal from Kolkata, a fellow Marwari and one of my most committed clients.

I meet many people in my office, and have lost count of those who were vegetarian by birth (and choice), but later turned into an egg-eater or meat-eater *kyunki health ke liye kuch toh karna hi padta hai na.* Welcome to the world of protein obsession!

Now, I have to stay loyal to my mission of unearthing the truth, so kindly allow me to clear the hullabaloo over non-vegetarian food protein. There is growing recognition that meat eaters are found to have higher levels of a compound called Trimethylamine-N-oxide (TMAO)—which is linked to greater risk of heart disease, stroke and heart attack—than their vegetarian peers. Ayurveda too considers eggs and meat as difficult-to-digest foods that should not be consumed regularly. So, what should you do?

If you are a vegetarian, you don't 'have to' start eating meat, fish and eggs just because you have started to work out or because you want to meet your daily quota of dietary proteins. Conversely, if you are a non-vegetarian, you don't 'have to' stop eating meat altogether. Only the obsession towards meat, fish and eggs should stop. Remember, moderation is always the best approach.

In TBBD, while we completely restrict red meat for phases 1 and 2 because of its pro-inflammatory nature, you are free to consume other non-vegetarian foods like eggs, fish and chicken in moderate amounts. In phase 1, you will have either fish or eggs or chicken only once per week. Avoid eating them twice in the same day. Also, make sure you choose grass-fed and antibiotic-free meat in its real, unprocessed form. No processed products, please!

Foods to Favour in Phase 1

Healthy eating isn't about filling your shopping cart with random healthy-sounding foods (like gluten-free, dairy-free, sugar-free, low-calorie, low-fat foods). In TBBD, you must specifically favour those foods that match the goals of each phase. *The foods you avoid in each phase aren't necessarily bad, but merely do not align with the goals.* Eating foods that I ask you to favour will help heal your inner garden, and as it heals, you will lose fat along the way as a perk.

The foods that you should favour in phase 1 are:

1. Antimicrobial foods that help cleanse, detox and clear out dysbiosis
2. Anti-inflammatory foods and drinks that help combat inflammation
3. Foods that rev up your metabolism
4. Foods that are easy to digest. The idea is to simplify your meals and lighten the load you put on your digestive system so it can heal and rejuvenate itself. This will help detoxify your body and lay the foundation for a faster, more efficient metabolism.

The following foods will help you achieve your goals:

*Millets:* Thanks to the gluten-free craze, millets are on being rediscovered in India. Possibly one of the oldest foods our forefathers ate, it is now making a comeback, and millets is one trend I am happy about! It is considered to be highly digestible and full of vitamins and minerals. Its high fibre content and low glycemic index makes it a great choice for those who are obese, diabetic, insulin resistant or have metabolic syndromes. However, as with all traditional foods, millets too should be consumed based on protocols derived from the time-tested practices of our grand-parents and the current farming practice. And this is one place where most of us are going wrong.

There are eight varieties that make up the family of millets. In Table 3, I have mentioned what they are called in English and their corresponding Hindi names. Based on the region you belong to, please check their vernacular names. Out of the eight millets, according to Ayurveda and grandma's experience, a few are known to be 'heating' and a few 'cooling' in their *'guna'* or nature. Needless to say, it is best to eat the heating grains like finger millet, barnyard, foxtail, etc. during winters, and the cooling proso and little millet in the hot summers. The native variety of the pearl millet (bajra), is smaller in size and considered to be cooling, whereas the modern varieties that are more prevalent everywhere are bigger and heating. But this is where things get rather interesting.

In times of yore, when food supply was limited, our ancestors devised ways of consuming whatever was available around the year. They not only knew but took advantage of the fact that intricate details—like what the millet is mixed with, how it is cooked, etc.—can change the overall guna of the resultant meal. These are things that neither Google nor Alexa can tell you. A few cases in point: Ragi (finger millet) is a staple in south India and Maharashtra. To reduce its heating effects, a small quantity of ragi is mixed with lots of coconut, which is known to be cooling, to make a traditional drink, so that one can consume ragi during the summer season too! Sprouting the grain also helps reduce the heating effect. Therefore, milk from sprouted ragi is used to feed small infants in the south throughout the year. On the one hand, bajra roti and bajra raab is eaten during the harsh cold weather of Rajasthan to keep the body warm, and on the other hand, the same bajra flour is mixed with buttermilk, fermented and turned into a refreshing drink, *rabdi*, that is consumed in the hot, humid summer months of Rajasthan and Tamil Nadu. Along with the addition of buttermilk, it is the process of fermentation that helps neutralize the intrinsic heating nature of bajra.

So, you see, when it comes to millets, it is incorrect to segregate them into winter or summer grains, because its physiological effect on your body is dependent on the overall meal preparation (the how, what and when). While in spite of decades of learning and practice, stories of how and why a certain meal evolved into what we see today continue giving me goosebumps, for you it essentially translates into the information below:

- During summers, consume more of the cooling millets (check Table 3). The heating millets can be consumed during summer, but only after combining them with sufficient amounts of cooling agents like ghee, moong dal (green gram), coconut, buttermilk (buttermilk only from phase 2 onwards) and milk (milk from phase 3 onwards). However, grandma's wisdom says it is best to avoid barnyard and finger millet for dinner during summer.

- During winters, consume more of the heating millets. If you live in a city like Mumbai, where winters are hardly *do char din ki mehmaan* and that too not quite harsh, then you can have the cooling millets all through the year, including winters.

- As millets gain popularity, it is not surprising to see multi-millet mixes and flours in the market. However, you should have only one kind of millet at a time. At best, you may mix two millet types. However, avoid random mixing of two heating or two cooling millets. It is OK to combine one heating and one cooling millet. For example, barnyard can be mixed with little millet, but it is not OK to combine barnyard with finger millet.

- What we choose to eat should depend not only on the nature of the food itself but also on our personal constitution. If you have a pitta-dominant body, you should entirely avoid eating the heating millets during summers or whenever the weather is hot. If consumed regularly, it can cause adverse effects. During cooler months or winter, you can have the heat-generating millets safely and regularly, but only after combining these with adequate amounts of cooling agents. The following conditions are related to high pitta in the body: hyperacidity, heartburn, gastric ulcer, ulcerative colitis, burning or heat sensation in any part of the body, heat boils, piles, redness in eyes, bleeding haemorrhoids, and frequent, heavy and prolonged menstrual periods.

Cooking with Millets

Millet rice: Out of the eight millet varieties, foxtail, little, kodo, proso and barnyard have a non-edible outer cover or husk. Like paddy rice, these millets need to be de-hulled and made into rice. That is why, technically, these millets are called millet rice. Similar to regular rice, they are also available in raw and parboiled form. The millet rice can also be ground and turned into rava or flour. When it comes to cooking millet rice, there is little difference between paddy rice (the usual rice) and millet rice. You can cook them the same way you cook rice—usually with 1:2 or 1:3 rice-to-water ratio—and eat it with sambar, dal, veggies, etc. You can replace paddy rice with millet rice in all your recipes and make khichri, pongal, pulao, biryani, kanji, etc. If you are new to millets, I suggest you start with any millet rice because it will taste quite similar to regular rice.

Millet grains: Similar to wheat; finger millet, pearl millet and sorghum are naked grains without a husk. These millets can be substituted for wheat in day-to-day cooking. These millet grains are ground to form flour, which is then used to make roti, stuffed paratha, bhakri, etc.

Versatility in Millets

Apart from what is mentioned above, millet grains and millet rice can both be used in various ways to make puttu, adai, chilla, neer dosa, idiyappam, porridge, etc. Millet flakes and pops (puffs) are also available and can be eaten as is, and can also be cooked to make upma, poha, etc. Based on the season and climate you live in, choose the millets and try traditional recipes and ways to incorporate this ancient superfood into your diet.

A Few Important Points

- If you have never had millets before, start by consuming them once a day. For other meals, you can have pseudo-cereals (check Table 4), rice and other rice products like puffed rice, poha, rice suji, etc. After three to four days or more, you can gradually increase the frequency of millets.
- Millets can be had throughout the day—breakfast, lunch, evening snack and dinner. However, it is important that you rotate between the different types of millets.
- Unlike rice and wheat, millets are coarse. For it to be digested and assimilated well in the body, it needs to be chewed well. Take time to chew your food and ensure you drink adequate water throughout the day.
- The reason why most of us find it difficult to make millet rotis is because millets are gluten-free. It is gluten that helps the dough bind. To make millet rotis, use warm or hot water as it will help knead the dough better.

## Table 3: The Eight Varieties of Millets Found across India

| English name | Hindi name | Heating | Cooling | Neutral | Note |
|---|---|---|---|---|---|
| Sorghum | Jowar | ✗ | ✗ | ✓ | Should be consumed sparingly by those with skin disease like itching, eczema, allergy |
| Finger millet | Ragi | ✓ | ✗ | ✗ | |
| Foxtail millet | Kangni | ✓ | ✗ | ✗ | Not recommended during the first trimester of pregnancy |
| Pearl millet | Bajra | ✓ | ✓ | ✗ | |
| Barnyard millet | Sama ke chawaal | ✓ | ✗ | ✗ | Not recommended for those with piles and severe stomach ulcer |
| Little millet | Kutki | ✗ | ✓ | ✗ | |
| Proso millet | Barre | ✗ | ✓ | ✗ | |

| English name | Hindi name | Heating | Cooling | Neutral | Note |
|---|---|---|---|---|---|
| Kodo millet | Kodon | Though this millet is nutritious, it has been found to have toxins (resultant condition is termed 'kodo poisoning'), because of which many Indian agricultural scientists do not advocate consuming it. This is one millet that I no longer use with my clients. | | | |

**Table 4: Other Gluten-Free Grains (Pseudo-cereals)**

| Name | Heating | Cooling | Neutral |
|---|---|---|---|
| Rajgeera (Amaranth) | ✓ | ✗ | ✗ |
| Kuttu (Buckwheat) | ✓ | ✗ | ✗ |
| Singhara (Water chestnut flour) | ✗ | ✓ | ✗ |

*Khichri*: Khichri is one of the most ancient foods of India that dates to the fourteenth century. Its name finds its origins in the Sanskrit word *khiccā*, which means 'a dish made with rice and pulses'. You may not know that in addition to the pre-eminent Kohinoor diamond, the British took the recipe of our invaluable khichri back to their country. It is said that the early colonists developed a taste for it. Since it is eaten across India, it rightly captures the distinctive 'unity in diversity' feature of our country. In its simplest interpretation, it is only rice and dal cooked together. But the versatility of this humble dish has led to each region—right from Kashmir to Kanyakumari—developing its own take on the khichri. If you consider it plain and boring, then you will be surprised to learn of the many interesting forms it assumes across our country.

*Wo sab toh theek hai, but what is khichri doing in a diet book? I mean, there's rice in it. All I see are CARBS!*

I don't blame you if the mention of carbs scares you out of your wits. That's the effect of the current diet trend. But science is never at the mercy of passing trends. The research is clear: You need carbs, we all do. Those who have tried going low-carb forever know how incredibly painful it can be. Apart from fuelling your body, carbs also feed your brain. Ever wondered why you feel satisfied after having a bowl of khichri? It's because carbs promote the production of serotonin, the happy hormone, and improves our mood. It's unfortunate that in recent times, we have demonized carbs and labelled them as fattening. Not all carbs are equal. The Belly and Brain Diet is based on high-quality carbs, the complex, 'slow-release' kind that will foster fat-burning and make you feel lighter in both your body and mind. Unlike modern comfort foods that leave you undernourished and overfed, khichri is so nutrient-rich, therapeutic and comforting that it's given to babies as their first solid food as well as to the elderly, frail and sick.

And let's not reduce khichri to just carbs. Because the lentils in it are smartly proportioned with the rice and there's a dollop of desi ghee that sits on it, it becomes a unique blend of protein, fats, carbs, dietary fibre, vitamins and minerals, making it a complete health food ready in a bowl. It not only nourishes the entire system, but also enhances the body's metabolism, is easily digestible and is incredibly easy to make. I encourage you to make different versions of it using rice–dal as well as millet–dal combinations. Play with different varieties and you will have many different ways of having this one-of-a-kind culinary boss.

*Indian spices and herbs:* In recent years, a variety of polyphenols, flavonoids and alkaloids exhibiting antimicrobial and anti-inflammatory properties have been isolated from a number of plants in the Indian subcontinent. This isn't surprising, because in ancient times, before the discovery of antibiotics, spices and herbs were used as food preservatives, medicines and natural remedies. Now with modern research, fortunately, we are able to revisit that area. Traditional Indian kitchens have long utilized the medicinal benefits offered by various plants and spices such as cardamom, cumin, nutmeg, coriander, saffron, turmeric, etc. A study published in the *Journal of Food Science* examined the chemical composition and antioxidant capacity of a few spice extracts, namely ginger, turmeric and cinnamon. All the extracts were seen to exhibit a high antioxidant capacity. They promoted the growth of beneficial bacteria and suppressed the growth of pathogenic bacteria, suggesting their potential role in the regulation of intestinal microbiota. Therefore, it is important to use a variety of these powerful spices in your daily meals while cooking.

You should not have them in large amounts either. Following traditional recipes will ensure that you strike the right balance. Traditionally, a well-kept spice rack has been a prominent feature of Indian kitchens for centuries. Indian food has always been treasured for its intelligent use of spices, but for the last few years, people authorized to give health or diet advice have started questioning this very heritage for the spices it contains. 'Too much masala in Indian food,' they complain, as they stick their knives and forks into sautéed and steamed food preparations with minimal to no seasonings. Little do they know that spiced foods can help burn fat by thermogenesis (generation of heat in the body), raise the body's metabolism, stimulate digestive juices and upregulate the body's built-in weight loss mechanisms. Not only do spices and herbs help fight bad bacteria, fungi, etc. and aid weight loss, most of them have also been known to enhance brain health, heart health, liver function, respiratory function, digestion and oral health. Therefore, honour the curative power of herbs and spices. Build and maintain a spice rack in your kitchen that covers the must-have spices I have listed next. Incorporating these functional foods into your food repertoire will help you burn fat faster and enhance your weight loss goals.


Must-Haves in Your Kitchen Spice Rack

Cumin, coriander, black pepper, cinnamon, nutmeg, cardamom, bay leaves, cloves, mint, saffron, yellow and black mustard seeds, ginger, fennel seeds, turmeric, dill seeds, Himalayan pink salt or rock salt, carom seeds, tamarind.

Apart from day-to-day meals, spices and herbs should also be consumed as the following:

- Herbal teas or Kadhas: India has a long-standing tradition of herbal teas. Made with plant leaves and spices, these teas have been in use for centuries. Therapeutic compounds and volatile oils found in herbal teas can offer benefits such as reducing bloating, strengthening immunity and calming your mind. Drinking hot, herbal teas aid in taming the bad kind of inflammation. Research tells us that including anti-inflammatory drinks in the diet may protect against obesity, depression, heart disease, diabetes, metabolic syndrome and a host of other diseases. Spices used to make herbal teas—mint, ginger, turmeric and others—have their own individual health benefits. They are infused with the goodness of all the antibacterial, antifungal and anti-parasitic properties of the constituent spices, but what makes these infusions a perfect means to beat inflammation is the fact that all benefits of these spices work synergistically to heal your body. That is why, every day throughout this programme, you will sip hot blends. Plenty of recipes of herbal teas are provided in Chapter 10 that are easy to make.
- Indian chutney: Chutneys are an excellent side dish that can be eaten with roti, khichri, rice, pongal, upma, etc. Phase 1 chutneys are made with anti-inflammatory herbs and spices, and will enhance the cleansing of the body. A few examples are listed below. The recipes for the ones in *italics* are can be found in Chapter 10.

## Table 5: Chutneys of Phase 1

| Lehsun (Garlic) chutney | Dhania (Coriander) chutney | Imli (Tamarind) chutney | Nariyal (Coconut) chutney | Drumstick leaves (Moringa) chutney | *Neem flower chutney* |
|---|---|---|---|---|---|
| Haldi (Turmeric root) chutney | Pudina (Mint) chutney | Sonth (dry ginger) chutney | Moongphali (Peanut) chutney | Mooli (radish) chutney | *Amla and curry patta (leaf) chutney* |

- Sherbets: Indian sherbets and drinks are seasonal, and most of them are teeming with spices and herbs that exhibit a range of different benefits. Favour these drinks as per the season. A few examples are given in the next table. The recipe for the one in *italics* can be found in Chapter 10.

## Table 6: Summer Sherbets and Drinks of Phase 1

| Jal jeera | Masala shikanji | Buransh sherbet | *Panakam* |
|---|---|---|---|
| Pudina nimbu sherbet | Dhaniya sherbet | Bael sherbet | Kokum saar |
| Imli sherbet | Aam panna | Phalsa sherbet | Variyali sherbet |
| Vasantha neer | Coconut water | Nannari sherbet | Neera |

## Table 7: Monsoon and Winter Drinks of Phase 1

| Rasam and soups | Kashmiri kahwa |
|---|---|
| Sugarcane juice | Amla sherbet |

- Soups: When I say soups, I mean the hot, homemade soups, not the creamy kinds you find in restaurants or the ready-to-make instant ones. There's a reason that soups are recommended by doctors and mothers alike when you feel under the weather. Even when both are made of the same ingredients, a khichri is known to be more therapeutic than a meal of rice and dal. Ever wondered why? That's because of the soupy consistency of the khichri. Soups are nutrient-dense, easy to digest and rich in flavour, and they boost healing, increase satiation and exhibit anti-inflammatory properties. I encourage you to indulge in warm, comforting, filling and nourishing soups that will keep you satisfied for hours. The following soups are recommended in Phase 1 as they are made with herbs and spices that will help bring anti-inflammatory and detox benefits to the table.

**Table 8: Soups of Phase 1** (Recipes for the ones in *italics* can be found in Chapter 10)

| | |
|---|---|
| Jowar (sorghum) soup | Onion soup |
| *Turmeric soup* | Lauki (bottle gourd) soup |
| *Drumstick soup* | Pumpkin soup |
| Neem flower soup | Moringa leaves soup |
| *Amla ginger soup* | Moong dal soup |
| Rajasthani mangodi soup | Rasam |

• Hot water: A simple yet very effective purifying technique is sipping on plain hot water. Drinking hot water throughout the day has a powerful influence in strengthening the GI tract. I urge you to adopt this habit not only for two weeks but for a lifetime. It may sound very simple, but it can help cleanse your system, rev up your metabolism, improve digestion and also help reduce food cravings. Instead of feeding and fuelling your metabolism, cold water and cold drinks slow the metabolism down. Hence, my advice to you is to avoid cold drinks and beverages, especially with meals. Because of their natural vasodilatory effect, warm liquids consumed during meals help in digesting food. They help open up or dilate blood vessels to allow blood to flow more easily. The blood circulation to the GI tract increases, and this in turn increases digestion efficiency, aids other metabolic processes and helps calm your nervous system, all at the same time.

To reap maximum benefits from this very special hot water technique, you will, however, have to keep a few things in mind. The water should be hot; you should ideally be blowing on it before you sip. The frequency of drinking the hot water is more important than the overall quantity consumed. Take sips of water every 30 minutes or every hour. I often ask my clients to invest in a good thermos. Fill it up with boiling water in the morning and then you can have sips from it throughout the day as you work. If you prefer, you can add flavours to your water, such as a squeeze of lemon, a slice of fresh ginger, a few mint leaves, etc. Do take note of my special 'magic mix' recipe in Chapter 10. If you are troubled by cravings for sugar or junk, bloating, constipation etc. then you MUST make use of this wonder recipe.

## More on Indian Herbal Teas/Kadhas

The Indian kadhas have seen a revival of sorts during the COVID-19 pandemic. On the one hand, making Dalgona coffee had become a fun new challenge to do at home during the lockdown in 2020, and on the other, every Indian next door was sipping on kadhas, consuming copious amounts of tulsi, black pepper, cinnamon, etc. in order to boost their immunity. Now here's the thing with kadhas: They are medicinal, and when it comes to anything medicinal, you can have too much of a good thing! As I explained before, if something is good, more of it isn't necessarily better.

Kadhas belong to the ancient collective traditional wisdom and hence, its mindless use should be discouraged. Herbs and spices like tulsi, black pepper, neem, ajwain, etc. are not meant to be consumed daily for months and years together. They act like strong, potent medicines and should only be had during certain seasons, or during certain ailments, in specific combinations with other herbs, and not for too long and not in huge amounts. Otherwise, they can get harmful in the long run. (Many news channels did report side effects in people consuming kadhas for immunity during COVID-19.) Whether you like it or not, there is a specific protocol for using kadhas, the invaluable knowledge of which can be found only with our ancestors and not online. For example, when ajwain (carom seeds) is put in warm milk and consumed, it exhibits cooling properties that works great for those with eye redness, ulcers, etc. but when you put the same ajwain in milk and then boil the milk, the drink becomes heating in nature and will have the opposite effects when consumed!

The recipes of herbal teas that I have provided in Chapter 10 aren't random combinations; they are time-tested recipes that have been proven to be beneficial. Teas with certain heating spices are specifically listed for the winter months, and those herbs and spices that are cooling are listed for the hot summer months. These recipes are safe for everyone to use, and wherever required, I have mentioned the duration for which they must be consumed. I insist that unless you know of certain kadha or herbal tea recipe that your grandma approves of, stay away from self-devised recipes, and also refrain from overdoing them especially during this 10-week programme.

## Table 9: The Three Fs of Phase 1 at a Glance: Foods to Forget, Have Few of, and Favour

| Forget | Few | Favour |
|---|---|---|
| All dairy except ghee, all dairy-based protein powders except whey isolate | Chicken, eggs, fish: only once per week | Millets |
| Whole wheat, maida, wheat suji/rava, daliya, barley, rye (gluten sources) | | Khichri/ Porridges/Kanji |
| Alcohol | | Homemade chutneys |
| Red meat | | Hot, homemade soups |
| NOVA ultra-processed foods | | Hot herbal teas, warm water |
| All beans and lentils except moong, masoor and toor (arhar) dal; certain tubers, namely potatoes, corn, turnip, beetroot, sweet potato, yam, cassava (sabudaana); deep-fried foods, raw foods like salads, raw sprouts (all these are difficult and heavy to digest) | | Homemade sherbets |
| Curd, vinegar, pickles and other such fermented foods | | Honey, ghee |

## Looking Ahead

With this, we have covered all the dietary basics for your first two weeks on the programme. In Chapter 10, you will find a detailed phase 1 meal plan that you can follow as is. Before you step on the plan, do check *the seven TBBD meal planning guidelines* explained in the same chapter.

## FAQs of Phase 1

Here are the answers to the top questions I usually get from my clients while they are on the programme. This will help you further solidify the concepts of TBBD and manage any challenges that you may have going forward.

1. Why are four different kinds of herbal supplements used?
   I encourage you to use all the four herbal supplements triphala, trikatu, chitrak and daruhald (unless contraindicated) together. That's because each herb contains its own unique combination of antibiotic compounds that target different types of bacteria, fungi and viruses. The synergy of combinations of medicinal plants will increase the antimicrobial spectrum and give the best results.

2. For how long do I need to take the four herbal supplements?
   Apart from having anti-microbial and anti-inflammatory effects, these herbal supplements also exhibit prebiotic benefits. Hence, you need to consume them in both phase 1 and phase 2, i.e., for a total of 8 weeks. Once you step into phase 3, you must discontinue trikatu, chitrak,

daruhald. That's because these three herbs are consumed only for a period of 2–2.5 months at a stretch. However, you may, if you wish, continue having triphala for another 4–5 months after the end of phase 2.

3.  What can I expect during phase 1?
    Phase 1 of TBBD is designed to help you kick-start your metabolism. Everyone is different. So, while fat loss responses will vary from individual to individual, you will see a steady drop in weight and/or body inches. Your clothes will fit better, your energy will increase, chronic symptoms will reduce, your cravings will disappear and you will feel a lightness in your belly.

4.  The body has its own detox system supported by the lungs, the colon, the liver, the kidneys and the lymphatic system, which are all programmed to detoxify the body constantly. Then why is a detox phase required? Isn't detox diet a fad or myth?
    Yes, the body removes inflammatory molecules, toxins and pathogens with its own self-cleansing mechanisms through the bowels, sweat, breath, urine, etc. But *only* when it is in a state of balance. If you are free from diseases, digesting everything well, eliminating effortlessly, sleeping soundly, waking up fresh and feeling energetic throughout the day, your joints and muscles feel strong, your hair is shiny and your skin looks clear and radiant, then you should head straight to phase 3 of TBBD, where you will only need to maintain the good health you already have. But when your microbiome is not in balance, your metabolism is weak

and your digestive organs debilitated—these show up as obesity, hormonal imbalances, blood sugar imbalances, mood disorders, chronic symptoms, etc.—then that's a sign that your body is unable to clear effectively on its own.

That is why TBBD is a step-wise plan wherein you will first encourage your body's natural cleansing mechanisms and clear the digestive sludge in phase 1. By the time you reach phase 3, your body will have attained balance. It can then use its own intelligent, self-cleansing mechanisms and function in the best possible manner to keep you healthy and fit. Those who call detox a fad must acquaint themselves with *kayakalpa* and *panchakarma*, which are ancient Indian treatment methods of detoxifying the body using oils, herbs, etc. (not salads and raw kale juice). Using detox as a means of transforming the body and health goes back a long way in our history, and it is plain foolish to think of it as a fad.

5.  Am I supposed to sip on hot water in summer too?
    Yes! In many places in south India, like Kerala and Tamil Nadu, it is a common practice to cook water with herbs and spices and have the water either hot or warm all through the year. In Ayurveda as well, it is believed that drinking hot water helps to prevent loss of appetite, bloating and other digestive problems that are common in the hot months. However, if you have difficulty drinking such hot water during summer, then adjust the temperature accordingly. You may also switch to room temperature water or earthen pot water during that time. Refrigerated water should never be consumed.

6.  I lost some weight initially once I stopped gluten and
    dairy. After some time, my weight plateaued. Why?
    That's because gluten or dairy is not causing the weight
    gain. The microbes that are using gluten and dairy are
    the real issue. Weight gain or obesity is associated with
    SCI and intestinal dysbiosis. In these cases, cutting down
    consumption of gluten and dairy in the short term can
    result in some weight loss. However, for long term weight
    loss and renewed health, you also need to work to shift the
    composition of the microbiome at the same time. There
    has to be a plan to reintroduce gluten and dairy foods in
    the long term. That's exactly what we do in TBBD.

7.  Why aren't all lentils, pulses allowed?
    Among all lentils and beans, moong (green gram) is the
    lightest and easiest to digest. After moong comes toor
    (pigeon pea) and masoor dal (red lentil). Considering the
    goals of this phase, you are therefore advised to consume
    only these three lentils for two weeks. The diet in phase 2,
    however, includes all kinds of lentils, beans and pulses. For
    this same reason, a few tubers and veggies are restricted in
    phase 1. These will be added back once you reach phase 2.

8.  What about millet cookies, pastas and noodles that are
    available in the market?
    Since millets don't have gluten, it's not possible to mass
    produce cookies, noodles and the likes without adding
    maida (or atta) to the millets. So, technically they are
    not gluten-free. At other times, instead of wheat, ultra-
    processed ingredients that act as a binder—like potato

starch, xanthan gum, etc.—are added to them, thus qualifying them as NOVA ultra-processed gluten-free foods that you must avoid.

9. They say that you must soak millets for six to eight hours before cooking, otherwise it does not get digested. Is that true?

No! That's not true. Whether the millet needs to be soaked or not depends on the recipe. A few recipes require the millet to be soaked for 15 minutes, a few will need three hours, a few overnight and a few don't need to be soaked at all. It is best to simply follow the traditional recipes as is.

10. Is there any restriction in the consumption of fruits? There is no mention of fruits in Table 9: The Three Fs of Phase 1 at a Glance.

For all practical purposes, know that the only foods you are expected to avoid completely in a given phase are those that are mentioned in the 'Forget' list of the said phase. Foods that are not mentioned in the 'Forget' list can be consumed.

There is no restriction in the consumption of fruits in any phase. Choose fresh, local, seasonal fruits and consume them between 10 a.m. and 4 p.m.

PHASE 2

Repair and Repopulate

Weeks 3–8

6

# Reseeding the Lawn

Now that we have prepared the soil of your gut in phase 1, it's time to reinoculate and repopulate your gut with healthy bacteria. Through the simple ways listed in the book, we will re-establish a thriving gut microbiome that will help develop a lean metabolism, support your health and achieve long-term weight loss. You will find that phase 2 offers much more flexibility compared to the previous phase. We will now add back a few of the foods.

## The Three Fs of Phase 2

Foods to Forget

1. Gluten food sources: Whole wheat, maida, wheat suji/rawa, daliya, barley, rye
2. Lactose food sources: Milk, soft cheese, paneer
3. Distilled spirits, i.e., brandy, gin, rum, tequila, whiskey, vodka and flavoured liqueurs
4. Red meat

## Foods to Eat Few of

Raising a Toast to Your Microbiome

Toasting with water or a non-alcoholic drink can result in seven years of bad sex. At least that's what the Spanish believe. So when I speak of raising a toast, I do intend to keep your toast alcoholic. After all, bedroom activities shouldn't be ruined, right? When it comes to the health of the microbial communities in your gut, what matters is not the number of calories in your drink, but how your alcohol is made. Not all alcohols are the same.

The Difference between Fermented Drinks
and Distilled Spirits

As I explained in the previous chapter, alcohol can cause potential gut wreckage. A direct corollary of it is that if you must drink, then your choice of beverage should be based not on calories but something called alcohol by volume (ABV) or volume per volume (V/V). These indicate the measure of alcohol in a given volume of an alcoholic drink. A label that reads 50 per cent V/V essentially means that 50 ml of alcohol is present in every 100 ml of that drink. Distilled spirits like whiskey have higher alcohol content (or ABV) than fermented beverages like wine, champagne and beer.

While fermented beverages like wine and beer are limited to a maximum alcohol content of about 20 per cent ABV, distilled liquor generally has an alcohol concentration higher than 40 per cent. Therefore, to save your microbiome from any damage, you must completely restrict hard distilled liquors in phase 2.

As long as you limit your consumption to no more than two glasses of wine or beer once every week or two weeks, these fermented beverages will not disrupt your microbiome. On the other hand, slamming down an entire bottle of wine, drinking multiple pints of beer or drinking too often will ultimately expose your gut to a high volume of alcohol that will shift the bacterial community to a state of dysbiosis. This will lead to weight gain (oh the beer belly!) and other health issues. The dose makes the poison! In fact, when taken in small amounts, these fermented beverages can fuel the microbes present in our system and enhance gut microbiota diversity—things that phase 2 is all about. *Huh? What? How?* Read on to find out!

Prebiotic Benefits of Beer and Wine

A team of researchers headed by Professor Tim Spector from King's College London explored the effect of red wine on our gut microbiota. The study, published in the journal *Gastroenterology* in August 2019, is one of the largest-ever studies to analyze the effects of red wine on the guts of nearly 3,000 people in three different countries, namely, the UK, the US and Belgium. They found that the gut microbiota of people who drank moderate amounts of red wine was more diverse, meaning it contained a greater number of different bacterial species. Increased gut microbiota diversity is a sign of good health. These people also had lower levels of obesity and bad cholesterol.

It has long been known that red wine is great for the heart, but now, we know why. The high levels of polyphenols in grapes used for fermenting wines have many beneficial properties. Most importantly, they act as food for the microbes in the gut and exhibit 'prebiotic' effects (more on prebiotics later in this chapter). Because the grapes for red wine are darker and carry more pigments, red wine has more polyphenolic content than white wine. In beer, the polyphenols come from 'hops'—flowers that impart bitterness, flavour and aroma to the beer. The hoppier the beer, the higher the polyphenol content, and the happier your gut will be. To find out how hoppy your brew is, do not go by its perceived bitterness. Instead, look for the IBU number—International Bitterness Units—listed by brands on their websites and/or on their bottles. The IBU is measured on a scale of 0–100; the higher the number, the hoppier the beer.

*Jan hith mein jari!* If you do not drink alcohol, then the prebiotic benefits of wine and beer are no reason to start. Remember, polyphenols are available in many fruits, vegetables and other foods besides wine and beer. We will be having a variety of them in this phase. If you must choose an alcoholic drink, then a Sunday brunch with either wine or beer is acceptable. Check the labels and opt for wine or beer that are lower in alcohol. Pale ales generally have alcohol content as low as 5.5 per cent and their IBU is 50–70. Light beers aren't necessarily low in alcohol content, so you must check the label. The market for low alcohol wines is on the rise, and thankfully, there are many flavours you can choose from. Cheers!

## Table 10: Alcohol Content in Various Alcohols

|  | Red wine | White wine | Beer | Distilled spirits |
|---|---|---|---|---|
| Average Alcohol concentration V/V or ABV | 5.5–20.5 per cent | 5.5–20.5 per cent | 4–7 per cent | over 40 per cent |
| Polyphenols (prebiotics) | Higher | High | More hops = more polyphenols | Absent |
| You should choose | ✓ | ✓ | ✓ | ✗ |
| Label check | Check for V/V or ABV value that is less than 12 per cent | Check for V/V or ABV value that is less than 12 per cent | Check for an IBU number between 50–70 and V/V value less than 7 per cent | ✗ |
| Frequency and dosage | One to two glasses once every week | One to two glasses once every week | One to two pints once every week | ✗ |

## Eggs and White Meat

See, I told you phase 2 is more relaxed! You can have more meat from now on. In phase 2, you can have either fish, or eggs or chicken two times in a week. However, we don't want to overdo it, so avoid eating them twice in the same day. Recent evidence says that any meat more than palm-size servings eaten twice weekly can cause disruption of the gut microbiome balance that can lead to many chronic symptoms.

## Foods to Favour

Now that it is becoming known that the gut microbiome is key to overall health, more and more people are interested in eating in a way that helps normalize a disturbed gut microbiota. Gut health and nutrition have become hot topics in the media, and rightly so. But when there is so much noise and too much contradictory information that lacks scientific evidence, then it becomes difficult to navigate through all those myths, false beliefs and reality. Not anymore! *What are probiotics and prebiotics? Do I need to drink kefirs and kombuchas? Does eating carbs lead to weight gain? What about high protein diets?* As you read on, all these questions will be answered and your confusions put to rest.

In keeping with the goals of this phase, the foods that you favour in phase 2 are:

1. Foods that heal a leaky gut
2. Fermented foods *with* live strains when consumed
3. Fermented foods *without* live strains when consumed
4. Probiotics
5. Prebiotics

Foods that Heal a Leaky Gut

We now know without a doubt that a bad diet can cause loss of tight junction integrity and increased intestinal permeability, and that this can show up in ways like weight gain, belly fat, migraine, acne, thyroid conditions, mood disorders and many more symptoms. The good news is that there are certain unique nutrients that can repair the gut lining; a couple of them have earned the trust of scientists globally. These two most essential nutrients are as follows.

a.   L-Glutamine

Considered a 'conditionally essential' amino acid, L-glutamine plays a vital role in fixing your gut wall. Apart from this critical role in healthy digestion, it also enhances brain function and helps you recover from exercise, reduce cravings and sleep better. L-glutamine is usually produced by the body in sufficient amounts, but in physiologically stressful conditions, the body's demand for it increases. Therefore, it must be obtained from the diet. Though it is naturally found in nuts, beans, yoghurt, chicken, fish and eggs, none of which is restricted in phase 2, I recommend (although it's not mandatory) that you consume it in a supplement form for the next six weeks. It is very safe and readily available online and in the market.

Supplement dosage: Mix 5 gm L-glutamine powder with 200 ml water at room temperature. Drink it once every day after any meal.

b.   Zinc

An essential mineral, zinc has been shown to improve mucosal inflammation and impaired immune system function. Apart from being involved in hundreds of biochemical reactions in the human body, it helps significantly in tissue repair and exhibits a protective effect on the intestinal epithelial barrier. Due to its myriad benefits, I recommend (again, not mandatory) zinc supplementation for the next six weeks. Available in capsule and tablet form, there are many zinc supplements available online and in the market today. Seeds like flaxseeds and sesame seeds, as well as meat, nuts, pulses and legumes are good sources of zinc, and all of these are foods you will favour in phase 2.

Supplement dosage: The recommended daily dosage of zinc is typically 10–30 mg of elemental zinc. It is best to take it after a meal.

As you begin working on the gut wall, it makes sense to simultaneously start seeding your inner ecosystem with live microbes, the number one source of which are fermented foods.

Fermented Foods

The act of transforming and preserving foods and beverages through the use of bacteria, fungi and enzymes is called fermentation. When we ferment any food, we allow beneficial bacteria to digest some of the carbohydrates and sugars in the food. Which means that consuming anything fermented is like eating food that's sort of 'predigested' by the bacteria before they have even entered our mouth. Interesting, isn't it?

That bacteria and other microbes are capable of transforming food substrates has been known for thousands of years. Fermented foods have been an integral part of Indian cultural heritage since the dawn of civilization. Like old folk songs, their recipes have been handed down from generation to generation. I have grown up hearing stories of my great-grandmother meticulously teaching the skills of fermenting and making achaar, murabba and kanji to my grandmother, and then seen my grandmother passing them on to my mother. Like the art of hand-weaving, this too is exquisite!

Moreover, if you look around you, you will find that almost all Indian communities have festivals—occurring during seasonal transitions—that revolve around feasting on day-old dishes. At the start of spring, Bengalis celebrate Sheetal Shashti with fermented rice gruel, while Marwaris also follow the tradition of Basoda around the same time of the year by eating foods cooked a day prior. Sindhis call this festival Shitala Satam around the Shrawan month, and in parts of Uttar Pradesh, the festival is called Sili Sat. But is this custom merely a religious observance? If you go by the word of microbiologists and scientists around the world, then there's more to it than meets the eye.

The discovery of many health-promoting and disease-preventing benefits of fermented foods—specifically those discovered over the last two decades—has put the focus back on ingesting these traditional delights. Depending on the raw materials (food ingredients) you use and the microbe(s) that ferment, there's a huge variety of these foods with equally varied health benefits. Rightly designated *naturally fortified functional food*, they not only preserve food, but also enhance the digestibility and vitamin content (especially B vitamins and vitamin K2) of foods, eliminate anti-nutrients naturally found in food and add a unique flavour and taste. Fermentation adds such benefits beyond those present in the pre-fermented food. We may ignore the age-old tradition of fermentation, calling it laborious or simply unnecessary, but it has caught the world's fancy. Owing to their desirable organoleptic properties, Michelin star chefs across the world are putting bacteria to work to produce foods that are fermented. With results that are delicious, to say the least. At the same time, microbiome science is fast gaining momentum and has forced scientists worldwide to study the possible health benefits of this so called 'rotten goodness'. And the verdict is out—our guts love fermented foods!

Though the interest in media and consumers alike has made fermented foods one of the hottest categories in a grocery store, there is still a lot of confusion going around. *Do we really know them? Aren't fermented foods the same as probiotics? Or are they different?*

By now, you may have realized that busting food myths and clearing confusions related to food is something that I proactively engage in. So, without further delay, allow me to set the record straight: *All fermented foods do not qualify as probiotic, and not all probiotics take the form of fermented foods.* We will gradually go into the details of what I just said, but first, let's gain more clarity about foods that are fermented.

Depending on whether microbes are alive at the time of consumption or not, fermented foods are divided into two groups:

1.  Fermented foods that RETAIN live microbes when consumed
2.  Fermented foods that DO NOT RETAIN live microbes when consumed

In order to favourably alter the gut microbiome balance, to enhance and diversify the gut microbiome, you should eat fermented foods from both the groups. It isn't about one being better than the other. Rather, it's about them being different from each other, and hence, exerting different health benefits in different ways.

Fermented foods are great natural sources of live beneficial bacteria like *Lactobacillus*, *Bifidobacteria* and others. But these microbes are heat sensitive. Live cultures are destroyed at around 115°F (46°C)—a basic microbiology fact. So while the dahi you set at home does have a good culture of live microbes, the moment you cook it to make *Punjabi kadhi*, *Kerala avial curry* or anything else, the live bacteria are killed and are no longer available in the final product. Cooking kills off the bacteria. Phew! I have heard celebrated nutritionists calling kaddhi, etc. a probiotic. Now, you know that that's just half-baked gyaan! Just because it's made out of curd doesn't mean it has live, active microbes. And it's not only cooking; every time food undergoes further processing like pasteurization, smoking, baking, etc. after fermentation, they are no longer sources of active microbes. The organisms in fermented foods that are subsequently heat-treated are inactivated. Examples of foods that undergo fermentation but do not contain live microorganisms at the time of consumption are kadhi, idli, dosa, khaman, sourdough bread, jalebi, bhatura, beer, wine, homemade ghee (made from white butter), etc. Since these are baked, cooked or treated after fermentation, the rich complement of microbes responsible for their transformation are killed.

On the other hand, there are many incredible fermented foods that contain good, friendly microbes that are still alive when we eat them, unless, of course, you subject them to high heat or cooking. *Ah, so these are the ones that we call probiotics, right?* Unfortunately, most fermented foods that contain living microbes—for instance, home-set curd and yoghurt—are wrongly termed probiotics not only by the media but also by nutritionists, health professionals and the like. This was one of the reasons I wrote this book. I wanted to bring to you scientific facts that often get blurred because of misinformation becoming commonplace. As you keep reading, you will learn what probiotics are, but for now, let's get to know more about fermented foods that retain live microbes when consumed. Broadly, these come in two varieties: fermented dairy products and fermented fruits and veggies.

Fermented Dairy Products

Fermented dairy foods are a common vehicle for live bacteria. That's because milk makes a great base in which good bacteria can multiply. One of the most significant groups of organisms that these cultured foods contain is the lactic acid bacteria (LAB) Lactobacillus. These live microorganisms feed on lactose, a naturally occurring sugar in dairy, and break it down. Fermented dairy is hence nothing but milk that has been pre-digested by bacteria, making it more digestible. *All types of fermented dairy, whether it's curd or hand-churned white butter or traditional, cultured buttermilk—are lactose free.* Cheese lovers can rejoice too! Unlike fresh, soft cheese—think paneer—hard aged cheeses go through a ripening process that range from three weeks to two or more years. As cheese ages, bacteria ferment the lactose over time, leaving the cheese with very little to no lactose and making it more digestible. A well-aged, artisanal cheese that doesn't go through pasteurization or processing (heat treatment) after it has been ripened is a microbial paradise, so to speak. As you can see, restoring the gut flora isn't only easy, it's delicious too! You will be surprised to see the phase 2 meal plan consisting of simple, homemade meals like curd rice, rabdi, ambali, makhan mishri, etc.

## Vegan: To Be or Not to Be

Animal agriculture results in exploitation of animals, deforestation, water and air pollution, biodiversity loss and climate change. Hence, veganism or eating a vegan diet is the 'single biggest way' to save the animals, our environment, our planet! Is it?

I am not an evangelist for going vegan. I am merely repeating the main reasons people cite for becoming one. Whether or not to turn vegan is your personal choice, just like deciding to stay single or marry. There is no right or wrong there. Simply put, to each his own. But when it comes to anything related to food, it is my responsibility to share the complete picture with you, without which you may end up making an uninformed decision. For instance, on the surface, the great war of the Mahabharata may appear as a genocide or mass slaughter instigated by Krishna. A few foreign scholars have misunderstood it as an act of violence, and hence call it unethical. But when one studies the scriptural text of the *Bhagavad Gita* under the guidance of a competent teacher and gains a broader view, one understands that the Mahabharata war was fought for the establishment of *Dharma*, i.e., righteousness, to redeem the society of *Adharma* and its dreadful consequences. That is why, even after millennia, the battle continues to be referred to as *dharamyudh*, the exact opposite of what it may appear to be from the outside. Hence, before you adopt militant veganism because it *appears* to be the ethical way of living life, I want to acquaint you with a few lesser-known facts, starting with the avocado.

The new-found love for avocados over ghee to save cows comes at a cost. If you live in India, then you should know that avocados are grown on a very limited scale and in a scattered way only in a few parts of south-central India. Most of the avocados in Indian supermarkets as well as those in America and UK are imported from Peru, Chile or Mexico, the major producers of avocados in the world. So the avocados that fuel your morning smoothie are transported, and transport does lead to greenhouse gas emissions. Moreover, while avocados add great value to your vegan or keto diet, it doesn't help the Mexican farmers; their lands have been seized by drug lords, who then force them to pay extortion money. In fact, the violence and problems in Mexico caused by the cartels have led to avocados being labelled 'the blood diamonds of Mexico'. It is hard to make the case for avocados when the nutritional benefits are readily available in products closer to home, one of which is ghee.

Now let's talk about almonds, one of the most water-intensive crops. It takes around 60 litres of water to produce just 16 almonds! If you're considering non-dairy milk because you are concerned about the environment, then you should note that in that sense, the dairy-free, vegan-friendly milk substitute that is almond milk isn't any different from dairy milk. It isn't the silver bullet you think it is. According to the United States Department of Agriculture (USDA), in 2018–19, increased almond production to meet the growing demands of almond milk and almond butter killed 50 billion bees. Veganism clearly isn't saving the planet.

In our enthusiasm to save one species, we are clearly not realizing that we are inflicting hardship on another. Yes, we should put a stop to industrialized dairy production. However, abstinence from dairy is not the answer. What we should do is favour sustainable farms that look after the cattle well and give high quality products. We cannot afford to forget that livestock is the most important economic security of farmers in our country. It doesn't just give them milk, but manure too. In the absence of this natural, organic fertilizer, farmers would add chemical fertilizers to soil, which would then flood our lakes, rivers and oceans, killing the very fish and marine life vegans are trying to save. Acclaimed Indian environmentalist Sunita Narain has said, 'Banning meat in India is cruel demonetization. It is stealing from the poor, nothing less.' *So how is saving animals more ethical than pushing millions of farmers and villagers into hardship?*

As you see, the story is more nuanced than you might have thought it is. Eating meat or consuming dairy is not the key issue, the overconsumption of foods is. In a country like India, the culture of eating food has always differed between communities, regions and religions for hundreds of years.

Some communities like mine stayed vegetarian, while a few other communities habitually ate meat. This helped maintain a balance and kept the entire ecosystem ticking. However, in the last few years, ignorance of optimal protein content in vegetarian foods has led people from vegetarian communities to consume meat. The current obsession towards protein—an obsession borrowed from the West—has resulted in more people eating more non-vegetarian food than the human body requires.

When it comes to the environment, animal welfare and human health, what really matters is the amount that is consumed and the manner in which the food is produced. When you buy fresh milk from local, sustainable farms, you cannot be assured of a fixed supply of milk delivered to your doorstep every morning. That's because the quantity and quality of milk produced by the cow changes based on the changing climate and diet of the cow. At an age where we look for instant gratification all the time, this may not be pleasurable to many.

All of this basically leads to my point: If there's anything that is destroying the world, it is *human greed*. Veganism will not save our planet. Curbing our greed will.

## Fermented Fruits and Veggies

Among all food items, fruits and vegetables are the most easily perishable. Our ancestors found an intelligent way to preserve them so that they could be relished all through the year. Age-old traditional recipes of achaar, kanji, murabbas were woven around the availability of fresh seasonal produce. Ask your grandma and she will tell you how every summer would be incomplete without making the yearly stock of *aam ka achaar*. During the rains and winters, when mango wasn't available anymore, these aam ka achaars would liven up the meal. The making of these heritage foods was almost like a community activity. Women would get together during summer afternoons along with the children of the house who would keep a watchful eye on all the preparations. Until a few decades ago, during winters, the making of the *Kaali Gajar Kanji* in huge *barnis* or jars was an annual ritual in most houses in the northern part of India. Contrary to today's day and age, where each recipe is documented and shared online, back then, fermenting fruits and veggies was rather a work of *andaaz*. How much water must submerge the carrots? How much mustard is required to kick-start the fermentation? All these details were all learnt with time and wisdom.

Little did our grandmothers know that their traditional fermented treasures would soon be recognized all over the world as 'functional foods'. Fermented fruits and vegetables are a potential source of live microbes as they harbour several lactic acid bacteria such as Lactobacillus plantarum, L. pentosus, L. brevis, L. acidophilus, L. fermentum and L. mesenteroides. That is why traditionally fermented achaar, kanji and murabba not only add a novel flavour to your meals but also provide health benefits.

Just as curd is obtained by lactic acid fermentation of milk, raw veggies are transformed into pickles through the same process. Bacteria occur naturally in the air, on your hands and on the raw fruits and veggies themselves. These bacteria gobble up the sugars in the fruits and veggies and produce lactic acid, which gives the characteristic sour tang to the pickles and at the same time, keeps pathogens in check so that the pickles don't spoil. The salt isn't added to give you high blood pressure, as most doctors believe. It is an important ingredient that helps the good LABs grow and multiply more rapidly than the bad ones so that they can have a competitive advantage. If not for salt, they would not quite win this race. The oil, jeera, dhania and methi daana are all added to control the microbial garden and make it less hospitable to spoilage microbes. The earthen pots and ceramic jars help maintain just the right temperature for the helpful microbes to thrive. And the muslin cloth covering the crocks helps seal out air and oxygen, thus creating an anaerobic environment that gives the good guys a leg up. What we perceive as nothing but a lump of oil and salt is in reality a carefully thought-out action plan that can give modern microbiologists a run for their money.

The disappearance of the quintessential tradition of making lacto-ferments in recent times is a curious case indeed. Considering the long list of benefits they offer, right from weight loss to improved immune response to modulating proper digestion, they should most definitely make a comeback in your kitchen.

Can I Buy My Lacto-Ferments Instead of Making Them?

*'Rasode mei kaun tha?'* This was probably the most burning question of 2020 that kept everyone busy looking for an answer. I too found one, *'Rasode mei sab kuch processed or packaged tha!'*

The busy lifestyles we lead make us hunt for easy and convenient foods. Adding to it is the explosion of interest in our inner ecosystem. What follows is pretty obvious: Significant commercial shelf space is now dedicated to fermented products. Canned, packaged and pasteurized varieties of yoghurts, pickles, sauerkraut and kimchi sit on the shelves of grocery stores. Kombucha, a fermented tea drink known to have originated in China in 220 BC, has begun to make an appearance at farmer's markets and health stores globally. All of them claim to have benefits that will change your gut microbiome for the better. Words like 'probiotics' are cleverly inserted on the label to increase brand value and sales. (Are they ferments? Yes! But are they probiotics? No!) Dr Michael Mosley, former medical doctor and BBC presenter, along with Dr Paul Cotter from the Teagasc Food Research Centre in Cork, Ireland, selected a range of homemade and store-bought fermented foods and beverages and had them tested in a lab. While a wide array of live and active microbes was found in the traditional, homemade varieties, the commercial products contained barely any. *Why is that so?*

Modern Processing and Pasteurization
Destroys the Live Cultures in Food

Commercial, off-the-shelf fermented foods and drinks that are typically found in most supermarkets are subjected to pasteurization (heat-treatment) after they are prepared. This helps to kill harmful bacteria, ensures the safety of the food and drink and extends their shelf life. But the process also kills off the live good bacteria and precious enzymes like lactase that are beneficial for us. Processed, packaged and canned versions of yoghurt, butter, pickles, sauerkraut and other fermented foods do not have the benefits of their homemade counterparts. In fact, most commercially-prepared pickles involve no fermentation. The fruits or vegetable is pickled in vinegar and then heated to high temperatures for sterility and long shelf life. Instead of natural fermentation, the pickles get their sour flavour from the added vinegar.

## Added Sugars and Chemical Additives Decrease the Nutritional Value

Most of the time, commercially sold fermented foods contain large amounts of sugars, including high fructose corn syrup (HFCS), corn starch and modified corn starch. The commercial yoghurts, kefirs and kombuchas in the market today are more like processed desserts than beneficial ferments with live cultures. And then there are the so-called 'all natural yoghurts' that are loaded with artificial sweeteners linked to dysbiosis, weight gain and poor health. Industrialized sugars feed pathogenic microorganisms and can elevate fungal and yeast infections.

## Plastic Packaging Can Kill Off Microbes

One of the main factors that affect the survival of LABs is the presence of oxygen. Lactic acid fermentation is an anaerobic reaction. Not only do the lactic acid bacteria not require oxygen for growth, but they may even die if free oxygen is present. Therefore, the level of oxygen inside the package during its storage until the end of its shelf life should be very low. The ceramic and earthenware containers used at home can easily control the process of fermentation. Glass and metal packaging materials have extremely low oxygen permeability. This means that they do not allow the passage of small gaseous molecules like oxygen through them. Glass and metal packages therefore favour the survival of live cultures. But the high cost of glass along with its handling difficulties makes it an inappropriate choice for packaging commercial fermented products. So, the most preferred material is plastic. However, plastic is permeable to oxygen, and hence causes toxicity and death of the microorganisms and the consequent loss of functionality of the product. This is also one of the reasons why many studies have shown low viability of beneficial bacteria in market preparations of fermented foods.

What Should You Do?

'I can't wait for the workshop to begin. Have always wanted to learn how to make that perfect puff pastry. It isn't all that easy, you know, Munmun,' Meera emphatically said while sipping on the fennel tea at my office. She had already lost some weight during phase 1 and now that she was in phase 2, we were talking about ferments that she could make at home. Instead, it was puff pastries that had captured her interest. The irony is that when it comes to French food, the challenges, such as the difficulty of making puff pastries, are perceived as aspirational. But people use the difficulty of making our indigenous foods as an excuse to not make them. Mass-produced fermented foods and beverages that mimic traditionally-made ones do not provide the same benefits of live microbes and enzymes that *real* fermented foods provide.

Although there are many ethnic fermented foods from different pockets of our country, I have listed a few such ferments that retain live microbes in Table 11. I encourage you to make a few of these, if not all. A study published in the *Journal of Economic Perspectives* might motivate you to wear the apron at home. The researchers of this study found that the amount of time spent cooking at home is inversely proportional to your risk of weight gain and obesity! If this still doesn't fascinate you, luckily, there are many home entrepreneurs these days who have taken it upon themselves to not let the valuable tradition of fermented foods die. It is worth finding one near you or online and get your regular supply of ferments from them. If you really have no choice but to buy from the market, then look for local sources. When buying something packaged, choose the ones with a short list of ingredients list—just milk and live active cultures in case of fermented dairy, for instance. The product should also be unsweetened, with no added sugar, and bear a label that says 'contains active cultures'. Although they are very few in number, some manufacturers add live cultures toward the end of the batch processing, and these microbes continue to be active during transit and make it all the way into your kitchen.

## How Many Ferments Should You Eat in a Day?

Since you will consume ferments every day for six weeks in phase 2, any one fermented food from Table 11 in a day is good enough to reverse dysbiosis and restore your gut flora.

However, you should rotate between these ferments and not stick to the same one every day.

A 2002 study published in the *European Journal of Clinical Nutrition* revealed that the amount and strain of useful bacteria in curd varies from place to place. The number and types of LABs that ferment the milk are likely to differ from household to household due to the lack of a standardized starter culture used to prepare curd. Likewise, with all other home ferments, bacterial content and composition varies depending on water activity, salt concentration, temperature, the composition of the food matrix, etc. Which means that when you add fermented foods to your diet, you will not know the exact species of bacteria you ingest. Your best bet would be to consume a variety of these foods, so that together, they provide a broad range of live microbes that will help rebalance your inner flora.

Table 12 also lists a few examples of fermented foods that retain live microbes when you consume them. The difference from the other list in Table 11 is that these are ferments of non-Indian origin. And that's exactly why we need to err on the side of caution. It isn't just speciality stores that are hoarding these foreign ferments. Restaurants and bars in cities like Mumbai, Delhi and Bengaluru are cashing in on the craze and serving kombucha in bottles. The last time I was in Goa, I came across a hipster cafe that had kombucha on tap! The truth is that most of the brewers pasteurize their products, killing all the live cultures—the key reason why you choose to consume them in the first place. You already know now that in order to receive live strains, you need to choose non-commercial, unprocessed, artisanal varieties made by a human and not a corporation. And since in case of fermentation, questions like how long you ferment your veggies or how you know when it is ready have no objective answer; you really do not want to trust a complete novice.

Ferments that are effective in delivering live, active strains are prepared by veterans who have learnt the skill with patience and over time. For foods like curd, murabba, kanji, etc., you will find enough people around you with the right expertise, right from your aunt to your neighbour to your *ghar ki bai*, but for foods listed in Table 12, you will most probably have a tough time finding someone knowledgeable. Just like a Russian grandma will not know how to manipulate the temperature of milk according to the changing climate to set dahi, we will not know how to use, make and consume the Russian kefir to our best advantage.

Additionally, most Indians experience gas, bloating and other mild stomach problems with kombucha, kefir, sauerkraut and the like, especially when they first start having these. On the other hand, as fermented indigenous foods—those listed in Table 11—have been traditionally serving Indian communities, microbiota associated with these foods is interconnected with healthy and safe attributes. To understand why, you will first have to know how live microbes benefit our microflora—their mechanism of action.

How Do Live Microbes Restore Our Gut Microbiota?

A common myth is that live microbes, when consumed either in the form of fermented foods or probiotics, colonize the digestive tract. The fact is that live microbes never colonize, i.e., they do not live permanently or even long-term in the human gut. It's the native, ancestral microbes that you were born with that reside in your gut permanently. Live microbes that you ingest are transient and comparatively fewer in number. So how do they confer health benefits even if they do not colonize?

As live dietary microbes pass through the gut, they adhere to the intestinal surfaces for some time, which varies from a day to a week. They interact with the resident microbes, influence them, educate them and synthesize some antimicrobial compounds, and that's how they exert their benefits in ways that are amplified throughout the body. But it isn't all that easy. The bacteria that are there inside the intestine don't simply move over and welcome the ones you consume from outside. The insiders–outsiders *ki kahaani* isn't just limited to Bollywood. Our guts are competitive environments too! The adhesion sites are open for competition, and the live microbes you ingest don't just go and cling to these sites. They need to fight for cellular attachments. If they win and take up the space, the bad guys have no choice but to leave. This effect is known as 'colonization resistance'. That's why when it comes to consuming foods with live microbes, the effectiveness of a strain in restoring normal flora is judged based on its ability to attach itself to the mucus covering the intestinal epithelium.

Whether or not the bacteria will adhere to the intestinal mucosa and be ahead of the game is dependent on quite a few factors, one of which is the presence of receptors. The gut lining has receptors that are like latches or anchors that the bacteria can adhere to. The kind of receptors that are present on the mucosa is largely dependent on an individual's genetics. Makes it clear why foreign live ferments, especially large amounts of kombucha, kefir, sauerkraut and the like, do not sit well with everyone's digestion, while that's rarely a case with Indian indigenous fermented foods.

The Bottom Line

Despite what social media tells you, if you are desi then you don't have to go around experimenting with all the international ferments in the world in order to have a healthy gut ecosystem. At the same time, if you really want to, you can. That's because, as I explained, dietary live microbes, irrespective of whether they are from Indian or non-Indian origin fermented foods, do not take permanent places in our gut, and members of our native gut microbiota do not really deal with them directly. As long as the international ferments are made the authentic way, are teeming with live microbes and are not causing any digestive distress to you, you can include them in your daily diet. To ensure safety and efficacy, make sure you buy them from someone who has many years of experience in fermenting them, rather than someone who is a mere one or two workshops old. To reduce the likelihood of any bloating, gas, etc., start with a small amount and slowly increase over a few weeks.

## Table 11: Indian-Origin Fermented Foods with Live Microbes

| |
|---|
| Curd |
| Hand-blended buttermilk★ |
| Hand-churned white butter★ |
| Bengali mishti doi |
| Pickle |
| Kanji |
| Murabba |
| Gulkand |
| Raw, unrefined and unfiltered fruit vinegar WITH mother ★★ |
| A few ripened cheeses like kalari, hard churpi, surti cheese, Kalimpong cheese |
| Fermented rice (Panta bhat) |

★ High-speed blenders create heat that can kill the live microbes. Use a traditional wooden *mathani* or stainless steel churner instead.

★★ Mother is the culture of beneficial bacteria that cause the process of fermentation to take place.

## Table 12: Non-Indian-Origin Fermented Foods with Live Microbes

| |
|---|
| Kefir |
| Kombucha |
| Sauerkraut |
| Kimchi |
| Filmjölk |
| Fermented soya like tempeh, miso, natto |
| Aged cheese like gouda, cheddar, feta, edam, brie, blue cheese, parmesan cheese, aged ricotta |

## Potential Health Benefits of Fermented Foods with Live Microbes

Providing our guts an ongoing exposure to a fresh source of microbes through dietary sources has been linked to a long list of benefits for your body and brain, including:

1. Enhances metabolism and accelerates weight loss
2. Improves immune response
3. Reduces stress and improves mood
4. Reduces risk of chronic illness including diabetes, elevated cholesterol levels, hypertension, cardiovascular disease, allergies and certain types of cancer
5. Downregulation of inflammation
6. Helps manage digestive discomforts
7. Decreases risk or duration of common infections, including respiratory, gut, vaginal and urinary tract infections

## Potential Health Benefits of Fermented Foods Not Retaining Live Microbes

Instant Gratification Syndrome or IGS—*naam toh suna hoga?* No? Oh dear! Let me explain. Every time you binge-watch a series instead of waiting a week for the next episode, let alone a year for the next season; every time you choose T20 cricket over a five-day test match; every time lasting relationships that demand investment sounds boring and Tinder romance sounds fun, you suffer from IGS, an under-diagnosed disease characterized by wanting everything right here, right now! In the world of quickies, food too has become a casualty.

Traditional recipes of dosa, bhatura, dhokla, khaman, idli, etc. that take around eight to nine hours of fermentation time have long been forgotten. No-hassle instant recipes that use commercial yeasts, baking soda, baking powder, ENO, citric acid and the like can help you whip up the same meal without fermentation in a quick 10–15 minutes. So cool, right?

Hate me all you want, but when it comes to food, love and life, an important thing we need to realize is, 'Good things come to those who wait.'

Here's an interesting question. Why should you let the batter rest and ferment when the live microbes in them will anyway die during the cooking process?

The old-fashioned way of hours of fermentation using lactic acid bacteria found in grains, legumes, utensils and naturally occurring yeast in the air improves the nutritional value of the food. Though the bacteria die because of the heat used in cooking, a few changes they bring about are retained in the final product. But when you use shortcut methods in the name of convenience, what you get is food with a similar number of calories but without many of the other invaluable benefits. This should give you another reason to think beyond calories, because when it comes to food, it's not always about what you eat but also about how it is made!

Ever wondered why globally, more and more people are deficient in vitamin B12 today? Our bodies cannot synthesize vitamin B12, i.e., there is no endogenous production. But the good LABs can! In fact, not just human beings, no plants and animals possess the key enzymes needed to form vitamin B12. They are found exclusively in bacteria. *Then why is it that doctors and nutritionists recommend animal foods as sources of B12?*

That's because cows, sheep and other herbivorous mammals absorb the B12 produced by bacteria in their own digestive system. The B12 is made not by their bodies, but by bacterial fermentation. Which makes me wonder if gradually shifting away from traditional recipes that allow fermentation—choosing an instant idli over the long-fermented one, for instance—is the reason why we see the rampant B12 deficiency today. Most probably yes! Fermenting synthesizes vitamin B12, and since the vitamin itself is not sensitive to heat, it is not destroyed during cooking. Additionally, fermentation also increases the bioavailability of amino acids, thus improving the assimilation and efficiency of protein in foods.

Another interesting property of several LABs is their ability to secrete something called exopolysaccharides or EPS (you can think of it as complex carbs) into the surrounding environment. The batter that ferments overnight or for a few hours has an abundance of these therapeutic compounds. And while the live microbes in the ferments aren't resistant to cooking, these beneficial compounds are. In your body, EPS are used as 'prebiotics' (food for bacteria) and are known to have health benefits such as lowering cholesterol and modulation of the immune response system. Lastly, when you subject the fermented batter to heat for cooking, yes, the live microbes do die. However, a body of evidence indicates that heat-killed bacteria, the dead cells and their components can exert broad biological effects such as enhanced barrier function, healing of a leaky gut and protection against pathogens. Phew! That's quite a list, isn't it?

The crux of the matter is that it is worth investing time and ferment foods in your kitchen. In order to support your ecosystem so that it can in turn support you, you should include both fermented foods that retain live microbes upon consumption and those that do not. In the recipes and meal plans of phase 2, you will see a mix of both these types. Keeping in mind the busy lives we lead, I have purposely made sure that most of the recipes are simple. And the few that are elaborate are so tasty that it is worth the extra time. One such recipe is chole bhature.

## Bhatura: Fried Junk or India's Sourdough Bread?

The thing with food is that it trends, just like fashion, movies and TV shows. When Google released its 'Year in Search' report for 2020, sourdough bread grabbed the third spot among the top 10 trending recipes globally. (Dalgona coffee was at the top, unsurprisingly!) It seems every 20-something Tom, Hardik and Hari's new obsession is sourdough bread. But long before it made its way to Instagram and Twitter, Ikarians— known for their high life expectancy—have been eating true sourdough bread. There's nothing new about sourdough. It has been around for millennia.

## Why Is This Ancient Process Becoming a Modern Trend?

Real sourdough bread is made with a long fermentation process—at least eight hours of fermentation time—without the use of any baker's yeast or commercial yeast. The breads are leavened by long-lasting fermentation of dough using naturally-occurring lactobacilli bacteria and yeast. The LABs break down the sugar in the dough and produce lactic acid, which contributes to the distinctive sour flavour of the bread. It is this method of prolonged fermentation that brings with it many health benefits, making sourdough bread one of the most sought-after superfoods among the health-conscious.

Unfortunately, most sourdough breads sold commercially in stores are fake; they contain fast-rising yeasts, ferment for only one to two hours and are devoid of many nutritional benefits. While there are artisanal bakeries in the metro cities of India that bake a true sourdough (I will still advise that you ask your baker how long the bread is fermented for), what if I told you about another traditionally-made, slow-fermented bread? Made from sourdough fermentation using a stable culture of natural lactic acid bacteria and yeast in a mixture of flour and water, this is India's very own sourdough that you can make easily in your own kitchen—the bhaturas!

Like real sourdough bread, a traditionally-made bhatura (not the instant kind that use baking soda, etc.) offers many health benefits.

1.  *It's gluten-free!* A long fermentation process (around seven to eight hours) gives enough time to the LABs to break down the gluten proteins in the wheat dough. In a 2011 study, researchers showed that when wheat undergoes a slow lacto-fermentation, it is possible to render it technically gluten-free. So, the bhatura that we think of as deep-fried junk has less gluten than even breads labelled 'gluten-free' and is sans chemicals and additives that are usually found in commercial breads.

2.  *It's rich in dietary fibre:* There's so much fuss about the maida in bhatura. '*OMG it doesn't have fibre! OMG it will*

*spike up sugar levels!'* What if I told you that your fears are unwarranted? Welcome to the world of resistant starch (RS). As its name suggests, RS is one that resists digestion. Our bodies cannot break it down to use for energy, but the good microbes in our gut love to feast on them. In the body, RS acts in a very similar way to dietary fibre, and has been associated with many health benefits. What we do not know—probably because we have never given enough importance to the tiny good guys living inside of us—is that maida has higher RS than whole wheat flour! A research study to estimate the RS content of selected, routinely-consumed Indian food preparations found that the bhatura contained more RS than whole wheat chapati! A long fermentation process enhances the levels of RS in breads. Additionally, the higher the fermentation time, the more the EPS produced. If you remember, EPS are complex carbs that also contribute to the dietary fibre content of the food. This increase in fibre slows the digestion of the bhatura and does not cause rapid blood sugar spikes like a commercially available white bread, also made from maida, would. In fact, the old-fashioned long fermentation process to make sourdough bread gives enough time to the wild yeasts and bacteria to break down the sugars in the dough, making them low on the glycemic index scale. A bhatura with more fibre and reduced sugars is, hence, slow burning, will keep you fuller for longer and help maintain steady blood sugar levels. It is not only safe but good for people who are diabetics and/or are obese.

*But bhaturas are deep fried and therefore unhealthy, right?*

It's 2021! Let's do away with stereotyping fried foods as unhealthy! Bhaturas are deep-fried but not necessarily unhealthy. It is best to deep-fry them in good old ghee, not refined vegetable oils that are inflammatory. The virtues of ghee would take up a book in their own right. The anti-inflammatory fat in ghee, along with the fibre and protein in chole, can help avoid the blood sugar roller coaster and increase satiation levels. Before any American restaurateur in Manhattan puts chole bhature in his menu, describing it as 'crispy Indian sourdough bread, slowly leavened with a live culture, gluten-free, lactose-free, rich in fibre and possessing prebiotic benefits, served with spicy chickpeas, pickled ginger and raw onions', let's wake up to the glories of our own food!

*Does it mean I can have chole bhature every day?* Of course not! You do remember the three Rs, don't you? Eat them once in a week as a treat meal, for lunch (not breakfast) and stop before you are full (eat five bites lesser). In Chapter 10, you will find a bhatura recipe using the traditional sourdough process.

Though you will continue to restrict gluten food sources like wheat, maida, barley, etc. in phase 2, I encourage you to slow ferment these gluten-filled grains and include a variety of such recipes, like barley dosa, wheat gulgula, etc., in your phase 2 meal plan. The long fermentation process will allow the bacteria to fully break down the gluten, making it desirable for this phase.

## Probiotics

Now that we know all about fermented foods, let's clear up the mystery around probiotics. The current definition of probiotics by the Food and Agriculture Organization (FAO) of the United Nations and the World Health Organization (WHO) is 'live microorganisms which when administered in adequate amounts confer a health benefit on the host.'

## Why Are Curd and Yoghurt Not Probiotic?

Curd, yoghurt and other fermented foods mentioned in Tables 12 and 13 contain a wide variety of living lactobacillus and/ or bifidobacterium that are beneficial to human health. But they do not qualify as probiotics. According to the universally accepted definition set by an international panel of experts, probiotics are live organisms that are characterized (known), have been scientifically studied and when consumed in amounts that have been tested provide a health benefit beyond basic nutrition. Let me explain what this means.

How many women called Munmun do you think exist in this world? Millions, likely. But what about Munmun Ganeriwal who lives in Mumbai, who is a celebrity nutritionist with 19 years' experience specializing in functional, microbiome medicine using traditional Indian foods along with Ayurveda and yogic techniques? There is only one. The point I am trying to make is that just as you cannot say all Munmuns are health and wellness specialists, you also cannot say that all lactobacilli or bifidobacteria are probiotics. Our surname, home address, qualifications, gender, age and other factors add to our characteristics and differentiate us from others. Similarly, bacteria also have a first name called genus, second name called species and a third name that adds even more specificity called strain. For example, for the bacteria Lactobacillus acidophilus

LA5, Lactobacillus is the genus, acidophilus is the species and LA5 is the strain designation.

In order to be a probiotic, the microorganisms in the food should be characterized (known) by all the three names, i.e., genus, species and strain. Strain specificity is important because different strains exist within the same species, and each strain can have specific health benefits. For cultures to be called probiotic, it is important that a food item or product is standardized in terms of the strain of bacteria and contains the studied strain at a dose that can confer a health benefit. On the other hand, the bacteria in curd, yoghurt and all other fermented foods mentioned in Tables 11 and 12 are not defined qualitatively or quantitatively. The number and type of bacteria in these foods vary from home to home. So fermented foods like these have an undefined, mixed microbial content.

The dahi you set at home does have live and active lactobacilli, but it is not a probiotic unless a specific probiotic bacteria is added to it. The benefits of probiotics are strain-specific; depending on the bacteria that gets added, the product—in this case dahi—will provide a specific benefit and be called a 'true' probiotic. Take the example of Danone's Activia Probiotic Yoghurt that's available widely in Western countries. Apart from the lactobacillus and streptococcus species that are naturally available in yoghurts, billions of the probiotic strain Bifidobacterium animalis lactis DN 173,010 are added to traditional yoghurt to make Danone's Activia yoghurt. At the given dose, this strain has been clinically shown to help reduce the frequency of minor digestive discomfort. This is why calling this particular yoghurt a probiotic is correct, but it would be wrong to generalize all yoghurts or dahi as one.

Not all fermented foods contain live cultures that meet the definition of a probiotic. Unless the strain has been tested and shown to be probiotic (displaying clinical evidence of a health benefit), and the same viable numbers are in that food, you can't call that fermented food probiotic.

## Why Is It Important to Distinguish between Fermented Foods and Probiotics?

It's not a bad thing that not all fermented foods meet the criteria required to be called probiotic. It's just important that we specify the difference and expectations from them. Targeted probiotic supplements allow us to control the types of strains introduced into the ecology, and are thus important. At the same time, you will never get very far if you don't have the foundation in place that the supplement is supposed to be supplementing. When you take probiotics, you're adding a small number of microbes to a very large pool, your native, indigenous gut microbiome; so it would be wrong to think that simply popping a probiotic will work some sort of magic and completely rebalance your inner garden and permanently shift you toward a lean metabolism. But when you do all the other things—kill the bad bugs, repair the gut lining, eat diverse kinds of fermented foods and prebiotics, etc.—then you can target a specific health concern, if any, with the probiotic supplements and witness how effectively it works in your favour. I do recommend them while working with my clients, if they require it.

In contrast to what TV marketers and social media influencers claim, if you have no chronic illness that can be addressed by the probiotics, there is no reason to take these supplements. Don't fix what isn't broken! And yet, there are a million claims out there and a million more probiotic supplements to buy. Probiotics make up a multi-billion-dollar industry that's projected to grow to US$65 billion by 2024. Available in powder, capsule and tablet form, the industry is evolving in tandem with quickly emerging research.

Dairy foods have long been the main delivery vehicle of probiotics, but now they are being incorporated into smoothies, nutrition bars and even chocolates. Products incorrectly labelled as probiotics and carrying unsubstantiated health claims are floating in the market globally. The current regulatory environment can easily be compared to the Wild West. Hence, irrespective of the form in which the microorganisms are consumed, scientific bodies demand that products labelled probiotics must strictly respect the definition and not confuse the general public with misinformation. This will allow the products to obtain the recognition they deserve, based on the research performed.

Until this happens, how do you know what a 'true' probiotic is? How do you know what to buy? Not all probiotics are the same, just as not all drugs treat headaches and not all vitamin supplements correct the same deficiency. Most people think they're the same but they all have different functions. Ideally, one should consult with an expert who specializes in probiotic therapies before taking a supplement. During consultations, I help people choose the right probiotics for them. But nevertheless, here's a checklist that you can use to buy probiotics.

Probiotic checklist:

- *Know your probiotic:* Not all strains of lactobacilli or bifidobacterium have been studied and found to be helpful.

Hence, before buying, look for the genus, species and strain for every microbe in the product. To know what probiotic you are getting, it is imperative that you know all three. More often than not, you'll simply see up to the species level—only two parts of the name—on a probiotic label. For instance, you'll see 'Lactobacillus rhamnosus' on the label instead of 'Lactobacillus rhamnosus GG'. The strain determines the benefit that you'll receive as the consumer. If it isn't listed on the label, chances are that it's either a poorly-studied strain or it doesn't do what the company is advertising it does. Simply put, if the label doesn't display strain's designation, steer clear!

- *Match the strain to the benefit you want:* 'The more the strains, the better it is' is a probiotic myth used as a selling point. It's not about more strains, but rather about matching the strain to the benefit you desire. Remember: The probiotic that will work for you won't necessarily work for someone else. Choose the one with the exact probiotic strain that has been proven to have the specific therapeutic action you desire. For example, the probiotic strain Lactobacillus casei Shirota (LcS), popularly known as Yakult, is a strain that has been scientifically proven to help alleviate symptoms of a few specific ailments. Contrary to what TV commercials have you believe, it is not for everybody.

- *Amounts matter:* The number of live microorganisms in each serving or dose of the supplement, all the way till the end of shelf life (not 'at time of manufacture', because such labelling does not account for drop of bacteria during storage), is denoted by colony forming units or CFU. The CFU is often the selling point for most marketers who try to convince you that their product is better because it has a higher number of healthy bacteria. While that may sound logical, it isn't always true. Instead, the CFU on the label should equal the amount shown to be beneficial in human studies for that particular strain. That's the best dose. A number greater than that doesn't equate with enhanced effects. Most often, effective doses range from 100 million to over 50 billion CFU per day.

- *Miscellaneous:* Probiotics that are labelled well ideally also carry the suggested serving size, proper storage conditions and safety guidelines. Probiotics are safe for most people, but pregnant women, infants, individuals with compromised immune systems, like AIDS or cancer, or the seriously ill may need to exercise caution before taking them.

## Table 13: Summary

|  | Fermented foods without live strains | Fermented foods retaining live strains | Probiotics |
|---|---|---|---|
| What they are | Contain no live microbes. | Contain live microbes. | Are live microbes that have been studied and found to confer specific health benefit(s) in specific amounts. |
| Examples of sources | Kadhi, idli, dosa, bhatura, dhokla, ghee, jalebi, appam, enduri pitha, gulgula | Listed in Tables 11 and 12. | Supplements in the form of drinks, pills, powders, functional foods with added probiotics like probiotic yoghurt, etc. |

| Health effects | Carry 'prebiotic' compounds. | Influence the resident microbes and exert many physical and mental health benefits. | Targeted effect, benefits are strain-specific. |
|---|---|---|---|
| Efficiency of live microbes reaching your gut alive | NA | The microbes have had to evolve in order to cope with the acidic environment in fermented foods. So they can naturally persevere through the acid-filled digestion process and reach the intestine alive. | Most supplements consist of inactive, freeze-dried bacteria so that they can go through the stomach acid. The bacteria activates only when it reaches the intestine. Moreover, a true probiotic will always go through an efficacy study before it is launched in the market. This ensures the bacteria in probiotic supplements always reach your gut alive. |

### Probiotic Myth: Probiotics Live in and on Us

'Probiotics live in and on us.' 'Probiotics are the friendly bacteria in our gut.' These are things I hear so often from the media and those who call themselves celebrity nutritionists. Nothing could be further from the truth. As I explained earlier, probiotics are 'live microorganisms which when administered in adequate amounts confer health benefits on the host'. A simple concept, but it so often gets misused. Probiotic strains do not live in and on you unless you have consumed them or applied them in the form of, say, cosmetics. They are found in the digestive tract only if you have consumed them. The lactobacilli and bifidobacteria that are present in the digestive tract are your ancestral, native, indigenous strains that you were born with, not probiotics!

The reason why we have so many incorrect concepts—not only about probiotics but about nutrition science in general—is because very few people are taking the effort to look for and follow people with true qualifications in their field. In today's social media world, if you're an effective communicator or have a decent body to flaunt, you can get people's attention. Anyone is free to write or say anything they want, and they are not necessarily constrained by scientific facts. Today, when headlines move faster than solid science, it's more important than ever to examine the source of your information. Separate myths from facts, find sources to trust and make well-informed decisions about your health.

## Prebiotics

When it comes to our biomes, you are more likely to see some new kombucha flavour or a local goat milk kefir grabbing headlines in a media article. But now you know that the microbes in these foods are just passing through and don't actually take up residence in our guts. These foods provide value to our health, yes, but no matter how many live and active bacteria they contain, they do not actually do much to re-establish your native gut bacteria that live permanently in our guts. It is easy to get distracted by these interesting, live, effervescent cultured foods, but if we focus solely on them, we will end up neglecting the upkeep of our native microbes. These foods cannot restore you to peak ancestral intestinal health. I hate to burst your highly-cultured bubble, but what our full-time microbes need is neither kombucha nor kefir but *fibre*!

Fibre is feed for our gut's ancestral microbes, and it also improves the implantation and survival of newly-added strains you consume. Rebalancing the gut microbiome is not only about consuming live microbes and adding numbers, but it's more about working on the complete habitat; that's how ecosystems flourish. Let me explain with an example. In order to pull the tiger back from the brink of extinction, during the St Petersburg declaration in 2010, the tiger range countries, including India, committed to double their tiger numbers by 2022. A target that we completed in 2018, four years early. Great news, right? Not quite if you ask the experts! While the number of tigers has increased, the number of prey has either stayed the same or even diminished in a few places. Predators need to have the right amount of prey, otherwise it will lead to increased competition for food and tiger–tiger conflicts. Additionally, when too many animals are packed into a small space, they start to migrate in search of new territory, often leading to man–tiger conflicts. Experts opine that our focus should have been simultaneously on the habitat and the abundance of prey—factors that they plan to consider now.

Similarly, in order to *restore the proper composition and function of the 'disappearing' gut microbiome*, we need to focus on foods that will help feed our native microbes. These foods will help them survive, grow, reproduce and will *prevent loss of beneficial bacterial species*. This is why diet is considered one of the most important contributors that can positively impact the composition and activity of our resident microbiota. Research has suggested that for every 10 grams of microbial food that reaches the lower intestine, about three grams of additional helpful bacteria blossom into life. That equates to about 3 trillion new microbes for just those 10 grams of fodder each day. Not a bad trade-off, if you ask me!

Along with the growing interest in the gut microbes, quite ironically, the low-carb diet or the keto craze has also been hitting the mainstream. I say it is ironic, because fibre, the very food we are interested in—and for good reason—is a carbohydrate. Fibre consists of long chains of carbohydrates. A big downside (oh, there are so many!) of the low-carb diet is the lack of fibre. It is nearly impossible to get natural fibre from dietary proteins and fats, or to get an adequate level of fibre intake from the fruits and vegetables that are often included in a low-carb diet.

In the fibre, the carb molecules are connected by complicated bonds. We humans think too highly of ourselves, but it's our microbiota that has developed metabolic capacities that we are unable to perform. For instance, we don't have the enzymes necessary to break down those bonds in a fibre molecule and digest the fibre, meaning these compounds reach the lower part of our large intestines intact. Once there, the good bugs can feast on them through the process of fermentation. They use these cast-offs for their own survival. When the bacteria ferment or break down these compounds and release by-products that positively impact human health and disease, the compounds are known as *PREbiotics*, and the by-products produced in the process are called *POSTbiotics*. While you may have seen your nutritionist dabbling in the former, there's a very good chance you haven't heard about the latter.

Postbiotics—an evolving term within the field of functional foods—are small, bioactive molecules that our little microbial factories reward you with when you feed them foods they like, i.e., prebiotics. I heard this term for the first time in a microbiome conference, and at that moment, I could almost visualize bacteria in Amrish Puri's Mogambo suit, saying in a high-pitched voice, *'Bacteria khush hua!'* It was only that these microbes who are happy to repay you are the tiny heroes of your body, not the villains of the plot. Depending on the microbes in your gut and the foods you eat, specific postbiotic metabolites (end products) from the microbiota are released. These then circulate throughout your body and affect key physiological signals that can have benefits ranging from weight loss to immune protection to better mood. For chemicals that are technically waste products, these are rather impressive feats. Had it not been for the microbes, our bodies would not have made them on its own.

Postbiotics are not the only way in which the prebiotic fibres found in rice, potato, banana, millet and mango—all carb rich foods that are incompatible with fashionable low-carb diets—exert weight loss benefits. That fibre is good for us has long been known. Now a new reality has taken hold; the major reason why they are so beneficial is because many fibres are in fact prebiotic. Since fibre is the bread and butter of our native microbes, so to speak, when we modify our diets and include sufficient carbs, the growth of good, beneficial bacteria is stimulated. The good guys can gang up and outcompete potential detrimental organisms, reverse dysbiosis and thereby contribute to the health of the host. In a recent Belgian study, when scientists fed prebiotic fibre to volunteers for two weeks, they found that their body was actually getting reprogrammed to reduce the size of fat cells. So much for all the 'carbs are fattening' junk floating around in the market! The prebiotics enhanced the numbers of intestinal microbes, which possibly induced genetic expression! If you remember, we explored in Chapter 3 how the bacteria in our body can 'talk' to our DNA. Now you see that they're not only talking but negotiating as well, 'Hey bro, how about reducing the size of the fat cells for this guy? A high five if you do that!'

Are All Dietary Fibres Prebiotics?

'What is wrong with my high-fibre cereals and biscuits? I mean, fibre is food for microbes—that's what you say, right?' said Rajeev, a high-flying businessman and a client of mine whose other interest was finding health in easy-to eat packed foods while carrying an expression on his face that said, 'Girl, do you even know what you're saying!'

'Not all fibre is created equal, Rajeev,' I replied. 'Fibre from different sources can be as similar as your LV belt is to your Jimmy Choo Shoes—that is, not very.'

Here's the thing. *Most prebiotics are dietary fibres, but not all dietary fibres are prebiotics.*

All fibres are resistant to the upper gastrointestinal tract, and therefore reach the colon—your microbial home—as is. Once there, the primary distinction between these nondigestible carbohydrates is their fermentability. Fermentability is the degree to which fibre, after resisting digestion, can be eaten, i.e., metabolized, by the microbes. *Not all fibres are accessible by our microbiota.* Compounds with high fermentability are the ones that the microbes are able to use as food substrates, and we benefit in the bargain. These are the best category of carbohydrates to focus on. They encourage the activities of your microbiota and promote our health.

On the other hand, fibres that are either not fermented or minimally fermented will not be utilized by the microbes, and hence these fibres cannot be termed prebiotics. This distinction is critical and often not taken into account by health professionals and consumers. That's why scientists recently proposed a more specific term in place of prebiotic fibre: Microbiota-accessible carbohydrate or MAC. When I told Rajeev about it, he exclaimed, 'That's also my wife's favourite brand of cosmetics!' We burst out laughing.

The first problem with the high-fibre biscuit and cereal that Rajeev was having is that they are NOVA ultra-processed foods. Secondly, the bran that is added to these products is a fibre, yes, but a minimally fermented one. Another example of such fibres is psyllium or ispaghula husk. The microbes don't feed on them, but I have met many new clients who were having ispaghula because they were wrongly told that it's a prebiotic. These non-fermentable fibres function mainly as bulking agents and help ease defecation. In phase 2, I would rather want you to focus on boosting the consumption of fermentable compounds that will help modulate your microbiota. The main candidates for prebiotic status reported in scientific literature are given next.

## Table 14: Prebiotics and Their Sources

| Prebiotic/MAC | Dietary Sources |
|---|---|
| Resistant starch | Green banana, lotus nuts, millets, rice, potato, white beans, peas, lentils, legumes |
| Beta-glucans | Barley, oats, edible mushrooms |
| Pectins | Fruits like apples, pear, guavas, plum, orange, amla |
| Inulin | Banana, onion, wheat, garlic, chicory root |
| Fructo-oligosaccharides (FOS) | Green banana, tomatoes, sugarcane, wheat, barley |
| Galactooligosaccharides (GOS) | Lentils, kidney beans, chickpeas, lima beans, cow's milk, human breast milk |
| Galactomannan | Fenugreek seeds, gawaar (cluster beans) |
| Tree gum exudates | Indian gond, gond kateera |

One look at Table 14, and you will realize how ironic it is that one is expected to restrict most of these fat-burning carbohydrate foods in a weight-loss diet. These diets say 'rice is bad', 'potatoes are fattening', 'sugarcane causes diabetes' and so on. Due to their high carb content, keto and low-carb diets also avoid lentils and legumes. One cup of cooked legumes generally provides around 40 gm carbs and 18 gm protein. 'Tch, tch, legumes may be healthy but not keto friendly!' A reputed lifestyle magazine once carried this as a headline to an article. Amusing world, isn't it?

How Can You Eat Your Way to a Healthy Gut Microbiome?

All plant sources have both fermentable and non-fermentable fibres in varying proportions. The current consensus on the definition of a prebiotic is 'a substrate that is selectively utilized by host microorganisms conferring a health benefit'. Until an adequate amount of MAC is present in a given food, it cannot cause a shift in colonic bacterial populations or elicit proven health benefits, and hence cannot be strictly called a prebiotic. Nevertheless, to some extent, most of the dietary plant foods have prebiotic effects, even though they are not exclusive prebiotics. Since different fibres have different effects, having a diet focused on a variety of whole grains, millets, pulses, legumes, beans, fruits, vegetables, nuts and seeds will help you naturally eat your way to a healthy and more diverse gut microbiome.

Having said that, you don't have to do anything drastic to meet your fibre requirements. Traditional diets of countries like India, Africa, China and of the Mediterranean have been found to be excellent at providing this expected fodder to our native microbes. Following an Indian diet with routine meals like rice dal or roti saag will take care of your fibre requirements without your having to count grams or even think about it. You will witness this first-hand in the phase 2 meal plans in this book! Moreover, these are foods that, over many years, your microbes have learnt to break down with ease. I have already made a case for traditional diets in Chapter 4. Archaeological investigations of sites inhabited by humans in ancient India suggest that our ancestors were eating enough prebiotics through their routine diets.

And it doesn't always boil down to the food source alone. Age-old recipes too have been intelligently curated to take care of the important inhabitants in your gut. Case in point: panta bhat. For centuries, it has been a practice in many parts of India, like Assam, West Bengal, Odisha, Tamil Nadu and

Kerala, to consume rice that has been left to soak overnight (fermented rice). Not only is it a great source of live microbes, but it's also a brilliant way to increase the prebiotic content of rice. *Ek panth, do kaaj,* if I may say so. Wondering how? That's because the act of cooling cooked rice increases the presence of resistant starch through a process called 'starch retrogradation'.

New research has revealed that the assumption that all carbs deliver four calories per gram is, at best, far too simplistic. It does not take into account how cooking and cooling changes the structure and chemistry of the food. The way we prepare and cook starchy foods like rice and potatoes can affect the calorie count and glycemic index, something that your hi-tech apps aren't aware of. Cooking and cooling potatoes or rice increases their RS content, and since RS is indigestible and isn't broken down into glucose in the stomach, it causes the calories and glycemic index to fall. Rice, when left in the fridge overnight, can contain up to 60 per cent fewer calories than when freshly cooked, even if you reheat it before consumption. Many popular recipes in India make use of day-old rice, without having any inkling about its extra health benefits. Falguni Shah, my Gujarati client from Ahmedabad, was overjoyed to learn of this, 'My hubby likes Vagharelo bhat so much. I specially cook extra rice so I can make it for him the next day. Chalo, at least something this man likes happens to be healthy too!' If men will be men, then wives will be wives too!

Also, let me clarify that I am no way undermining the nutritional importance of freshly cooked meals, including rice and potatoes, but simply trying to drive home the point that it is important to include a variety of recipes in your day-to-day meals, because that's how your microbes will produce the various compounds beneficial for you. By the way, I am already imagining you moving the calorie calculator app on your phone to the trash bin. Am I right or am I right?

*What about supplements?* There's a new wave of prebiotic and postbiotic supplements and functional foods, and I am not surprised. Fermentable fibres are being added to foods like yogurts, infant formula, cereals, breads, cookies, desserts and drinks. Instead of using the word 'prebiotic' on the label, what shows up most of the time is any one of the names listed in the left column of Table 14. Now the question is whether they are necessary.

First of all, a specific prebiotic will increase only a specific strain of bacteria. It won't increase the number of different types of bacteria. Microbiome diversity is hence achievable not by swallowing supplements, but rather by eating a well-rounded diet consisting of a variety of foods that are naturally rich in prebiotics. Apart from supplying you with a concentrated amount of prebiotics, these foods, unlike supplements, are also rich in health-promoting vitamins, minerals and antioxidants. Secondly, research on the ideal dosage of prebiotics needed to gain health benefits is still ongoing. Until we have those results, it's difficult to determine just how much of a supplement one should take. The extra fibre in prebiotic supplements or multigrain, high-fibre foods simply gets excreted, but it may also lead to pain, bloating, diarrhoea and flatulence due to excess production of methane and hydrogen in the intestines. As I keep saying, if something is good, more of it isn't necessarily better.

Potential Health Benefits of Prebiotics and Postbiotics

Studies indicate that increasing your intake of prebiotics leads to a laundry list of benefits.

1.  Modulates satiation and accelerates weight loss
2.  Decreases risk of allergy
3.  Stimulates production of antibodies that have critical roles in immune protection
4.  Regulates hormone and insulin levels
5.  Regulates gut–brain communication
6.  Manages autoimmune symptoms better
7.  Positively affects levels of LDL cholesterol, triglycerides and blood glucose
8.  Increases serotonin production
9.  Increases absorption of dietary minerals like calcium and magnesium and protects bone health

## What No One Told You about Low-Carb, High-Protein Diets

When researchers based in the UK, Poland, Sweden and Greece presented the results from new and pooled research on low-carb diets at the European Society of Cardiology's 2018 Congress, they concluded that low-carbohydrate diets (LCD) can be effective for short-lived weight loss, but they are not suitable or safe in the long term. Due to the size of the group in the experiment (4,47,506 participants) and the length of time the individuals were followed (average of 15.6

years), we cannot afford to brush the results under the carpet. *People who consumed a diet low in carbs were found to be at greater risk of premature death, including death from heart disease and stroke.* Additionally, a significant link was found between low-carb or high-protein diets and death due to cancer. At a time when several health gurus across the world have been promoting LCDs, this large study could very well mark the first in a series of critical blows about to hit the low-carb movement.

When you go low on carbs and restrict roti, rice, idli, bhakri, etc., you are essentially starving your gut microbes. As a result, you lose these healthful microbes, reduce microbiome diversity and also suffer from postbiotics deficiency. The river of short chain fatty acids or SCFAs (postbiotics) that your microbiome produces when you give it a constant supply of MACs protects and impacts many metabolic processes. However, in a low-carb situation, this can get altered due to the low production of SCFAs, and can tip us towards metabolic syndrome—obesity, high blood pressure, abnormal cholesterol levels and type 2 diabetes. However, something far more detrimental happens when you start panicking over every gram of carbs in the name of 'eating clean'.

When MAC-loving microbes go hungry, they begin to eat you from within! Can't blame them. *Paapi pet kaa sawaal hai*; after all, you didn't give them the food they want. The natural layer of mucus that lines our gut is an endogenous source of carbohydrates. When the good microbes are starved of dietary carbs—fibrous, complex and rustic kinds—they begin to munch on the mucus. The more you don't feed them, the more frequently they eat away the mucus barrier, as it is their only other major source of nutrients. Sounds bad? Well, it is. Deficiency of dietary carbs leads to the proliferation of these mucus-digesting bacteria strains in your gut, and they gradually erode the vital intestinal barrier and grow the mucus layer thinner. The immune system responds as if under threat, leading to SCI (explained in pathway 1 in Chapter 3) and diseases including but not limited to obesity. Not only this, if you now encounter a pathogen, say a COVID-19 virus, your response to the infection will be worse. Remember, it's the mucus layer that acts as a protective barrier and keeps out pathogens. A thin, eroded layer increases your susceptibility to pathogens, and becomes a wide-open door for pathogenic microorganisms to invade, causing the infection to accelerate more rapidly.

During my Instagram live chat with Rakul Preet Singh this year, one of the questions asked by an Instagram follower was, 'A lot of people I know got on Keto diets, fasting diets etc. in order to use the lock down time "productively" and lose weight. Unfortunately, most of them got infected with the virus. Is there a correlation?' Since I couldn't take up all the questions my Insta family posted due to time constraints, I hope the lady is reading this book and figured out the answer herself!

Now let's look at what happens when you supplement your LCD with high-dietary proteins—the ultimate formula frequently used for weight loss. Yeah, you got it right. What I mean is meals with no carbs: Only grilled chicken or an egg biryani that looks as if someone was gracious enough to drop a few rice grains in a sea of yellow, white eggs. And then there are those veg warriors who have only dal or sprouts but no grain or rice with it. Little do people know that excess protein survives past the small intestine and enters the colon. Proteins that reach the large intestine no longer supply you with amino acids and build your muscles; they only contribute to smelly gases out your backdoor. Carbs are the preferred food source for microbes in the gut, but in a low-carb high-protein situation, microbes turn to proteins and start digesting them. Unlike carbohydrate-based fermentation in the colon, the colonic microbial protein fermentation—called putrefaction—produces an array of toxic metabolic by-products, including ammonia, sulphides and phenols, which can increase intestinal permeability and induce inflammation. A groundbreaking study conducted in the United States and Italy revealed that high protein intake increases the risk of overall mortality in amounts that is analogous to the risk imposed by cigarette smoking! So much for all the low-carb high-protein meals!

So how do you reduce the putrefaction that leads to detrimental shifts in your microbiota profile? Firstly, by not over-consuming and obsessing over proteins. What many don't understand is that the adequate amount of protein can be obtained from routine meals that consist of plant sources, legumes, nuts, seeds, whole grains and even dairy. You can eat meat too, but not every day. Secondly, adding adequate carbs to your diet reduces putrefaction. Your microbes will not be forced to forage on the extra proteins that escape into your colon. To cut a long story short, if your next-seat neighbour on a flight is letting out a cloud of smelly gases, offer them a piece of bread or cracker, before taking assistance to change your seat, of course!

Unlike what many believed, during her prep for *Rashmi Rocket*, Taapsee's diet had an adequate balance of dietary carbs and protein. When she ate fish, it was with rice, chicken was paired with rotis, and eggs with sourdough bread and mashed potatoes. On balance, going low on carbs is not the way, neither to a lean, toned and athletic body nor to a healthy microbial ecosystem.

## The Three Fs of Phase 2 at a Glance

### Table 15: Foods to Forget, Have Few of, and Favour

| Forget | Few | Favour |
|---|---|---|
| Whole wheat, maida, wheat suji/rava, daliya, barley, rye (gluten sources) | Wine, beer (once per week) | Fermented foods |
| Milk and fresh, soft cheese like mascarpone, paneer, etc. (lactose sources) | Egg, fish, white meat (twice per week) | Lentils, millets, rice, pulses, legumes, beans, fruits, vegetables, nuts, seeds |
| Distilled spirits, i.e., brandy, gin, rum, tequila, whiskey, vodka and flavoured liqueurs | | |
| Red meat | | |
| NOVA ultra-processed foods | | |

## Dietary Diversity: Expanding Your Food Horizons

According to the Food and Agriculture Organization of the United Nations (FAO), there are 20,000–50,000 edible plant species that have been discovered, of which humans regularly consume only 150 to 200. In fact, rice, maize and wheat alone contribute to around 60 per cent of the calories from plants in the entire human diet. Except for the times you occasionally go out to eat, if you take a close look at what you eat every day, chances are that you will find yourself having the same meals habitually, or at best, three or four different main dishes that are eaten for a whole year.

Let's take an example. In spite of having many varieties of fish to choose from, pomfret, surmai, rawas and prawns remain the four most commercially-exploited species in India, showing up on way too many menus, both at home and restaurants alike. There may be a few more varieties on offer at certain high-end eateries, but still, the number of fish varieties we consume can be literally counted on our fingertips. There's an abundance of beautiful fishes like Indian mackerel, red snapper, trevally, cobia, barracuda, tuna, mahi-mahi, leather jacket fish and so on in our coastal waters, continental shelf and deep sea, but we are largely unaware of them. This is leading to overfishing of a few popular species and putting them at the risk of extinction. This monotony in our diets is linked to a decline in the diversity of plants as well. For instance, the 1,10,000 varieties of rice once cultivated in India have dropped to just 6,000 varieties in the last few decades.

Relying on a narrow range of foods threatens the resilience of our ecosystem to pests, climate change and extreme weather.

What dietary monotony also does is that it leaves your inner ecosystem vulnerable, making you prone to obesity and diseases. That's right! Recent findings from the American Gut Project have revealed that the diversity of foods that a person consumes is associated with microbial diversity. Which simply means that *even if you are eating a wholesome, balanced diet with whole grains, lentils, fruits, veggies, etc., but if they are the same few kinds all the time, the diversity of your microbiome and your health will not improve. Variety is key.* For example, if you have fish regularly, make sure it isn't always a basa variety.

Unlike phase 1, this phase is all about consuming a variety of lentils, pulses, beans and seeds. Each food variety supports different microbial species. So, ditch your routine of constantly eating the same thing. Eating a varied and diverse diet helps build an equally diverse microbiome that is associated with lean metabolism and prevention of diseases. A diverse gut microbiota is a synonym for health.

Foods, particularly in India, have evolved according to the climate, culture and cropping practices of a particular region. Hence, there's a lot of regional diversity. Though the meal plans for this phase consist of a wide range of foods from different parts of our country, it is not possible to do justice to the many exotic, regional and heirloom varieties of incredible India in the few pages of a book. Moreover, many recipes are passed on from generation to generation in a rather secretive manner and have never been documented. For example, many do not know that people in Manipur have been fermenting meat and fish, while those in Sikkim prepare bamboo shoot-based ferments. Fermented soya bean forms an intrinsic part of the diet of people in Meghalaya and so on. While the phase 2 meal plans I have created are sufficient to replenish your microbiome diversity, I would love for you to bring back the joy of discovering and cooking a variety of your traditional foods that you may have not known or eaten before.

Additionally, you must combine food sources of live microbes with prebiotics. Scientists have named such food items 'synbiotics'. Another term added to your newly-acquired microbiome vocabulary, right? Factually, synbiotic meals are nothing new, and Indians have been unknowingly consuming them for many years. Case in point: curd rice. When you have both curd and rice together, the curd will seed your biome with friendly flora and the resistant starch in the rice will act as a nutrition source for them and help them thrive. This makes curd rice a synbiotic meal! Add a dose of achaar to it and you just increased its synergistic value even further. Kanji vada, roti with makhan, dahi poha and jowar rabdi are a few of the many synbiotic meals that you may be familiar with. Research says that consuming prebiotics and live microbes at the same time offers the most benefits due to how prebiotics support the growth of the bacteria. Therefore, this is also one of the things that we will do in this phase.

## More about Pulses, Legumes and Beans

India has thousands of lentil varieties, but unfortunately, most of us eat only a few. Eating a variety of different pulses is important because your microbes love to feed on them. And while doing so, they produce gases. Pretty much explains the after-effects—farts, flatulence, bloating, etc.—of eating that scrummy chole masala. However, this should not hold you back from eating them more often. After all, the superstars of phase 2 are beans, seeds and lentils. So here are my tips that will help reduce pulses-related flatulence.

## Tips to Make Beans and Lentils Less Gassy

*Check for size and cooking time:* In general, there are two thumb rules to ascertain the gas-producing capacity of any lentil or pulse. Rule number 1: The bigger the size of the lentils, the harder it is to digest and the more gassiness it will lead to. For example, compared to moong dal that is smaller in size, lobia produces more gas. Rule number 2: For lentils that are of similar size, check for the cooking time. The longer a bean takes to get cooked, the more flatulence it will induce once consumed.

*Soaking:* Before you cook, you should soak the pulses. Soaking times vary depending on the type. Use the two thumb rules above as a guide. Let the bigger and more gas-producing beans soak overnight, while the smaller ones can be pre-soaked for about 30–60 minutes. The soaking water should always be discarded and the pulses rinsed well before proceeding further.

*Sprouting:* Sprouting not only reduces the gassiness but also makes it easier for the body to digest the beans and whole pulses. Again, use the two thumb rules above as a guide. Sprout the bigger and longer-cooking-time beans before you cook, especially if you are prone to bloating.

*Cooking:* Cooking enhances digestibility. So, avoid eating sprouts, beans, etc. in their raw forms. When the water in which you are cooking reaches boiling point, the foam that forms on the surface should be scooped out.

*Tempering:* Once cooked, add a tempering of garlic, ginger and hing (in ghee) to it. All three have carminative, i.e., anti-flatulence properties, and they will also lend a special flavour to your meal.

*Timing and variety in recipes matter:* Consume the bigger and longer-cooking-time beans and lentils during the day, preferably for lunch. Think rajma, chole, kulthi, etc. For dinner, it is best to consume moong, toor and masoor dals.

Include pulses and lentils in many different ways like sabzi, dals, parathas, laddu, vadi, soups, chutneys, etc.

*Note:* You can have pulses throughout the year. However, among them, horse gram (kulthi) is particularly heating. Hence, during summer and monsoons, make sure you do not consume horse gram with a heating millet like ragi, foxtail and barnyard. A meal of little millet rice and kulith dal works well for hot afternoons. Apart from combining it with cooling millets, you can also combine horse gram with other cooling foods like ghee, moong dal, coconut, buttermilk and milk (milk from phase 3 onwards) during the hot, summer months.

Those who are pitta-dominant should use horse gram in the same manner as advised for heat-generating millets in Chapter 5.

A Few Varieties of Lentils, Beans to Include in Your Diet

| | |
|---|---|
| Chana dal (Split bengal gram) | Chole (Kabuli chana) |
| Kulith (Horse gram) | Vaal (Lima/Fava bean) |
| Bhatma (Soybean) | Vatana (White, black and green peas) |
| Urad (Black gram, white gram) | Chow-dhari (Winged bean) |
| Tuvar (Pigeon peas) | Masoor (Red lentil) |
| Red chori (Adzhuki/red beans) | Chow-dhari (Winged bean) |
| Moong (Green gram) | Naurangi dal (Ricebean) |
| Rajma (Red kidney beans) | Lobia (Black-eyed beans) |
| Matki (Moth bean) | Kala chana (Black chickpeas) |

## Looking Ahead

With this, we have covered all the dietary basics for weeks 3–8 on the programme. In Chapter 10, you will find detailed Phase 2 meal plans that you may follow as is. Now let's go through some FAQs.

## FAQs of Phase 2

1.  I am diabetic. Can I eat the carbs and be on this programme?

Yes! You can (in fact, you should). If you are diabetic, PCOD or insulin resistant, chances are you have been told to watch your total carb intake and avoid high glycemic-index foods, whether they're rice, mango or summer sherbets. Now here's a fact: In the largest study of its kind, called the Personalized Nutrition Project, blood sugar levels in 800 people were continuously monitored for a week. What the researchers found was surprising. Individuals responded differently in terms of their glycemic response to identical meals that also had the same number of calories. That's because each individual harbours a unique set of bacteria that is specific to them. Predicting blood sugar response to foods based on total calories or total carbohydrate intake has led to falsely name-shaming many foods that can, in reality, increase the diversity of microbiota in both type 1 and type 2 diabetes and help in reversing them. Your gut microbiome is the driver of the glycemic response, but this has been largely ignored. Until now. Following the TBBD as explained in this book will help your gut flora influence chemical pathways that help regulate blood sugar and insulin balance. Excluding foods in the name of carbs has never helped, including them will.

2.   What about soups, sherbets, chutneys in phase 2?

In phase 2, you will continue having the soups, sherbets and chutneys, but the kinds that are more aligned with the Three Fs of this phase. So, favour those that are lentil or seed-based, fermented (with or without live microbes) and are made from prebiotics. You will find these in the meal plans in Chapter 10.
     A few examples are given below.

Sherbet: Sattu sherbet, gajar kanji, *buttermilk*, *thandai*, *gond kateera sherbet*, etc. (The recipes for the ones in italics can be found in Chapter 10.)

Soup: Horse-gram soup, soup with sprouted beans

Chutney: Til chutney, flaxseed (alsi) chutney, dahi ki chutney, garden cress seeds (aliv) chutney

# PHASE 3

## Reintroduce and Renew

## Weeks 9–10 and Beyond

7

# Your Lifetime Tune-Up

Congratulations! You have made it to the last phase of TBBD. You should be feeling different from the way you did when we started—looser clothes, restful sleep, radiant skin, fewer cravings, more energy, better mood, less painful periods? Coming to phase 3 doesn't mean the weight loss stops or you don't get any better! This chapter serves as both an end and a beginning. Phase 3 is not a diet. It is a sustainable way of eating that will keep you fit and healthy for the long run. It is a beginning to a new way of living that is in tune with your inner ecology as well as the broader ecology around you.

## Reintroducing Foods

Gluten Dietary Sources

As explained in Chapter 5 (in the section Gluten Isn't the Problem, Bad Microbes Are), once the microbiome is restored, consuming gluten foods, i.e., wheat and barley, poses no threat to your health. But what if you want to stay gluten-free for life? Why do you need to consume them? That's because wheat and barley aren't all gluten, they are also prebiotics (Table 14 in Chapter 6) that help you build a healthy and diverse microbiome. They provide nutrients like folic acid, magnesium, iron, B vitamins, calcium and zinc.

A long-term, gluten-free diet can have adverse effects on your gut microbiome, which you now know plays a critical role in promoting lean metabolism and immune function. A gluten-free diet should not be for life. Hence, unless you have Celiac disease (autoimmune reaction to gluten), it is important to bring these grains back into your daily diet.

The Green Revolution in India and Wheat

The wheat that you eat now is very different from what your great-grandparents ate before the Green Revolution commenced in India in the late 1960s. For the sake of easier harvesting and higher yields, the food grain that has suffered the highest manipulation is wheat. There's been an irrevocable change in the structure of wheat caused by decades of cross-breeding, hybridization and adding chemicals and herbicides while growing and processing. Modern wheat varieties laced heavily with pesticides have been shown to cause inflammation and create havoc within our digestive and immune systems.

On the other hand are the ancient or heirloom varieties of wheat. Being naturally hardy, they are grown without pesticides; they have a higher nutritional value and carry impressive merits. Although chances are that you have heard only about khapli (emmer) wheat in wellness farmer's markets, our country boasts of many desi varieties, like chandausi, lokwan, paigambari, bansi, sharbati, kathia, etc., that when consumed can leave you feeling light. Medical trials have shown that traditional varieties of wheat can help reduce inflammation and improve outcomes for chronic diseases like diabetes, heart disease, and IBS.

The wheat used in a typical store-bought cookie or bun is the modern variety, so a good solution for you is to first bypass processed foods. Choose ancient or heirloom wheat varieties as far as possible. They are available online, at offline wellness markets, at kirana stores and not impossible to procure. Apart from the higher nutrition profile, the rotis made out of them are softer and tastier. You can have wheat once every day through all seasons, not because it is bad to have it twice (or more) but simply because I want to make sure you eat enough of other grains too. Remember, diversity is key!

### Oats vs Barley

Barley has the same prebiotic fibre called beta-glucan that is found in oats. Hence, even though it isn't backed by aggressive marketing activity like oats, in terms of nutrition, both offer the same benefits, i.e., they beneficially affect cholesterol levels, reduce the risk of heart disease, control blood pressure and help you lose weight. But the fact that barley has been around since the Neolithic Age started in India around 7000 BCE, while the branded oats brigade is a mere 15–20 years old here, I cannot help but have a bias for barley. Additionally, barley's higher compatibility to desi taste buds and its versatility in terms of cooking makes it the better choice. Most of my clients prefer barley to rice or millet for dinner because it feels very light in the tummy, making it ideal for an evening meal. You can have barley in many forms like soup, roti, porridge or kanji, khichri, pulao, barley water, barley sattu sherbet, upma, etc. Again, consume barley only once a day, and for other meals, continue having different varieties of millets, pseudo-cereals and rice.

## Lactose Dietary Sources

The only dairy you were having in phase 1 was ghee. In phase 2, though you were consuming ghee, curd and hard-aged cheese, milk and paneer were restricted. Now that we are in phase 3, you are encouraged to have milk and all kinds of fresh, soft cheese including paneer. Hurray!

We have always known that dairy is the most bioavailable form of calcium in our diet. It is mostly enriched with vitamin D, and unlike nut milks, animal milks are complete sources of protein. Various studies have found an association between calcium/dairy intake and weight loss. At this time, milk is one of the most controversial foods, but considering that good old-fashioned cow's milk is one of the important sources of prebiotics (Table 14, Chapter 6), it should not be restricted or banned. Milk of most farm animals, including buffalo, goat and sheep, has been found to be prebiotic and effective for human nutrition.

Raw Milk vs Pasteurized Milk

The milk sold in packets and tetrapacks (industrialized milk) is pasteurized (including the ones that are branded as 'organic'). In the pasteurization process, milk is heated and then immediately cooled to get rid of germs and impurities before it is packaged and shipped to grocery stores. However, there are many downsides to this: Pasteurization destroys many of the vital enzymes (that help digest the lactose in milk), essential fatty acids and essential proteins that raw milk is naturally rich in. For these reasons, fresh, raw milk from local sources is becoming increasingly popular in Western countries. While it is still illegal to sell raw milk in half of the United States, in a country like India, where we have access to locally-sourced, raw milk, there isn't any solid reason to buy pasteurized milk. All you have to do is take the raw milk and boil it before consumption to get rid of any germs—a practice prevalent in most Indian households. But the question is, 'Are you boiling the milk correctly?' In order to have the right balance of safety and nutrition, warm the milk slowly over medium heat, and stir it while it comes to a boil. As soon as you see bubbles forming around the edges of the vessel and just a few in the middle—indicating that the milk is boiling—turn off the heat. Avoid bringing the milk to a boil too quickly.

Many of the risks that people associate with consuming milk (asthma, allergies, acne, etc.) are largely due to having pasteurized milks and not the raw milk of our indigenous breed of cows. Although I see Gujarat's Gir cows being hailed as the best breed, this really isn't the case. The Gir breed of cows is good, no doubt, but so are others like Karnataka's Hallikar,

Andhra's Ongole, etc. You will be surprised to know that our desi cows are in huge demand in the Western countries and are referred to as 'Zebu Breed' by them. Ironically, Brazil is the biggest exporter of the Indian breed, and they supply these especially to African and Southeast Asian countries. Raw milk from our local, indigenous breeds of cows will help you sustain the robust microbial community that you have built over the past few weeks and will favour your health in the long run.

Red Meat

Though you can now include red meat in your eating plan, ensure that it is only once a week. It is important to not have too much of red meat because of its pro-inflammatory nature, so avoid eating it twice in the same day. The great thing about Indian red meat preparations is the intelligent use of anti-inflammatory spices such as cumin, fennel, turmeric, ginger, garlic and onions in cooking. Apart from being anti-inflammatory, these spices increase the digestibility of the meat too! You can either make a well-spiced curry to have with rice or roti for lunch, or indulge in a warm paaya or shorba on a cold, winter evening.

Distilled Spirits

The extent to which alcohol can mess up your microbiome has already been discussed in Chapter 5. And let me be honest—consuming it in phase 3 is not going to make it any less detrimental. But for a country that quaffs almost half the whiskey produced worldwide, it is only logical that I give you guidelines that will help you drink better, instead of expecting you to avoid your whiskeys and vodkas for life. So, without further ado, here's my take on better drinking.

- *Form a ritual:* If you must drink, then it's important to have a ritual in place for how often you will be drinking. It could be weekly or fortnightly or even monthly. Ritual helps cultivate self-discipline and allows you to be in charge of your decisions. If you are adult enough to drink, you should be adult enough to say 'no'. Yes, you've got that right. 'I didn't want but my friends were forcing yaa, what to do!' doesn't count as a great explanation for random drinking episodes. Adult up!
- *Ask yourself, 'Who's consuming who?':* Whenever you drink, you should be consuming the alcohol, and not let the alcohol consume you. The focus of your evening should be about friends and the company you are with, rather than about the alcohol itself.
- *Drink wisely:* I cannot emphasize enough the importance of sipping on your drink slowly and staying well-hydrated. To pace yourself, have no more than one standard drink per hour, with water as 'drink spacers' between your alcoholic drinks. For every 30 ml of the drink, consume 500 ml water. Make sure you do not drink on an empty stomach. Eat while you drink.
- *Damage control:* The best way to cure a hangover is to not have one. If you have followed all the previous points, it is unlikely that you will wake up with a throbbing headache or a dry mouth the next morning. But what if you fail to do

so and cross the Laxman Rekha? All is not lost. Prioritizing rehydration and detox the next day will get you feeling better. Sugarcane, black-seeded raisins, pomegranate and neera are excellent at liver detoxification and breaking down of toxins. Hence, along with the necessary fluids to help you replenish and rehydrate, I make use of them while suggesting a hangover remedy plan for my clients. Wondering what the plan looks like? You will find one in Chapter 10.

## The Seven TBBD Lifetime Guidelines

Ever heard of 'blue zones'? These are regions in the world—five places precisely—where people report high levels of well-being and live extraordinarily long lives. The world's highest concentration of centenarians is in these places. Over the years, many studies have investigated what they eat and found that people in blue zones do not 'diet'. Instead, they have a few simple, healthy habits, a constellation of little things, that add up and keep them in balance. You see, a healthy long-term eating programme is never a diet; it is rather an approach that is more realistic, flexible and applicable in our daily lives. Therefore, I have designed phase 3 around seven principles. There are no Three Fs for this phase, but what I'm offering you now is a roadmap that you can use to make wise decisions about what you eat. If you understand and follow these principles, *you will be able to maintain the rich and diverse gut flora that you have cultivated in the last few weeks.* Not only that, it will help you create a sustainable, healthy eating plan for life.

## Guideline 1: Say 'No' to Diets

Blue zones don't follow diets, they do not count calories, and they don't single out a nutrient and eat more or less of it. What they do instead is eat a variety of wholesome foods, stay true to their traditional practices, eat slowly and joyfully in the company of their loved ones until they're 80 per cent full, and they never eat late in the evening. Similar to Ayurveda that advises to leave at least a quarter of the stomach empty after meals, these long-lived individuals in the blue zones practise the 'hara hachi bu' principle that recommends eating until you are eight parts (out of ten) full. We, on the other hand, have an eternal food fight going on in our bodies: full-fat against low-fat, sugar against sugar-free, animal protein against plant protein and what not! This reflects in our achy joints, tired bodies and clogged minds.

Long-term restrictive diets have been found to be associated with a decrease in microbial diversity. Instead of focusing on nutrients (because the omega 3, vitamins, minerals, etc. are never consumed in isolation) or designer dietary trends (because diets that are low-carb, low-fat, high-protein, etc. only lead to yo-yoing), we need to start thinking about our diet in the broad sense. Scientists are moving from individual foods and ingredients towards healthy eating patterns that can be woven into a lifestyle to modulate the intestinal microbiota. The Three Rs of TBBD—right quality, right quantity, right timing—and the seven TBBD meal-planning guidelines (you will learn these guidelines in Chapter 10) are the best tools to achieve a long-term healthy gut microbiome in the most realistic, practical and sustainable way.

## Guideline 2: Make Plant Foods and Dairy the Star, Let Meat Be the Supporting Actor

Increased intake of diary and plant-based proteins—lentils, beans, nuts, legumes, seeds, cereals and millets—and reduced intake of non-vegetarian foods are associated with reduction in inflammation and lower risk of diseases. Too much non-vegetarian food can upset the gut microbiome balance. If you are non-vegetarian, limit meat, fish and eggs to twice a week, and avoid eating them twice in the same day. Instead of consuming more and more seafood for its protein and omega 3, think of consuming more varieties of seafood. It's important to diversify your choices, and this is exactly what the next guideline is about.

## Guideline 3: Diversify Your Food Choices

'Don't look where you fell, look where you slipped,' says an African proverb. When it comes to eating right for weight loss, we often fail to recognize exactly where we go wrong. This is why I ask my clients to spend some time logging their meals. This can clue you in to a lot of areas where you need to focus more, one of which is how diverse your diet is. Most of the time, we feel that we are eating a variety of foods, but when we track our food intake, we realize it isn't so. 'Oh god! As if keeping up with a variety in fashion wasn't enough, now I have to stress about variety in food too!' complained one of my south Delhi clients. Stress too can alter the composition of the microbiome, so the last thing I want is stress you out about what you are eating. Instead, I will suggest a simple and easy way to create a more diverse diet. You see, real change comes with small, simple steps, not with anything drastic.

Every new season—summer, monsoon, winter—include in your diet just two new seasonal foods that you have never eaten. That's six a year. It could be a grain or lentil, fruit or vegetable, or just a different variety of fish. Without it seeming like a lot of effort, you will have introduced at least 20 new foods that weren't in your diet four years ago. Isn't that awesome? Changing your diet seasonally not only helps in naturally bringing a variation to your foods, but it also equips you to deal with the seasonal changes. That it is good for the planet, your wallet and your waistline is an added bonus too. To help you know what's in season, I have provided a *seasonal food guide* in Chapter 10. However, visiting your local market and talking to the farmers about what's in season will help you discover many more regional and 'not so popular yet' leafy greens, fruits, veggies, etc.

Did you know that every two months there's a season of different fishes? That's right! It is wrongly assumed that fish breed only during the monsoon. You may have also heard a few nutritionists claiming the same. But the truth is that different fishes breed at different times of the year. Know Your Fish and In Season Fish are doing fabulous work in this area. On their websites, you can find season-wise seafood guides for both the west coast and east coast of India. The core principle of these organizations is to avoid consuming fish during their breeding season so that they can be left to mate and reproduce. For every month of the year, the websites have a list of fish species they recommend and ones they ask you to avoid. Which essentially means that you can enjoy eating fish all through the year, just a different variety each month. How cool—or should I say eco-friendly—is that!

Eating right, whether for weight loss or good health, requires one to go beyond the concept of 'this food is good, and that is bad'. There's much more to healthy eating, and I hope by now you agree.

## Guideline 4: Make Use of Fat-Burning Spices and Herbs

A distinctive feature of Indian cuisine is the delicate balance of many spices. Herbs and spices are digestives, anti-inflammatory and fat-burning, have nutraceutical properties and are filled with phytonutrients. Continue consuming hot water with the blend of spices throughout the day. Favour hand-pounded chutneys, homemade sherbets, herbal hot teas and soups in your day-to-day meals. Have porridge, kanji or khichri at breakfast and dinner for most days of the week.

## Guideline 5: Ferment your food Sometimes, Not Too Often

By the time you come to phase 3, you should have reseeded and repopulated your intestinal community effectively, but for the long haul, the goal should be to include fermented foods in the diet to continue to nourish and evolve a healthy microbiome, as well as help prevent a recurrence of dysbiosis. You can continue consuming ferments but only once a week is now good enough.

## Guideline 6: Get Rid of 'Food Guilt'

'It's not what you eat between Christmas and New Year; it's what you eat between New Year and Christmas.' I read this while scrolling through my social media feed and found it apt. Once your gut microbiome and metabolism has been rehabilitated, indulging in an occasional cake, some chips, fries or any other processed food will not really affect your weight or long-term health. Periodic indulgences do exert a change in the microbiome, but as soon as you go back to healthy eating, the microbiome goes back to its original state. That's because the microbiome overall is stable and resilient over time. It is the long-term dietary habits that help shape the microbiome, not only over the lifetime but also over generations. Beating yourself up for an occasional slip is unnecessary; it is the daily assault of inflammatory, processed foods that sets you up to regain weight and lose health. More often than not, however, it is these occasional splurges that morph into a regular habit. A friend's wedding tonight, a party at office tomorrow, and then weekend movie night the day after and so on—never-ending reasons that sound very reasonable, don't they? But then, that's life. It asks you to make decisions every step of the way, some of which may be harder than others. This or that? Today or tomorrow? Yes or No?

My advice to you is that you think of these decisions in terms of shreyas and preyas (from Chapter 4). If the good decisions trump the not-so-good ones most of the time, pat yourself on the back. You don't have to feel guilty about indulgences that are few and far between. In fact, when you associate guilt with eating, it can cause you to actually gain weight. Two researchers conducted an interesting experiment and found that participants who associated eating a chocolate cake with guilt were less successful at losing weight compared to those associating the cake with feelings of celebration. It all boils down to having the right attitude. You can either feel guilty and helpless or accept the occasional splurges as they are and get back to your life the next day. I would say go for the latter!

Guideline 7: Reboot When the Season Starts to Change

Come back to TBBD (phase 1 and phase 2) twice a year, preferably at the start of a season change—once in the spring month of March and again in the autumn month of September. As the seasons shift, we tend to become vulnerable to allergies and sickness. Going through the eight-week cycle all over again will help cleanse your system and ease you into the new season. You can also repeat this eight-week protocol anytime you feel you have gone too far off track—for example, after a long holiday, an extended period of increased stress, etc.

In Chapter 10, you will find detailed phase 3 meal plans. I have designed these specifically to consist only of preparations using wheat, barley, milk, paneer and red meat, i.e., the foods that have been reintroduced in this phase. The idea is to give you a sense of how and at what time of the day you can reintroduce these different meals.

However, when you start with phase 3, mix up the phase 3 meal plan with meals from both the earlier phases. For instance, if you choose a breakfast meal from a phase 3 meal plan, then you can choose lunch from phase 2 and dinner from phase 1 for that day. This is how you will be able to sustain and maintain your microbiome health for life.

## Going Ahead

While diet does play the most significant role in rebalancing your inner flora and keeping you healthy for life, the connections between diet, stress, lifestyle and the overall health of the body and mind cannot be undermined. Taking an ecosystems approach to weight loss is important. The epidemic of weight gain and chronic illness that we see today is largely because we no longer connect food, stress, exercise, sleep and other factors with each other, much less with the health of our inner community. In the next chapter, we will explore these connections. I will provide you the necessary tools that will help you live a healthy, gut-balancing lifestyle for good. Excited? So am I, so let's go!

8

# The Gut-Balancing Lifestyle

I was waiting for Anisha, my client from Bengaluru. We were scheduled to meet at my office, and it was 15 minutes past the scheduled time. A few minutes later, she showed up, regretfully said, 'I am so sorry, my darling,' and hurriedly removed her footwear at the door. After settling into the chair, she reached for the glass of water kept on the table for her and gulped it down. A couple of minutes later, her back gave in. She was now slouching, yawning intermittently and trying hard to keep her eyes open and herself awake. She was there with me, but still not quite 'there'.

Now, you may be thinking of Anisha as an uninterested client, but in reality, this meeting meant a lot to her. She had been in touch with my office, trying to get an appointment for months. And when the day finally came, alas, she just didn't have enough energy to sustain her through it. The Bengaluru–Mumbai early morning flight, back-to-back work meetings throughout the day, coordinating with her maid on the phone about the kids and many other things had clearly left her exhausted and, if I may add, dehydrated. But isn't this the norm in our modern day lives? We are perpetually overworked, overstressed and under-slept. When it comes to exercise, we almost never have time. Our bodies are more stagnant and our minds more restless than ever before. All of this is impacting our health, weight and inner ecology. In this chapter, you will learn about small switches to make in your lifestyle that will offer a protective and buffering action towards healthier bodies and healthier minds.

## Exercise

It has been rightly said, 'If exercise was a pill, it would be the biggest blockbuster in the history of medicine.' I know I am not the first to tell you that exercise enhances our fat-burning machinery and that it can be a great antidote to most chronic health issues. But only in the past decade have we really been able to appreciate the extraordinary role of exercise in improving mental fitness. It has been found that physical activity can be as effective as antidepressants in reducing symptoms of anxiety and depression.

What we also know now is that many of the benefits of exercise, from the physiological to the psychological, are due to its impact on our gut microbes. Because exercise can help reverse dysbiosis and thus improve the status of our physical, mental and emotional health, a new term 'muscle–gut–brain axis' has been introduced. But do you need to become a triathlete to reap these benefits? What exercise and how much of it should you do? Let's read ahead for the answers, because the thing with exercise is that we know it is good, but more often than not, we find it difficult to turn it into a habit.

## What Exercise and How Much of It?

'Give me a hardcore strict plan, haan. I have strong willpower, so you don't have to get lenient with me.'

Meet Amit. His doctor had recently told him to knock off 20 kg to clear up his sleep apnoea and control his cholesterol and blood pressure. Since then, he has been working out for two hours a day, every day of the week. Impressed with Taapsee's transformation for *Rashmi Rocket*, he had now signed up with me and was expecting an exercise regime harder than what he was already following. 'You see, drastic situations call for drastic measures,' he said assertively. Amit was an investment banker and had been sedentary for most of his adult life. His current exercise was way too challenging for him, and therefore unrealistic. Instead of feeling good, it made him feel tired all the time. I could see that there was no way this would last. In just a matter of a few days or weeks, Amit would be back to square one. He had clearly fallen into the 'not enough fallacy'.

The 'not enough fallacy' is when you believe that small steps are futile or insignificant, and only something much more demanding can result in real change. So you would rather sign up for a half marathon instead of simply including more movement and being more active at work. Let me explain with another example. Suppose you want to take care of your teeth. To accomplish this goal, would you rather visit a dentist for some high-end treatment or simply decide to brush your teeth for two minutes twice a day, every day? Is brushing your teeth twice a day for two minutes substantial enough? No. Unless you do it twice a day for two minutes *every day*. If you stick with the course of action, no matter how small the action is, it will eventually result in a dramatic change.

Similarly, when it comes to exercise, it's not about doing too much, but rather, doing often. It's not about intensity, it's about consistency. Going to the gym for five hours will not get you into shape, but working out for 20 minutes every single day will. *Consistent, regular physical activity is associated with weight loss and health benefits; sporadic, high-intensity workouts are not.* Hence, the most important rule is to choose exercise(s) that you enjoy and can incorporate easily into your schedule over those that feel overwhelming. If you like what you do, you are most likely to stick to it and turn it into a long-term habit. The best exercise is one that you can look forward to on most days of the week, not one that is trending on Instagram Reels.

## The Dose Makes the Poison

The calories-in–calories-out theory of losing weight has inadvertently gotten us to believe that we need to almost kill ourselves exercising to reap the many advantages of moving our body. Time for a reality check? Hell yes! The truth is that exercise is good, but more is not better. Too much of exercise leads to metabolic adjustments that can make fat burning difficult! Modern science is now revealing that just as not exercising is harmful, training to exhaustion is also associated with negative consequences. We need to take the *madhyam marg* or middle path—that which Krishna calls essential—if we want to succeed in our physical, mental and spiritual journey of well-being (*Bhagavad Gita 6.17*). Instead of clinging to the extreme end of any ideological spectrum, Krishna urges us to recognize moderation as an important discipline.

The good news is that the National Health Service in the UK and the American College of Sports Medicine both have outlined recommendations for the amount of exercise that one should be doing.

- *150 minutes (2.5 hours) of moderate aerobic activity OR 75 minutes (1.25 hours) of vigorous activity a week.* Examples of aerobic activities are: cycling, walking, running, jogging, swimming, skipping rope, dancing, walking up the stairs, martial arts, kickboxing, gymnastics, sports like football, badminton, etc.
- *Complement moderate or vigorous activity with strength exercises twice a week.* Examples of muscle-strengthening activities are: yoga asanas, pilates, lifting weights, body weight exercises, working with resistance bands, weight machines, etc.

*Notes*

1. You know you are working at a moderate intensity level when you can still talk, but not sing. At vigorous intensity, you will not be able to speak more than a few words without having to pause for breath.
2. Exercises like yoga asanas, kickboxing, martial arts and gymnastics can be both cardio (aerobic) and strength. For

example, a couple of rounds of Surya Namaskars or sun salutation can increase your heart rate enough to produce cardiovascular health benefits. On the other hand, when you are holding your body in a yoga pose, you are using your own body weight to develop strength. More on yoga and a sample yoga plan later.

3. If you are an absolute beginner, you don't have to do aerobic plus strength training all at once. The most important thing is to be consistent with what you are able to do now. Gradually, you will feel capable of taking on more and ramp up.

## Sample Weekly Calendar

Table 16 is a sample of how a week can look for you. I encourage you to use the weekend or any one day of the week to bring your workout outdoors. Also, note that it is important that you take one day off a week. This will allow optimal recovery from exercise.

## Table 16: Sample Weekly Workout Plan

| Mon | Tue | Wed | Thu | Fri | Sat | Sun |
|-----|-----|-----|-----|-----|-----|-----|
| Aerobic | Strength | Aerobic | Aerobic | Strength | Either rest or any outdoor activity like a cycle ride, leisure walk, hike, etc. | Rest |

Sample Strength Plan for Beginners (Home Workout Plan, No Weights, Full Body)

Home workouts have taken on a new role since the COVID-19 pandemic closed gyms almost everywhere across the world. Therefore, I am providing a home workout plan with exercises that use your own body weight and require no equipment. For the form and technique, you can search for these exercises on www.exrx.net.

**Table 17: Sample Strength Plan for Beginners**

| Exercise | Sets | Reps |
|---|---|---|
| Spot marching + Jumping jacks + High knees + Butt kicks (warm up) | | 4 minutes (1 minute each) |
| Squats | 1–2 | 15 reps |
| Knee pushups | 1–2 | 15 reps |
| Superman | 1–2 | 15 reps |
| Mountain climber | 1–2 | 30–40 seconds |
| Plank | 1–2 | 30 seconds |
| Child's pose and/or stretches (cool down) | | 5 minutes |

*Note*: Machines at gyms are an effective and safe way to train if you are a beginner. If you have access to a gym, then use machines to work all the major muscles (legs, back, glutes, chest and core).

## What You Must Learn from the Vamana Avatar

If you go by the Vedic texts, then Vamana, the fifth avatar of Lord Vishnu, covered the universe in just three steps. In his own creative way, he thus protected humanity against evil. *Why am I telling you this?* To assert that taking steps (and movement) can sound like small things to do, but they can have a large impact on protecting you from the evils of disease and weight gain. We tend to underestimate the positive effects of small bursts of movement throughout our day. That's because we are conditioned to believe: 'No pain, no gain'. On the contrary, getting exercise isn't about all or nothing.

Public Health England's 'Active 10' campaign was launched in March 2017 to promote the efficacy of being active for, guess what, just 10 minutes a day! That's one-sixth the time you may be spending scrolling through pictures of people you don't know on Instagram. The campaign highlighted that a 10-minute brisk walk each day 'counts as exercise' and 'can reduce your risk of serious illnesses like heart disease, type 2 diabetes, dementia and some cancers'. If 150 minutes a week is too much for you presently, adding just 10 minutes of brisk walking into your day is a good place to start an exercise habit. And while it won't turn you into an athlete or make you look like one, it can definitely increase your life span. The world's longest-lived populations—people in the world's Blue Zones—don't join classes, run marathons or push weights in gyms. *The environments they live in, instead, constantly push them into moving without thinking about it.* Instead of spending time seated at desks, they walk several miles throughout the day, grow gardens and don't use mechanical conveniences for house work. Irrespective of whether you meet the guidelines of 150 minutes per week of exercise or not, it is important that you move naturally throughout the day. In a recent Canadian health study, the authors discovered that exercise does not cancel out the ill-effects of too much sitting during the day. They found that individuals who met the physical activity guidelines but remained seated for longer durations in a day had increased chances of death from all causes.

The bottom line is that exercise alone will not save you! Our bodies were designed to move. Build movement opportunities into your daily life, like taking the stairs, taking the long route to the restroom at work, standing up and talking on the phone, etc. When I was appointed as a Movement Expert by the *Huffington Post* founder Arianna Huffington's company Thrive Global to work virtually with Accenture USA employee populations for two consecutive years, I started off by asking the employees to incorporate more movement into their day. Instead of sending an email to a co-worker, walk over and talk to them. Do squats at your desk and take short walks around the office whenever you can fit it in. The more you do, the stronger you will feel—and the more you will want to do!

## Sleep

*'Shekhar, tula kaya jhale? Tumhi khupa vajana kami kele'* ('What happened to you, Shekhar? You lost so much weight!') questioned Ratna, my house help. Shekhar is my cook and he had just returned from his native place. Going home meant a lot of pampering from his mom and wife—read more food, less physical activity—and the last thing Ratna expected to see was a thinner Shekhar. Contrary to everyone's expectations, something was working in his favour. Every time he travelled home, he returned lighter and thinner, in spite of the fact that at home, he was eating more food and working lesser. What was it? Just like you, I too was keen to find out. And so, I did. It was his circadian rhythm (term explained in Chapter 4)!

What we have lost in modern life is our right to darkness. In the good old days, the sun was the major source of lighting, and people spent their evenings in relative darkness. Today, however, our evenings are illuminated. The bright light from fluorescent light bulbs, computer screens, smartphones and TV screens confuses our circadian clock, throws the circadian rhythm out of whack and makes us less sleepy. For Shekhar too, it wasn't anything different. In Mumbai, he would not sleep before 1 a.m. What we also know now is that sleep, circadian rhythm and the gut microbiota are closely connected. Scientists suggest that sleep of good quality and duration—seven to nine hours a night—supports healthy gut microbiota composition, and can help us lose weight, get healthier and stave off depression and anxiety. This is exactly why my cook always returned thinner and fitter. Back in his village, there would be no electricity after eight in the evening. As a result, he would have an early dinner and retire to bed before it got completely dark. The absence of any bright light in the evening helped build natural melatonin, a hormone that promotes deep sleep. Both the quality and quantity of his sleep would thus improve. *Shekhar lost weight every time he went home simply because his circadian rhythm wouldn't be misaligned anymore!*

Sleep is a biological necessity—a non-negotiable one—and not an optional lifestyle luxury. It is unfortunate that we wear sleeplessness as a badge of honour. We are proud of not sleeping in the name of being productive, when in reality, the disruption of our sleep-wake functions has been associated with both physiological and psychological health consequences. Chronic sleep problems, in time, can lead to weight gain, inflammation, metabolic diseases and mental health disorders. It is during deep sleep that the lymphatic system (waste removal system) of the brain is at its peak. You can think of sleep as that which helps detoxify the brain. It is one of the best things you can do for your mental health.

## How Can You Know If You Sleep Well and What Can You Do If You Don't?

Sorry to burst your bubble, but you don't have to invest in some hi-tech gadget or app to know how well you are sleeping. It's no rocket science. We all know when we sleep well and wake up fresh. Moreover, according to the guidance published by the National Sleep Foundation, if you can fall asleep in 30 minutes or less and do not wake up during the middle of the night—called wakefulness after sleep onset or

WASO—then you are said to have a healthy sleep pattern. But what can you do if you're stuck in a sleepless rut? Here are some tips to help you improve your sleep hygiene.

1. *Regularity is king:* Go to bed and wake up at the same time (within an hour's difference) each day, irrespective of whether it's the weekday or the weekend.

    Stick to a sleep schedule. Every. Single. Night.

2. *Optimize light:* Expose yourself to as much bright light as possible during the day, as little light as possible in the evening, and absolutely no light when you sleep, i.e., complete darkness. Catching some natural sunlight, which is the richest and cheapest source of blue light, for at least 30 minutes a day can make you more alert, improve your mood and regulate your sleep patterns. Towards the evening and night, the same blue light, now produced by gadgets, screens, fluorescent lightbulbs and LED lights, can affect your sleep. Avoid blue light exposure beginning two to three hours before bed. Instead, use the old-fashioned incandescent light bulbs we grew up with. They produce much lesser blue light. If you must work with gadgets after sundown, change their displays' background colour to a dimmer orange or red. That's because red and orange light have the least power to suppress melatonin, your sleep hormone. You may also consider wearing blue light-blocking spectacles or installing a blue-blocking app on your PC that allows your computer to adapt its display colour to the time of day.

3.  *Cultivate bedtime yogic rituals:* Practise guided meditation
    like Yog Nidra or pranayama such as Anulom Vilom 10
    to 15 minutes before bed. Such practices can help activate
    your parasympathetic nervous system (explained in the
    neural retraining section) and induce rest and recovery. I
    also recommend practising Yog Nidra as a post-workout
    cooldown. Most of my clients, including Taapsee and
    Rakul, have been benefitting from this practice. My
    personal favourite is Yog Nidra by Swami Niranjanananda
    Saraswati from the Bihar School of Yoga. You can practise
    the same from this link: https://youtu.be/E4fO1istXvo

4.  *Avoid sleep-disturbing elements:* Caffeine and nicotine
    interfere with the process of falling asleep and affect your
    ability to reach deep sleep. Avoid coffee, tea and energy
    drinks five to eight hours before bedtime. Also, avoid
    alcohol and large dinners late at night. While regular
    exercise is excellent for getting more of deep sleep,
    exercising too late can interfere with it. Avoid exercising
    three to four hours before your bedtime.

5.  *Optimize your body temperature:* Take a warm bath an hour
    or two before bedtime. Your body needs to drop its core
    temperature to initiate and stay asleep. Though it sounds
    counterintuitive, a warm bedtime bath triggers sleepiness
    by cooling the body's core temperature.

6.  *Create the right sleep environment:* Do not lie in bed awake
    for too long, hoping you will finally drift off. Use your
    bed only for sex and sleep. If you do anything else in it,
    your brain will associate your bedroom with wakefulness.
    If you are unable to sleep after about 30 minutes of laying

in bed, go to a different room and do anything that's mentally relaxing. Return to your bed only when you're sleepy. Make sure you get up at your usual time the next day. Sleep scientist and author of international bestselling book named *Why We Sleep* (2017), Matthew Walker says, 'You would never sit at the dinner table waiting to get hungry. So why would you lie in bed waiting to get sleepy?' Makes sense.

7. *Eat right:* Our body starts to produce melatonin a few hours before bedtime to help us feel sleepy, and eating during this time disrupts its production. Eat two to three hours before you hit the sack. I cannot emphasize enough how important it is to eat carbs for dinner if you want to sleep well. Certain bedtime drinks also help induce sleep. For recipes, check Chapter 10.

## Sleep Strategy for Night Shift Workers

If you work nights, then you should know that any form of night shift compromises the circadian clock function. It's no wonder then that WHO has classified shift work as a probable carcinogen. However, if you are left with no choice, then follow the strategy below. It will help reduce the damage.

# Table 19: Sleep Strategy for Night Shift Workers

| Day of First Night Shift | | |
| --- | --- | --- |
| Goal: Minimize sleep debt | | |
| Sleep until you wake naturally (don't set an alarm). | Avoid morning coffee, tea, nicotine and other stimulants. | Take a nap of around 1.5 hours between 2 p.m. and 6 p.m. |

| During Night Shift | | | Last Few Hours and Way Home | |
| --- | --- | --- | --- | --- |
| Goal: Improve performance | | | Avoid caffeine and nicotine. | Avoid exposure to bright light (wear sunglasses when you step out). |
| Stay active. Move as much as possible. | Take naps of 10 to 20 minutes during the early part of the shift. | Take caffeine only during the early part of the shift. | | |

| Days between Night Shifts | | | |
| --- | --- | --- | --- |
| Goal: Minimize sleep debt | | | |
| Try to get to sleep as early as possible. | Before trying to sleep, avoid bright lights, alcohol and caffeine. | Sleep in a quiet, cool, darkened room. | Know that any sleep is better than none. Maximize sleep time. |

| Resetting after Night Shifts | | | |
| --- | --- | --- | --- |
| Goal: Re-establish normal sleep rhythm | | | |
| Take a 90 to 180-minute nap immediately following the shift. | After waking up, go outside and catch some sunlight. | Aim to go to bed close to the normal time. | Avoid daytime naps on subsequent days. |

*Source*: Adapted from BMJ Publishing Group Ltd.

## Sleep and the *Upanishads*

In deep, dreamless sleep, the *Upanishad* says, you experience nothing. You are unaware of the fears, insecurities, worries and stresses that you otherwise carry through the day when you are awake. You may be going through a lot of problems, but they are all suspended when you are sleeping. Dreams too aren't sweet every time. For example, you may sweat profusely in your sleep, dreaming of a lion chasing you through a forest. However, in deep, dreamless sleep, your mind is as though it's dissolved. The whole world continues but the experience stops for you. In the state of deep sleep, a king and a pauper both are the same. You no longer identify as a doctor or a teacher or anyone else. Individuality and our ego get resolved. This experience is devoid of any worries and is hence called *ananda* (happiness) and *sukha* (relief), and can be had only when one is in *sushupthi avastha* or deep sleep state.

Now, let's turn to modern science, which states that sleep switches between two phases: non-REM (dreamless) sleep and REM (with dreams) sleep. In sync with the *Upanishads*, sleep experts consider the dreamless NREM—to be precise, NREM stages 3 and 4—as the deep sleep stage. This is why they opine that the less we remember our dreams, the better our sleep likely was—because it's a sign that you spent more time in the stage that's most valuable!

## Neural Retraining

'You can drink that green juice, hit the gym and take all the supplements. But if you don't deal with the shit going on in your head, you are going to have a tough time losing that weight,' said Swamiji while sipping on jaggery tea.

I was at the Sivananda Yoga Vedanta Meenakshi Ashram in Madurai, studying the Yoga Siromani diploma course, and realized that Swamiji had made an important point. Most of us are not ready to embrace it, but factually speaking, mind–body medicine is an important piece of the weight-loss puzzle. *How?* A rudimentary understanding of the sympathetic and parasympathetic nervous systems will help explain how stress can affect your health.

Your sympathetic nervous system is called the 'fight or flight' system, and gets activated when you are feeling fear, pain or when you are tense or stressed. The breathing speeds up and the heart rate increases. For instance, for many of us, the sympathetic nervous system can turn on in the presence of our boss. The parasympathetic nervous system, also called the 'rest and digest' system, has the opposite relaxing effect, almost like your best friend telling you to simply ignore the boss and chill out. If you end up staying in the constant company of your boss without your best friend watching your back, which means that if your fight and flight system stays switched on for a long time without an effective parasympathetic system to turn it off, then dysbiosis sets in. Your body becomes prone to chronic diseases, a few of which are weight gain, high belly fat, sugar cravings, anxiety, depression, suppressed immune response, high blood pressure, heart disease and inflammation.

This is exactly what is happening to most of us in the modern world.

Therefore, it is crucial to employ neural retraining techniques to calm the chronic stress response by shifting the nervous system into a state of parasympathetic dominance. Retraining the nervous system is a crucial aspect in preventing and treating dysbiosis, and should be integrated into our daily life, along with diet, exercise and sleep hygiene, if you want to lose weight and stay healthy physically, mentally and emotionally.

## How Do You Retrain the Nervous System?

The principal component of the very important parasympathetic nervous system is the vagus nerve, part of your gut brain axis (discussed in Chapter 3). Certain practices can help strengthen and stimulate the vagus nerve and counteract the stress response. This can help produce a range of health benefits, including long-term weight loss. One such practice is *yoga*.

### Patanjali's Ashtanga Yoga: Eight-Limbed Yoga

Most of us tend to believe that yoga is simply a set of postures. The truth is that yoga is a complete system, of which asana is only one limb. The Patanjali's *Yoga Sutras* divide the complete practice of yoga into '*asht*' (eight) '*anga*' (limbs), namely:

Rules of conduct
1.  Yama
2.  Niyama

Physical postures

3.   Asanas

Breathing exercises

4.   Pranayama

Contemplative practices of meditation

5.   Pratyahara
6.   Dharana
7.   Dhyana
8.   Samadhi

Contrary to prevalent belief that views these as rungs of a ladder, the eight limbs of yoga should be simultaneously practised. These are not steps, but limbs—would you say your legs are more important than your hands? Same answer. You would rather, depending on your need, decide whether to use your right hand or your left. In the same way, based on your physical or mental need, you must decide which limb of yoga to use first. You may want to start off with meditation and then go to asana practice, and that is completely fine. Or going by your temperament and liking, you may want to focus more on the pranayama, which is again all right. *All the eight limbs can individually help promote parasympathetic nervous system activity in varying degrees.* Classical schools of yoga follow the ashtanga system and teach yoga with an integrative approach. This very fact sets them apart from the innumerable styles of yoga existing today.

Different Yoga Styles: Which to Choose?

Wherever you choose to practise yoga, in India or abroad, it is important to know if yoga is being taught as a complete system or just a physical exercise. That's because we are not just physical bodies. We are also minds, emotions, thoughts, senses, breath and many more. The yoga classes we have today can sound pretty exotic—a few examples being nude yoga, goat yoga, beer yoga and tantrum yoga—but they deviate from the true purpose and principles of yoga. It is important that you learn from living traditions where you can study about all the eight limbs of yoga. Three such traditional schools of yoga are: Sivananda by Swami Sivananda, Iyengar by Guruji BKS Iyengar and Mysore style by K. Pattabhi Jois. As a student, you must seek these living traditions or learn from authentic sources that are connected to these traditions.

The Practice

Swami Sivananda has said, 'An ounce of practice is worth a tonne of theory.' So, no matter how much I write, this (or any other) book cannot teach you what your own practice will. The best way to start your practice is under the guidance of a competent teacher. Online yoga classes have also become a reality owing to the pandemic. So, if you live in a place where you do not have access to a traditional class, you can always sign up for classes online. If neither option is available, then there are excellent yoga books written by the highest authorities in the field, and you can use them to start your practice. A few of these books that are available at bookstores and online are *The Complete Illustrated Book of Yoga* by Swami Vishnudevananda, *The Illustrated Light on Yoga* by BKS Iyengar and *Yoga in Action: A Preliminary Course* by Geeta Iyengar.

Asana Sequence

Your workout at the gym or your morning run is primarily a sympathetic nervous activity. Unlike any other physical workout, classical yoga traditions follow meticulously-planned sequences, so that if one asana stimulates your sympathetic nervous system, then the asana immediately afterwards will help trigger the parasympathetic response. For instance, in the below sequence, child's pose and other restorative poses along with brief periods of shavasana (dead body pose) are used after difficult and tiring postures to launch the rest and digest branch of your nervous system. In yoga, if there are postures that move the body in a certain direction, then there are counter-positions to move the body in the complete opposite direction to maintain harmony and balance. In the sequence below, for example, incline plane which is a backbend pose follows immediately after the forward bend pose. All of this increases parasympathetic activity, promotes relaxation and makes yoga truly unique compared to most other forms of exercise.

I have presented below the sequence from the basic class in Sivananda style. The sequence addresses all the limbs from the ashtanga system, and hence represents yoga as a complete system of total well-being for body, mind and spirit.

## Table 20: Basic Sivananda Class (Suitable for Beginners)

You can follow the class here: https://youtu.be/iUKjuni-6l8.

| Sequence | Basic Class | Ashtanga |
|---|---|---|
| Prayer, breathing exercise and meditation | Shavasana (Initial relaxation: 5 minutes) | Yama/Niyama |
| | Starting prayer | |
| | Kapalbhati | Pranayama |
| | Anulom Vilom | |
| | Meditation (5–10 minutes) | Pratyahara, Dharana, Dhyana, Samadhi |
| | Shavasana (1 minute) | |
| Warm-up exercises | Surya Namaskar/Sun salutation | |
| | Shavasana (1–2 minutes) | |
| | Single Leg Raises | |
| | Double leg raises | |
| | Shavasana (30–60 seconds) | |
| Mental prep for headstand | Balasana (Child's pose) | Asanas |
| Inversion | Sirshasana (Headstand) OR Dolphin (preparatory exercise for headstand for those who are new to it) | |
| Relaxation | Shavasana (30–60 seconds) | |
| Inversion | Sarvangasana (Shoulderstand) | |
| | Halasana (Plough) | |
| Back bend (Counter-pose) | Matsyasana (Fish pose) | |
| Relaxation | Shavasana (30–60 seconds) | |
| Forward Bend | Paschimothanasana (Forward Bend) | |
| Back bend (Counter-pose) | Purvottanasana (Incline plane) | |

| Restorative pose | Makarasana (Crocodile pose) | |
|---|---|---|
| Back bend | Bhujangasana (Cobra pose) | |
| Restorative pose | Makarasana (Crocodile pose) | |
| Back bend | Salabhasana (Locust pose) | |
| Restorative pose | Makarasana (Crocodile pose) | |
| Back bend | Dhanurasana (Bow pose) | |
| Relaxing (Counter-stretch) | Balasana (Child's pose) | |
| Twisting pose | Ardha Matsyendrasana (Half Spinal Twist) | |
| Balancing pose | Kakasana (Crow pose) OR Mayurasana (Peacock pose) | |
| Standing pose | Pada Hasthasana (Standing forward bend) | |
| | Trikonasana (Triangle pose) | |
| Relaxation | Shavasana (Final relaxation: 10 minutes) or Yog Nidra | |
| Prayer | Closing prayer | Niyama |

# 9

# Taapsee Pannu

## The 'Unstoppable' Rocket

**September 2020**

Taapsee was scrolling through pictures on an iPad and sitting beside her, I was looking through them. We were in a meeting along with the producers of *Rashmi Rocket*. Pictures of great and powerful female sprinters from across the world had been collected and were being shown to us as reference.

'So, Munmun, this is the transformation we are aiming for.'

'How much time do we have?' I asked.

'Exactly after two months, the shoot begins. And after about three months from now, we will start shooting the final race scenes that will be the climax of the movie,' Taapsee said, looking at me.

When I got back, a montage was playing in my head: A woman athlete exploding off the starting block on the athletic track, another one sprinting towards the finish line, a stadium filled with fans holding placards that said, 'Stop her if you can!'

It quickly dawned on me that for the purpose of the movie, not only was an aesthetic transformation required, but it was also imperative to turn Taapsee into a 'running rocket' for real! The challenge was huge, but I was quite confident of making it. No, wait, before you label me as arrogant, hear me out. Over my 19 years of practice, I have come to realize that my success with my clients isn't all about what I do for them. It's about the clients who choose to work *with* me. That's because I can only give them guidance; it's they who execute it and turn it into a success story. I had already been working with Taapsee for a few years before *Rashmi Rocket* came along, and knowing her, I had no doubt that she would give 100 per cent to this project. There was no reason for me to doubt the results. Female actors taking up a challenge of this kind is rare, and that itself speaks volume about Taapsee's courage and grit. My confidence came not from me but from our partnership. As they say, you are only as good as your team, and looking back over the years, I could confidently say, 'Oh boy! She and I make a bloody good team!'

*Arre yaar, chalo maan liya, teamwork makes the dream work and all that jazz, par sirf do mahine? Do mahine mei kiski body banti hai?* For me to answer this question, allow me to take you back a couple of years. *Flashback! Ab kya karu, thodi filmi toh mei bhi hu!*

## Year 2018

It was a Monday morning. The clock was about to strike 9 a.m., so I hurriedly planted myself in my chair and reached for my phone. In the next minute, I was on a FaceTime call with Taapsee, my very first consultation with her. Casually dressed in a pink tee and matching PJs, her hair tied into a bun and no trace of make-up on her face, her look complemented the non-starry attitude she exhibited while getting in touch with me for her first appointment. It is well known that managers of stars make the first call, take appointments, etc., and this is considered business as usual. But Taapsee likes to stand out from the crowd in just about everything. Instead of having her manager facilitate the call between us, she chose to be on it herself. The next hour flew by with her talking about herself and me registering every minute detail in my head. For instance, she explained, 'See I am a sardarni. I love food, and I just cannot bring myself to eat something that doesn't appeal to my taste buds.' This was music to my ears. *Why?* Because today we live in a world where a guy can convince millions of people that putting butter in their coffee will help them lose fat. Whether it tastes horrible or not, doesn't really matter! The man created a business from it. But here was this girl who wanted to ensure her meal plan consisted of only foods that she liked to eat. And then she would follow the plan to a T, no matter if it's the weekend or she's on a holiday.

When your routine diet is tailor-made based on what you like to eat, there is no reason to look for a cheat meal. Contrary to most others who decide to eat anything to lose weight—all in the name of willpower—and then fall off the wagon after just a few weeks, Taapsee has been quite sensible, and this is something that I love the most about her. In an industry where for an actress, being skinny is directly proportional to being successful and in demand, she refuses to burden herself with the pressure of how much she weighs on the scale. Weight loss is the by-product of a healthy lifestyle—or a healthy gut, so to speak—and I was glad that she was ready to work on her gut health, metabolism and digestion instead of chasing a number on the scale.

For the next few months, we decided to work on the following areas:

a) *Her sensitivity to gluten and dairy*, due to which she was on a self-devised diet that was devoid of wheat, milk and milk products.
b) *Sluggish metabolism*, which she believes she got genetically from her mom.
c) *Acid reflux*, which was chronic and persistent, was affecting her work productivity and quality of life.
d) *Inefficient digestion*, in spite of being extra-conscious of eating everything 'healthy'.
e) *Not knowing what, how much and when to eat*, with long shoot hours, shooting in different places and countries, night shoots, continuous travels further adding to the confusion.

## Getting Started

Before I start working with my clients, apart from a few other things, I also ask them to note down their food intake, exercise details (if they are working out) and activities of daily living (referred to as ADLs), and send these details to me. This simple tool provides a great starting point from where both my client and I can take off on the TBBD journey together. On the day before our conversation, Taapsee too had shared her details with me, and this is how a general day in her life looked like.

**Table 21: A Day in the Life of Taapsee Pannu, circa 2018**

| On rising | Ujjayi Pranayama |
|---|---|
| **6.30–7.30 a.m.** | 1 litre of warm water, 1 cup of green tea, 10 soaked almonds, 2 walnuts and 4 dry figs |
| **Breakfast (9–10 a.m.)** | Vegetable juice (cucumber + celery + amla/ mint), masala omelette made of 3 full eggs, with gluten-free granola in almond milk/Pao bhaji (gluten-free bread)/Poori aloo (gluten-free flour) |
| **10–10.30 a.m.** | Freshly brewed coffee |
| **Lunch (2–3 p.m.)** | 'I usually don't feel very hungry at this time, so will have something as light as just some dal or veggies cooked at home, or will just avoid eating until I feel hungry.' |
| **Post lunch** | Freshly-brewed coffee |
| **Workout (3–5 p.m.)** | 45–60 minutes of squash or cardio (treadmill, cycle, cross trainer) followed by 60 minutes of weight training. |
| **Dinner (8–8.30 p.m.)** | Usually ordered from outside. 'I try to eat chicken or fish at this time.' |
| **Bedtime (11 p.m.)** | 1 cup of green tea before sleeping |

## The Plan of Action (POA)

At the outset, I explained to her about the Three Rs (right quality, right quantity and right timings) of TBBD. The plan was to reset her microbiome using the three-phased approach explained in this book that would help address and gradually resolve all her concerns. A few of the changes we brought about in her plan were:

Dietary Modifications

1. *Everything processed and packaged was eliminated.* Gluten-free granola, gluten-free bread, gluten-free flour, tetrapacked almond milk—like most of us, Taapsee thought that these were all healthier options. But no matter how healthy they sound, they all qualify as NOVA ultra-processed foods. Consuming these foods, as you have learnt by now, is associated with decreased beneficial gut microbes.

2. *The SPAR technique of eating was employed.* The simplest way to know how much to eat is to employ the SPAR technique. 'This sounds so fuss-free, I mean, no measuring in spoons and katoris! I'll get right on it,' Taapsee said joyously. After a few days of practising it, she texted me, confessing that she was unconsciously eating lesser than her usual portion sizes. Till today, she sticks to the basic principle of taking time to chew the food well, and eating till only 80 per cent full.

3. *Lunch was deliberately made the biggest meal of the day.* Research tells us that disruption of circadian rhythms induces changes in the intestinal microbiota community. And an important step in restoring gut health is to time your meals according to the circadian clock. Taapsee's pre-breakfast and breakfast meals were so huge that she didn't feel hungry enough for lunch. And not eating for long hours during the day got her famished by dinner time. I asked her to reduce the size of her breakfast, and that got her hungry for a hearty lunch. Eating well around noon ensured she could wind up her eating window with a light, homemade dinner around sunset.

4. *Moderation in consumption was encouraged.* Tea and coffee both have great anti-inflammatory properties, but it's important not to overdo them. 'No more than two cups a day. Avoid having it first thing in the morning, on an empty stomach and after sunset,' I cautioned. Though the Punjabi in her wasn't too happy on not getting meat and fish every day, I did advise her to exercise moderation in its consumption, and so she did!

**Table 22: Taapsee's Modified Diet**

| Meal timings | Meal plan—Phase 1 | Meal plan—Phase 2 |
|---|---|---|
| On rising: 6–7 a.m. | Fennel tea | Hot herbal tea |
| Breakfast: 9 a.m. | Porridge | Millet upma |
| Lunch: 12–1 p.m. | Millet roti and rice, dal, sabzi with garlic chutney (non-veg food only once a week) | Nachni roti, millet rice, dal, sabzi with homemade pickle (non-veg food only twice a week) |
| Mid-meal: 4 p.m. | Lentil (moong dal) soup | Artisanal aged cheese or buttermilk |
| Dinner: 6–7 p.m. | Khichri with ghee | Jowar khichri with kadhi |

## Exercise Modifications

1. *Exercise duration and frequency were reduced:* This was new to me. I usually had to lecture people on why it is important that they move their butts. I was used to people asking me, *'bees minute treadmill kiya toh weight loss toh hoga naa?'* or *'sirf weekends par gym karu toh chalega naa?'*. With Taapsee, it was the opposite. With around two hours of workout every single day, she was clearly over-exercising—a

reflection of her go-getter attitude in life in general. But when it comes to exercise, more is *not* better. Exercising appropriately can lessen inflammation and damage done to your gut microbiome, but exercising too much can lead to inflammation and gut (hyper)permeability. The dose makes the poison! Taapsee often got heartburn in the middle of her workout sessions, and she was completely taken aback when I explained to her that the heartburn was exercise-induced.

2. *Exercise structure was altered:* There are three energy systems in our body—adenosine triphosphate–creatine phosphate or ATP–CP, anaerobic glycolysis and aerobic—that work simultaneously to fuel the body during exercise. However, depending on the exercise duration and intensity, one of the three systems predominates. Taapsee was working out pretty hard, but because her exercise sessions consisted of both squash or cardio (predominantly aerobic) and weight training (primarily anaerobic glycolysis) one after the other, she wasn't reaping as much benefit as she should have been. An altered regime was planned for her, with aerobic and anaerobic activities alternating with each other. Doing so leads to better fuel utilization, enhanced muscle recovery and greater fat burn without spending hours and hours exercising. Additionally, a day of high-intensity interval training or HIIT workout (10 seconds of maximum effort followed by a two-minute rest) that predominantly trains the ATP–CP system was introduced. Targeting each of our energy systems by different types of exercise is important, as it maximizes fitness benefits and results in a leaner, more toned body.

## Table 23: Taapsee's Modified Workout Plan: A Weekly Calendar

| Days | Exercise | Duration |
|---|---|---|
| Day 1 | Lower body strength training (anaerobic glycolysis) | 45–60 minutes |
| Day 2 | Cardio (aerobic) | 45–60 minutes |
| Day 3 | Upper body strength training (anaerobic glycolysis) | 45–60 minutes |
| Day 4 | Squash (aerobic) | 45–60 minutes |
| Day 5 | HIIT workout (ATP–CP) | 15 minutes |
| Day 6 | Cardio or Squash (aerobic) | 45–60 minutes |
| Day 7 | Rest | |

## Table 24: Exercise Plan: Lower Body

*Note:* Use weights that make you hit failure (volitional fatigue) at the 15th repetition for each set and exercise

| Exercise | Sets | Reps |
|---|---|---|
| Squats | 3 | 15 |
| Sumo squats | 3 | 15 |
| Lunges | 3 | 15 |
| Stiff-legged barbell deadlift | 3 | 15 |
| Leg extension | 2 | 15 |
| Leg curl | 2 | 15 |
| Calf raise | 2 | 15 |

## Table 25: Exercise Plan: Upper Body

*Note:* Use weights that make you hit failure (volitional fatigue) at the 15th repetition for each set and exercise

| Exercise | Sets | Reps |
|---|---|---|
| Deadlift | 3 | 15 |
| Lat pulldown | 3 | 15 |
| Seated row | 3 | 15 |
| Bench press | 3 | 15 |
| Cable flyes | 2 | 15 |
| Overhead press | 3 | 15 |
| Plank | 3 | 1 minute each |

Taapsee was bang-on with the plans. She was eating and exercising as advised, keeping up with her morning pranayama and practising good sleep hygiene. She had started to feel better in just a few days. The acid refluxes had reduced, and she had started feeling lighter and more active in her body. After about six weeks, when she was in Pune with her Premier Badminton League (PBL) team, I received a text from her, 'Hey, I feel terrific. Though I did feel initially that working out for just about an hour would not be enough for my body, but surprisingly, I do see that my strength and stamina has increased. My metabolism has for sure fired up. You please now start working with my mom also.'

A few weeks later, *Manmarziyaan* was to be showcased at the 2018 Marrakech International Film Festival and the River to River Florence Indian Film Festival. Taapsee was to fly to Morocco and then to Florence, and I felt it was just the right time to transition her to phase 3 and reintroduce gluten and dairy back into her diet. So, while her Morocco plan consisted of couscous, in Florence she ate bagel and pasta with great relish. Her gut microbiome had been restored, and she was getting leaner and fitter by the day and looking absolutely stunning. From there on, I only wanted to maintain her gut ecosystem in an incredibly beautiful way with many different types of microbial strains and communities. The best known way to do it is to eat a wide variety of different foods.

So, from role to role, movie to movie and location to location, Taapsee's diet underwent a change. She ate white cheese in Azerbaijan, Danish blue cheese in Denmark and the famous churpi in Darjeeling. When she was shooting for *Game Over* in Chennai, there was rice with coconut-based curries, and while shooting for *Thappad* in Lucknow, she fearlessly ate kebabs, naan and biryani. Her co-actors and people on the sets labelled her diet a '*khata peeta*' diet, and wondered how it could make her look the way she did. We often mistakenly assume that a great body comes from deprivation, but the truth is that it comes from a robust metabolism—that is, to be able to eat, digest and enjoy all kinds of food—and *Taapsee* was certainly leading by example. From *Game Over* to *Saand ki Aankh* and then to *Thappad*—with each passing year—*Taapsee*'s fitness game was getting stronger. And then one fine day, she signed on for *Rashmi Rocket*.

## Back to September 2020

To make her look like an athlete on screen, I now had to plan her regime in a way that helped her lose body fat even further and gain lean muscle mass at the same time—a transformation that is called 'lean bulk' in the fitness world. 'Let's do this!' she exclaimed. Getting out of her comfort zone to do something extraordinary is like fuel for Taapsee. She thrives on it.

I was excited too. She wasn't starting from zero in terms of gut health, body aesthetics or overall fitness. For instance, the redistribution of blood during high-intensity training—away from the gut to working muscles—usually causes GI distresses like reduced digestion, diarrhoea and nausea. You will know this from the nauseated feeling that you may have had during heavy workouts. But I was sure that over the years, her gut had been trained and conditioned, and she was ready to take her fitness game a notch higher. Two months looked just right. The only challenge was her long working hours, hectic schedule and frequent travels.

In September, she was shooting in Jaipur for the film *Annabelle Sethupathy*. Her day would begin at 5 a.m. with a workout at the gym, followed by a 12-hour shoot. Her diet was neither low-carb nor low-fat, and was planned around three interconnected priorities—recovery, immunity and muscle gain. Her routine teas and sherbets were replaced with protein shakes and recovery drinks. Sports supplements were now introduced. Instead of counting calories or macros, we continued focusing on the basics of the Three Rs: eating clean, eating on time and eating intuitively. Instead of resorting to packaged protein bars that scream high protein, we kept our faith in humble, homemade meals. People around her insisted that a diet that consisted of rice, ghee, potatoes, buttermilk, paneer and parathas was fattening, but she remained unfazed.

And then just like that, a month passed, and Taapsee's 'Biggini shoot' video took the internet by storm. Wearing a bikini and her charisma with equal ease in beautiful Maldives, she looked fit and fabulous, and it was difficult for the world to ignore. Texts exclaiming 'she looks so hot' accumulated in my phone from colleagues, clients, family and friends. The media suddenly became interested to know what Taapsee ate.

By the time the shoot of *Rashmi Rocket* commenced in November, Taapsee had gained 2.5 kilos of lean muscle mass, no easy feat by any means. Dressed like an athlete ready to face the camera, her pictures resembled those that had been shown to us as reference. The real test, though, came in December, when she had to shoot for the races in Ranchi. Then, apart from looking like an athlete, Taapsee also had to perform.

At Ranchi, the temperature was somewhere around 8–10 degrees Celsius, quite a contrast for us Mumbaikars. Mumbai usually gets down to 27–28 degrees in December, and that's enough for the high-end junta to take their winter fashion-wear out from the cupboards and onto the skin! In Ranchi, while I was wrapped in all possible woollen wear, Taapsee was bravely bearing the cold in the sleeveless sports jerseys that she was supposed to wear for the race scenes. The focus of my work had become manifold. On the athletic front, I had to ensure that she had enough explosive strength required for the sprints. That's because during sprints, the body predominantly engages the ATP–CP system for energy. Alongside, I wanted to make sure her muscle-pump was boosted for the sake of aesthetics. Her muscles also had to get adequate recovery between back-to-back runs throughout the day (unlike a real sprint race that gets done in a few seconds, an actor in a shoot has to go through multiple retakes and run repeatedly throughout the day), and be ready to fire up consecutively for the next six days that we were there. At the same time, I wanted to consider the dipping temperature that, along with her insufficient clothing, could result in discomfort, chills, seasonal cold, increased muscle soreness, etc.

My weapons of choice to accomplish these myriad goals were foods like ghee, garlic, mustard, bajra, makai and herbal coffee. Apart from being warming in nature, they all have their individual benefits. For instance, in many ancient cultures, garlic was traditionally used to provide strength, enhance the working capacity of labourers and reduce fatigue. In fact, it was one of the earliest performance enhancing agents, and was given to Olympic athletes in ancient Greece. Human studies have confirmed that exercise-induced fatigue, systemic fatigue due to cold or physical fatigue of any kind can be resolved with garlic through a variety of actions.

In Ranchi, we were both anxious and excited, and looking forward to start the shoot of the final, big races. It was time to put the months of hard work to the test. The shoot finally began. Taapsee took to the starting block, the director called out 'Action,' and she exploded off the block. As she sprinted towards the finish line, I watched her, my heart filled with pride, and in my mind, I said, 'Stop her if you can!'

## Table 26: Taapsee's Meal Plan for *Rashmi Rocket*

| Meal timings | Mumbai meal plan: October–November | Ranchi meal plan: December | Bhuj meal plan: January |
|---|---|---|---|
| Meal One: On rising | Pre-workout meal (refer to Table 26) | Pre-race meal (refer to Table 27) | Pre-workout meal (refer to Table 27) |
| Meal Two | Banana (or any fruit) and post-workout meal (refer to Table 27) | Banana (or any fruit) and post-race meal (refer to Table 27) | Banana (or any fruit) and post-workout meal (refer to Table 27) |
| Meal Three: Breakfast | Sweet potato tikki with chutney | Sourdough bread and omelette | Khandvi with chutney |
| Meal Four: Lunch | Rice, dahi, veggies or chicken curry and homemade achaar | Litti with ghee, aloo chokha, baingan chokha and garlic chutney, tomato chutney | Fresh haldi sabzi, Kaju gathiya nu saag with roti, jaggery and ghee |
| Meal Five: Evening meal | Buttermilk with sattu powder, flaxseed powder and methi seed powder | Mixed nuts and Chukku kaapi | Besan and coconut laddu |
| Meal Six: Dinner | Apple cider vinegar (ACV) with ginger, turmeric and methi seeds. Dinner after 15 minutes. Jowar roti with paneer bhurji | ACV with ginger, turmeric and methi seeds. Dinner after 15 minutes. Bajra roti and curry | ACV with ginger, turmeric and methi seeds. Dinner after 15 minutes. Gujarati khichri and kadhi, jaggery and ghee |

## Table 27: Taapsee's Supplement Plan for *Rashmi Rocket*

| Supplement | Duration | Timing | Benefits | |
|---|---|---|---|---|
| | | | Aesthetic | Performance |
| Carbohydrate powder | September–January | Pre-workout/Pre-races | Optimizes sculpting by maximizing training effort | High-octane fuel for muscles to train hard |
| Creatine HCL | October–January | Pre-workout/Pre-races | Gain in lean muscle mass, muscle volume, muscle size | Enhances performance during short, high intensity strength training and sprints that rely on the ATP–CP energy system |
| Whey isolate | September–January | Post workouts/Post races | Increases protein synthesis for muscle building and repair | Improves muscle recovery and restoration |
| Casein protein | September–January | Bedtime | Increases muscle strength and muscle growth. Promotes fat loss. | Slow-digesting protein prevents muscle breakdown overnight |
| L-glutamine | September–December | Post workouts/Post races | Promotes muscle growth and fat loss | Immune system strengthening, improves recovery, enhances glycogen replenishment |

| | | | | |
|---|---|---|---|---|
| BCAA | November–December | Between races | Replenishes amino acids to build and maintain muscles | Muscle recovery, helps avoid fatigue, improves endurance during races |
| L-arginine | December–January | 20 minutes before shoot | Boosts muscle pump, increases vascularity | Increases immune system defence, enhances endurance through increased blood flow to the working muscles |
| Potassium | November–December | Post dinner | Muscle tissue growth | Reduced muscle soreness, prevents excessive cramping |
| Calcium/Magnesium | September–December | Alternatively, at bedtime | Improves fat loss | Speeds recovery, enhances muscle contraction |
| CLA | September–January | Post meals | Improves body composition, improves lean muscle tone | Fuels energy and fat metabolism |
| Omega-3 and vitamin D3 | September–December | Post lunch | Increases protein synthesis | Reduces inflammation and immune health |

| Vitamin C and vitamin E | September–December | Post workouts | Promotes muscle growth, inhibits muscle breakdown | Minimizes oxidative damage that may occur from exercise |
| --- | --- | --- | --- | --- |
| Vitamin B complex and zinc | September–January | Post breakfast | Increases anabolic hormone and muscle strength | Energy metabolism, immunity and repair |

# 10

# Meal-Planning Guidelines, Meal Plans, Seasonal Food Guide, Recipes

## The Seven TBBD Meal-Planning Guidelines

The following guidelines are based on Ayurveda as well as modern science. They stay valid throughout the three phases of TBBD. You can use these and the Three Fs of each phase to create your own phase-wise meal plans too! I would like you to follow these guidelines from Day 1 and gradually make them a part of your lifestyle forever.

1. *On rising: Soon after you wake up—within 30 minutes—have a warm drink (not tea or coffee; recommended recipes are given below).* Those who exercise first thing in the morning can take a mix of soaked raisins and soaked almonds after the warm drink. After 15 to 20 minutes of having this, you can begin your workout. *Unless you work out first thing in the morning, and that too, at a respectful intensity, you should not rush to eat, not even a fruit.*

2.  *Breakfast: Eat a light breakfast, not later than 9 a.m. Smoothies and warm, soupy porridges, kanji and khichri are preferable to solid breakfast foods.* You may take time to get used to this new routine, especially if you have been in the habit of eating a big breakfast, but once cultivated, it is a ritual you will thank yourself for. Try incorporating liquid or semi-liquid breakfasts on most days of the week (five days a week), if not every day.

3.  *Lunch:* Most of us are in the habit of starting our day with a buffet breakfast, followed by remaining seated all day. So when lunchtime arrives, there is neither any real hunger nor any real time for it. And then suddenly, we find ourselves ravenous for the evening *papdi chaat, paanipuri* and the like. Dinner, of course, is a banquet of food along with some drinks, because we think that after working so hard all through the day, *itna toh banta hai na.* We then wake up with a heavy, congested feeling that worsens with the heavy breakfast, before again staying seated all day. When we keep doing this day in and day out, unrestrained inflammatory pathways are kept active, and it ultimately leads to weight gain, chronic illness and mood disorders.

    So how do you avoid this vicious cycle? It's quite simple. *Make lunch the most substantial meal of the day. Avoid delaying it. Have it between 11 a.m. and 12 p.m. or latest by 1 p.m.* But what if you don't get hungry? Following steps 1 and 2 above will ultimately lead you to step 3. Taking a light breakfast in the morning will ensure that you are hunger-ready for lunch! And having a wholesome lunch will, in turn, prevent cravings for junk in the evening. Sounds like a plan, right? Lunch is also the time when you can have roti and rice together, something that you should avoid doing at other meals.

4.  *Mid-Meal:* Food provides nourishment, but it is not the
    only nourishing thing that we put into our bodies. The
    relationships we nurture, the air we breathe, the water we
    drink are all feeding us. We need to rise above the idea that
    food is the only fuel source. Your body metabolizes not
    just calories but all of the experiences that you consume.
    Food is a vital energy source, but just one among many.
    Making this mental switch will help you get over the
    constant need to graze and depend on a continual supply
    of food throughout the day.

    In fact, most of the time, we eat because of a false sense
    of hunger. Technically, it's not even hunger, it's rather an
    appetite. I want you to differentiate between appetite and
    hunger. Is it really your belly hungry or your tongue that's
    craving some salt (snack) or your boredom making you
    resort to something interesting and sugary? Is it really hunger
    or your appetite that's stimulated merely because your
    colleague opened a pizza box in front of you? I want you
    to recognize one from the other and let true hunger build
    in between meals. One of the most important principles
    of TBBD is that you eat *only* when you are hungry and
    pause when you feel satisfied, not full; following this alone
    will put your body into a fat-burning zone. *A gap of four
    hours between meals is ideal, and hence an evening meal around
    4 p.m. is just about fine.* You don't *have to* eat every two
    hours. However, if you do feel hungry, feel free to eat.
    True hunger is a sign that your body is ready to digest food.
    But when you only rely on the external clock on your wall,
    not on your body's internal hunger signals, and go on eating
    every two hours, you are simply dumping food that will stay
    undigested, accumulate toxins and set the stage for SIBO.

5. *Dinner:* To keep a fire going, it needs some kindling, but throw too much on it and the fire will be smothered. The same is true for the digestive fire or the metabolic fire inside us. Eating light will maintain it at a slow burn, but too much food can dampen the digestive fire, cause the metabolism to become weak and ultimately lead to weight gain. Therefore, *the most important guideline is to keep dinner as light as possible.* I favour a warm, soupy khichri, porridge or kanji the most at this time, although from phase 2 onwards, you will have more options in the meal plans given in this book. The timing is important too. Ensure you finish your last meal around sunset, before 7 p.m.

6. *Post-Dinner/Bedtime:* 'What if I get hungry post-dinner?' is a question that most of my clients ask. Ideally you should maintain a 12-hour fast between dinner and your early morning drink. And it isn't daunting at all, unless you keep yourself awake late into the night. The only times we feel hungry at odd hours in the night is when we stay awake. If you retire to bed by 10.30 p.m. and sleep by 11 p.m. latest, the chances of your getting hungry post-dinner is minuscule, to say the least. *Maintain a regular sleep routine. It will help you stay committed to your diet.* If you feel hungry, then a cup of herbal tea (in phases 1, 2 and 3) or milk (in phase 3) taken any time after dinner or at bedtime is completely fine. Towards the end of the chapter, I have shared a few recipes that are known to be calming and aid a deep, restful sleep.

7. *Miscellaneous:* Every 30 minutes, every single day, sip on hot water. You can choose to sip on plain hot water or add fresh ginger and lemon slices. Here's one spice blend—I call it the 'magic mix'—that I prefer to use. Boil water. Take it off the stove. For every one litre of water, add half

a teaspoon each of cumin seeds, coriander seeds, fennel seeds (you may grind these into powders instead of using the seeds based on your preference) and freshly-grated ginger. Squeeze into this the juice from half-a-lemon, roughly about a tablespoon. Transfer it into a thermos. The seeds need not be strained out. Let it steep for 15 minutes. Sip on it all day. You can even make this in the morning and carry it in a thermos flask to work so that it lasts you the entire day. This helps reduce inflammation, allergies and hyperacidity, and improves skin health and calms the nervous system too! What about tea and coffee? *Tea and coffee are great beverages to have, but make sure you do not exceed two cups a day.* Avoid having them first thing in morning and after 4 p.m. The best times to have them are 15 to 20 minutes after breakfast and your evening meal.

Now that you have understood the core principles, let's get to the meal plans.

## Important Points

- The meal plans for each phase are divided based on the seasons and regions (east, west, north, south) of India. Depending on the region you belong to and the season, you can choose the plan and follow as is.
- Meals in *italics* are those whose recipes can be found towards the end of the chapter.
- For breakfast, I have given two options. Option A is a liquid or semi-liquid that you should favour most of the time. Option B is solid breakfast options for days you feel you need more.

- For evening meals between 3 and 5 p.m., I have again provided two options. Option A is the lighter meal option and Option B is the relatively heavier one. Depending on how hungry you get and how early you can anticipate your dinner time, pick between the two options. On days you know you cannot have dinner at or before 7 p.m., go for meals listed in Option B.

## Phase 1 Meal Plans

*For the dosage and usage of herbal supplements, refer to Chapter 5.*

| Meal timings | North region | | |
|---|---|---|---|
| | **Summer** | **Monsoon** | **Winter** |
| Meal 1: On rising | *Any one summer tea from Table 31 below* | *Any one monsoon tea from Table 31 below* | *Any one winter tea from Table 31 below* |
| Daruhald and chitrak tea 30 minutes before breakfast | | | |
| Meal 2: Breakfast, by 9 a.m. latest | Option A: *Millet porridge/Coconut smoothie/Post-workout protein smoothie*<br><br>Option B: Moong dal chilla with chutney/ Poha/Millet flakes poha/*Millet rice pancake* | Option A: Bajra raab/*Millet porridge/Coconut smoothie/Post-workout protein smoothie*<br><br>Option B: Moong dal chilla with chutney/ Poha/Millet flakes poha/ Buckwheat chilla/*Millet rice pancake* | Option A: Bajra raab/*Millet porridge/Coconut smoothie/Post-workout protein smoothie*<br><br>Option B: Moong dal chilla with chutney/ Poha/Millet flakes poha/ Buckwheat chilla/*Millet rice pancake* |
| Trikatu after breakfast | | | |

| Meal 3: Lunch, 11 a.m.–1 p.m. | Rice dal sabzi/ Millet roti, dal, sabzi/Chawal ki roti, dal, sabzi/ Veg pulao and curry/Millet rice, dal, sabzi/Stuffed millet paratha with chutney | Rice dal sabzi/ Millet roti, dal, sabzi/Chawal ki roti, dal, sabzi/ Veg pulao and curry/Millet rice, dal, sabzi/Stuffed millet paratha with chutney | Rice dal sabzi/ Millet roti, dal, sabzi/Chawal ki roti with sabzi, dal/Veg pulao and curry/Millet rice, dal, sabzi/ Mooli jowar paratha with chutney |
|---|---|---|---|
| | Add eggs/fish/ chicken to the above only once a week | Add eggs/fish/ chicken to the above only once a week | Add eggs/fish/ chicken to the above only once a week |
| Meal 4: Evening meal, 3 p.m.–5 p.m. | Option A: Cashews and jaggery/Fresh fruit/Sprouted green moong chaat (not raw)/ Any one sherbet from those mentioned in Chapter 5/Spicy millet puffs | Option A: Cashews and jaggery/Fresh fruit/Spicy millet puffs/Kashmiri kahwa/Sprouted green moong chaat (not raw)/ Any one soup from Table 8, Chapter 5 | Option A: Cashews and jaggery/Fresh fruit/Spicy millet puffs/Sugarcane juice/Kashmiri kahwa/Amla sherbet/Any one soup from Table 8, Chapter 5 |
| | Option B: Any meal from Option B breakfast | Option B: Any meal from Option B breakfast | Option B: Any meal from Option B breakfast |
| Daruhald and chitrak tea 30 minutes before dinner | | | |
| Meal 5: Dinner, by 7 p.m. latest | Chicken congee/ Khichri with ghee/*Millet khichri* | Chicken congee/ *Millet khichri/* Khichri with ghee | Chicken congee/ Bajra khichri/ *Millet khichri/* Khichri with ghee |
| Trikatu after dinner | | | |

| Meal 6: After dinner, if hungry | *Any one summer tea from Table 31 below* | *Any one monsoon tea from Table 31 below* | *Any one winter tea from Table 31 below* |
|---|---|---|---|
| Triphala at bedtime | | | |

| Meal timings | South region | | |
|---|---|---|---|
| | **Summer** | **Monsoon** | **Winter** |
| Meal 1: On rising | *Any one summer tea from Table 31 below* | *Any one monsoon tea from Table 31 below* | *Any one winter tea from Table 31 below* |
| Daruhald and chitrak tea 30 minutes before breakfast | | | |
| Meal 2: Breakfast, by 9 a.m. latest | Option A: *Millet kanji*/Rice kanji/ Ven pongal/ *Coconut smoothie/ Post-workout protein smoothie*<br><br>Option B: Pesarattu with chutney/Rice (arisi) upma/ Idiyappam or Shavige with coconut milk or chutney/ Rice, ghee and jaggery/*Millet neer dosa* | Option A: *Millet kanji*/Rice kanji/ Ven pongal/ *Coconut smoothie/ Post-workout protein smoothie/ Amaranth porridge*<br><br>Option B: Pesarattu with chutney/Rice (arisi) upma/ Idiyappam or Shavige with coconut milk or chutney/ Rice, ghee and jaggery/*Millet neer dosa* | Option A: *Millet kanji*/Rice kanji/ Ven pongal/ *Coconut smoothie/ Post-workout protein smoothie/ Amaranth porridge*<br><br>Option B: Pesarattu with chutney/Rice (arisi) upma/ Idiyappam or Shavige with coconut milk or chutney/ Rice, ghee and jaggery/*Millet neer dosa* |
| Trikatu after breakfast | | | |

| Meal 3: Lunch, 11 a.m.–1 p.m. | Millet mudde with curry/ Puttu and green gram curry/Rice and dry veggies, veg curry/Rice and green gram curry/Rice and sambar, chutney, sabzi | Ragi mudde with curry, chutney/Puttu and green gram curry/Rice and veg curry/ Rice and green gram curry/Rice and sambar or rasam, sabzi and chutney | Ragi mudde with curry/ Puttu and green gram curry/ Rice and green gram curry/Rice and veg curry/ Millet rice and sambar, sabzi and chutney |
|---|---|---|---|
| | Add eggs/fish/ chicken to the above only once a week | Add eggs/fish/ chicken to the above only once a week | Add eggs/fish/ chicken to the above only once a week |
| Meal 4: Evening meal, 3 p.m.–5 p.m. | Option A: Peanuts or dried coconut and jaggery/Fresh fruit/Sprouted green moong chaat (not raw)/ Any one sherbet from those mentioned in Chapter 5/Spicy millet puffs | Option A: Peanuts or dried coconut and jaggery/Rasam/ Fresh fruit/Spicy millet puffs/ Sprouted green moong chaat (not raw)/Any one soup from Table 8, Chapter 5/*Ragi payasam* | Option A: Peanuts or dried coconut and jaggery/Rasam/ Fresh fruit/Spicy millet puffs/ Sugarcane juice/ Sprouted green moong chaat (not raw)/Any one soup from Table 8, Chapter 5/*Ragi payasam* |
| | Option B: Any meal from Option B breakfast | Option B: Any meal from Option B breakfast | Option B: Any meal from Option B breakfast |
| Daruhald and chitrak tea 30 minutes before dinner | | | |

| Meal 5: Dinner, by 7 p.m. latest | Chicken congee/ Bisi bele bath/ Ven pongal/ Tamarind khichri/Rice kanji/*Millet kanji*/*Millet Khichri*/Pulagam | Chicken congee/ Bisi bele bath/ Ven pongal/ Rice kanji/ *Millet kanji*/*Millet khichri*/Pulagam | Chicken congee/ Bisi bele bath/ Ven pongal/ Rice kanji/ *Millet kanji*/*Millet khichri*/Pulagam |
|---|---|---|---|
| Trikatu after dinner | | | |
| Meal 6: After dinner, if hungry | *Any one summer tea from Table 31 below* | *Any one monsoon tea from Table 31 below* | *Any one winter tea from Table 31 below* |
| Triphala at bedtime | | | |

| Meal timings | West region | | |
|---|---|---|---|
| | **Summer** | **Monsoon** | **Winter** |
| Meal 1: On rising | *Any one summer tea from Table 31 below* | *Any one monsoon tea from Table 31 below* | *Any one winter tea from Table 31 below* |
| Daruhald and chitrak tea 30 minutes before breakfast | | | |
| Meal 2: Breakfast, by 9 a.m. latest | Option A: *Millet porridge/ Coconut smoothie/ Post-workout protein smoothie*<br><br>Option B: Moong dal chilla with chutney/ Poha/Khichu/ Rice upma/ Rice, ghee and jaggery/*Millet neer dosa*/Rice Shevaya with veggies | Option A: *Millet porridge/ Coconut smoothie/ Post-workout protein smoothie/ Amaranth porridge*<br><br>Option B: Moong dal chilla with chutney/ Poha/Buckwheat chilla/Goan patoleo/Khichu/ Rice upma/ Rice, ghee and jaggery/*Millet neer dosa* | Option A: *Millet porridge/ Coconut smoothie/ Post-workout protein smoothie/ Amaranth porridge*<br><br>Option B: Moong dal chilla with chutney/ Poha/Buckwheat chilla/Khichu/ Rice upma/ Rice, ghee and jaggery/*Millet neer dosa* |
| Trikatu after breakfast | | | |

| Meal 3: Lunch, 11 a.m.–1 p.m. | Rice bhakri or millet bhakri, dal, bhaaji/Rice, amti, bhaji/Mug ni dal-bhat-rotla-saak/Vaghareli khichri | Rice bhakri or millet bhakri, dal, bhaaji/Rice, amti, bhaji/Mug ni dal-bhat-rotla-saak/Vaghareli khichri | Rice bhakri or millet bhakri, dal, bhaaji/Rice, amti, bhaji/Mug ni dal-bhat-rotla-saak/Vaghareli khichri |
|---|---|---|---|
| | Add eggs/fish/ chicken to the above only once a week | Add eggs/fish/ chicken to the above only once a week | Add eggs/fish/ chicken to the above only once a week |
| Meal 4: Evening meal, 3 p.m.–5 p.m. | Option A: Peanuts or dried coconut and jaggery/Sprouted green moong chaat (not raw)/ Fresh fruit/Spicy millet puffs/Any one sherbet from those mentioned in Chapter 5 | Option A: Peanuts or dried coconut and jaggery/Fresh fruit/Spicy millet puffs/Sprouted green moong chaat (not raw)/ Any one soup from Table 8, Chapter 5/*Ragi payasam* | Option A: Peanuts or dried coconut and jaggery/Fresh fruit/Spicy millet puffs/Sugarcane juice/Sprouted green moong chaat (not raw)/ Any one soup from Table 8, Chapter 5/*Ragi payasam* |
| | Option B: Any meal from Option B breakfast | Option B: Any meal from Option B breakfast | Option B: Any meal from Option B breakfast |
| Daruhald and chitrak tea 30 minutes before dinner | | | |
| Meal 5: Dinner, by 7 p.m. latest | Chicken congee/ *Millet khichri/* Moong dal khichri | Chicken congee/ *Millet khichri/* Moong dal khichri | Chicken congee/ *Millet khichri/* Moong dal khichri |
| Trikatu after dinner | | | |

| Meal 6: After dinner, if hungry | *Any one summer tea from Table 31 below* | *Any one monsoon tea from Table 31 below* | *Any one winter tea from Table 31 below* |
|---|---|---|---|
| Triphala at bedtime | | | |

| Meal timings | East region | | |
|---|---|---|---|
| | **Summer** | **Monsoon** | **Winter** |
| Meal 1: On rising | *Any one summer tea from Table 31 below* | *Any one monsoon tea from Table 31 below* | *Any one winter tea from Table 31 below* |
| Daruhald and chitrak tea 30 minutes before breakfast | | | |
| Meal 2: Breakfast, by 9 a.m. latest | Option A: *Millet porridge*/Rice kanji/*Coconut smoothie*/*Post-workout protein smoothie*<br><br>Option B: Poha/Rice pitha/Rice, ghee and jaggery/*Millet rice pancake* | Option A: *Millet porridge*/Rice kanji/*Coconut smoothie*/*Post-workout protein smoothie*<br><br>Option B: Poha/Rice pitha/Rice, ghee and jaggery/*Millet rice pancake* | Option A: *Millet porridge*/Rice kanji/*Coconut smoothie*/*Post-workout protein smoothie*<br><br>Option B: Poha/Rice pitha/Rice, ghee and jaggery/*Millet rice pancake* |
| Trikatu after breakfast | | | |
| Meal 3: Lunch, 11 a.m.–1 p.m. | Rice, dal, saak/Rice and curry, sabzi and chutney/Millet rice, dal, bhaja, chutney<br><br>Add eggs/fish/chicken to the above only once a week | Rice, dal, saak/Rice and curry, sabzi, chutney/Millet rice, dal, bhaja, chutney<br><br>Add eggs/fish/chicken to the above only once a week | Rice, dal, saak/Rice and curry, sabzi and chutney/Millet rice, dal, bhaja, chutney<br><br>Add eggs/fish/chicken to the above only once a week |

| Meal 4: Evening meal, 3 p.m.–5 p.m. | Option A: Peanuts or dried coconut and jaggery/Fresh fruit/Spicy millet puffs/Bengali chire bhaja/ Sprouted green moong chaat (not raw)/Any one drink from those mentioned in Chapter 5 | Option A: Peanuts or dried coconut and jaggery/Fresh fruit/Spicy millet puffs/Bengali chire bhaja/ Sprouted green moong chaat (not raw)/Any one soup from Table 8, Chapter 5 | Option A: Peanuts or dried coconut and jaggery/Fresh fruit/Spicy millet puffs/Sugarcane juice/Bengali chire bhaja/ Sprouted green moong chaat (not raw)/Any one soup from Table 8, Chapter 5 |
|---|---|---|---|
| | Option B: Any meal from Option B breakfast | Option B: Any meal from Option B breakfast | Option B: Any meal from Option B breakfast |
| Daruhald and chitrak tea 30 minutes before dinner | | | |
| Meal 5: Dinner, by 7 p.m. latest | Bengali khichri/ Rice kanji with veggies/*Millet khichri* | Chicken congee/ Bengali khichri/ Rice kanji with veggies/*Millet khichri* | Chicken congee/ Bengali khichri/ Rice kanji with veggies/*Millet khichri* |
| Trikatu after dinner | | | |
| Meal 6: After dinner, if hungry | *Any one summer tea from Table 31 below* | *Any one monsoon tea from Table 31 below* | *Any one winter tea from Table 31 below* |
| Triphala at bedtime | | | |

## Phase 2 Meal Plans

Diversity on your plate is important from phase 2 onwards. In order to bring variety to your meals, make use of the Seasonal Food Guide that I have compiled for you on pages 311–314.

| Meal timings | North region | | |
|---|---|---|---|
| | **Summer** | **Monsoon** | **Winter** |
| Meal 1: On rising | *Any one summer tea from Table 31 below* | *Any one monsoon tea from Table 31 below* | *Any one winter tea from Table 31 below* |
| Daruhald and chitrak tea 30 minutes before breakfast | | | |
| Meal 2: Breakfast, by 9 a.m. latest | Option A: *Bajre ki khatti rabdi/* Rice or millet flakes with dahi/*Makhana smoothie/Jau ki ghaat* | Option A: Rice or millet flakes with dahi/*Makhana smoothie/Bajre ki khatti rabdi* | Option A: *Millet porridge/Makhana smoothie/ Amaranth porridge* |
| | Option B: Rice or millet chilla/ Besan chilla/ Whole wheat sourdough bread toast and white butter | Option B: Foxtail millet upma/Besan chilla/Rice or millet chilla/ Whole wheat sourdough bread toast and white butter | Option B: Foxtail millet upma/Besan chilla/Rice or millet chilla/ Whole wheat sourdough bread toast and white butter |
| Trikatu after breakfast | | | |

| Meal 3: Lunch, 11 a.m.–1 p.m. | Chana dal phaanu with millet rice/ Rajma chawal/ Chane chawal/ Singhare ke paratha with dahi, sabzi/Rice, dal, sabzi and achaar/Millet roti with dahi/ Roti and gatta sabzi/Whole wheat sourdough bread, eggs, veggies, white butter, pickled olives and aged cheese | Gahat phaanu with millet rice/ Rajma chawal/ Chane chawal/ Kuttu paratha with dal, sabzi, chutney/Rice, dal, sabzi and achaar/Millet roti with dahi/ Roti and gatta sabzi/Whole wheat sourdough bread, eggs, veggies, white butter, pickled olives and aged cheese | Makai roti and sarson saag/Til ki khichri with curd/Gahat phaanu with millet rice/Millet roti with dal, sabzi, chutney/ Horse gram paratha with dal, sabzi, chutney and achaar/Roti and gatta sabzi/ Whole wheat sourdough bread, eggs, veggies, white butter, pickled olives and aged cheese |
| | Add eggs/fish/ chicken to the above only twice a week | Add eggs/fish/ chicken to the above only twice a week | Add eggs/fish/ chicken to the above only twice a week |

| Meal 4: Evening meal, 3 p.m.–5 p.m) | Option A: Roasted chana and jaggery/ Chana jor garam/Bhel/ Sattu sherbet/ *Buttermilk/ Thandai/ Gond kateera sherbet/* Murabba/ Roasted makhana/Fruit and aged cheese | Option A: Roasted chana and jaggery/ Chana jor garam/Horse gram soup/ Bhel/Millet laddu/Roasted makhana/Fruit and aged cheese/ *Kulthi laddu* | Option A: Roasted chana and jaggery/ Chana jor jaram/ Horse gram soup/Gajar kanji/Besan gond laddu/Roasted makhana/ Shakarkandi chaat/*Kulthi laddu* |
|---|---|---|---|
| | Option B: Any meal from Option B breakfast | Option B: Any meal from Option B breakfast | Option B: Any meal from Option B breakfast |
| Daruhald and chitrak tea 30 minutes before dinner | | | |
| Meal 5: Dinner, by 7 p.m. latest | Khichri with kadhi/Millet rice with dal/Kaddhi chawal/*Millet khichri*/Millet roti and sabzi | Khichri with kadhi/Kaddhi chawal/*Millet porridge/Millet khichri*/Millet roti and sabzi | Khichri with kadhi/Millet roti with dal/*Millet porridge/Millet khichri* |
| Trikatu after dinner | | | |
| Meal 6: After bedtime, if hungry | *Any one summer tea from Table 31 below* | *Any one monsoon tea from Table 31 below* | *Any one winter tea from Table 31 below* |
| Triphala at bedtime | | | |

| Meal timings | South region | | |
|---|---|---|---|
| | **Summer** | **Monsoon** | **Winter** |
| Meal 1: On rising | *Any one summer tea from Table 31 below* | *Any one monsoon tea from Table 31 below* | *Any one winter tea from Table 31 below* |
| Daruhald and chitrak tea 30 minutes before breakfast | | | |

| Meal 2: Breakfast, by 9 a.m. latest | Option A: Rice or millet flakes with curd/*Ellu juice/Jau ki ghaat* | Option A: Rice or millet flakes with curd/*Ellu juice/Uluva kanji* | Option A: *Millet porridge/Uluva kanji* |
|---|---|---|---|
| | Option B: Barley idli with chutney/ Paniyaram and chutney/Appam and stew/Millet idli and chutney/ Whole wheat sourdough bread toast and white butter | Option B: Foxtail millet upma/ Paniyaram and chutney/Appam and stew/Millet idli and chutney/ Sundal/Whole wheat sourdough bread toast and white butter | Option B: Foxtail millet upma/Appam and stew/Millet idli and chutney/ Paniyaram and chutney/Whole wheat sourdough bread toast and white butter |
| Trikatu after breakfast | | | |
| Meal 3: Lunch, 11 a.m.–1 p.m. | Barley dosa with sambar and chutney/Rice, pachadi and lentil curry/Adai and curry/Puttu and Kadala curry/ Vishu kanji and jackfruit/ Hyderabadi biryani with raita/Curd rice/ Whole wheat sourdough bread, eggs, veggies, white butter, pickled olives and aged cheese | Rice, pachadi and lentil curry/ Adai and curry/ Puttu and Kadala curry/Millet dosa, sambar and chutney/ Vishu kanji and jackfruit/ Hyderabadi biryani with raita/Whole wheat sourdough bread, eggs, veggies, white butter, pickled olives and aged cheese | Adai and curry/ Puttu and Kadala curry/Millet dosa, sambar and chutney/Millet rice, lentil curry and veggies/ Hyderabadi biryani with raita/Rice and kalan/Whole wheat sourdough bread, eggs, veggies, white butter, pickled olives and aged cheese |
| | Add eggs/fish/ chicken to the above only twice a week | Add eggs/fish/ chicken to the above only twice a week | Add eggs/fish/ chicken to the above only twice a week |

| Meal 4: Evening meal, 3 p.m.–5 p.m. | Option A: Roasted chana and jaggery/ Chana jor garam/ *Buttermilk/Gond kateera sherbet/* Murabba/ Roasted or boiled jackfruit seeds/Fresh fruit/ Fruit and aged cheese | Option A: Roasted chana and jaggery/ Chana jor garam/Horse gram soup/ Coconut laddu/ Roasted or boiled jackfruit seeds/Fresh fruit/ Fruit and aged cheese/*Kulthi laddu* | Option A: Roasted chana and jaggery/ Chana jor garam/Horse gram soup/Fresh fruit/Sesame chimili/Fruit and aged cheese/ *Kulthi laddu/* Murabba |
|---|---|---|---|
| | Option B: Any meal from Option B breakfast | Option B: Any meal from Option B breakfast | Option B: Any meal from Option B breakfast |
| Daruhald and chitrak tea 30 minutes before dinner | | | |
| Meal 5: Dinner, by 7 p.m. latest | Lemon rice/ Tomato rice/ *Millet khichri/* Coconut rice/ Ven pongal | Millet pongal, sambar, chutney/ Millet roti, sabzi/ Ven pongal/Rice and lentil curry/ Khichri | Millet pongal, sambar and chutney/Millet roti, dal sabzi/ Ven pongal/Rice and lentil curry |
| Trikatu after dinner | | | |
| Meal 6: After bedtime, if hungry | *Any one summer tea from Table 31 below* | *Any one monsoon tea from Table 31 below* | *Any one winter tea from Table 31 below* |
| Triphala at bedtime | | | |

| Meal timings | West region | | |
|---|---|---|---|
| | **Summer** | **Monsoon** | **Winter** |
| Meal 1: On rising | *Any one summer tea from Table 31 below* | *Any one monsoon tea from Table 31 below* | *Any one winter tea from Table 31 below* |
| Daruhald and chitrak tea 30 minutes before breakfast | | | |

| Meal 2: Breakfast, by 9 a.m. latest | Option A: Rice or millet flakes with dahi/ Tandalachi ukad/ Ragi ukad/*Jau ki ghaat* | Option A: Rice or millet flakes with dahi/ Tandalachi ukad/ Ragi ukad/*Millet porridge* | Option A: Ragi ukad/*Millet porridge*/Millet raab/*Makhana smoothie*/Gond raab |
|---|---|---|---|
| | Option B: Khaman/Rice or millet chilla/ Besan chilla/ Dhokla with chutney/Idli with chutney | Option B: Foxtail millet upma/Rice or millet chilla/ Besan chilla/ Dhokla with chutney/Idli with chutney | Option B: Foxtail millet upma/Rice or millet chilla/ Besan chilla/ Dhokla with chutney/Idli with chutney |
| Trikatu after breakfast | | | |
| Meal 3: Lunch, 11 a.m.–1 p.m | Sodyachi khichri/ Amboli with chickpea curry/ Valachi khichri/ Jhunka bhakri/ Usal bhakri/ Phodnicha bhat with koshimbir/ Curd rice with pickle/Sandage and bhakri/ Whole wheat sourdough bread, eggs, veggies, white butter, pickled olives and aged cheese | Amboli with chickpea curry/Valachi khichri/Jhunka bhakri and rice, dal, sabzi/ Usal bhakri/ Phodnicha bhat with koshimbir/ Curd rice with papad/Sandage and bhakri/ Whole wheat sourdough bread, eggs, veggies, white butter, pickled olives and aged cheese | Amboli with chickpea curry/Valachi khichri/Jhunka bhakri and rice, dal, sabzi/ Usal bhakri/ Phodnicha bhat with koshimbir/ Curd rice with papad/Sandage and bhakri/ Whole wheat sourdough bread, eggs, veggies, white butter, pickled olives and aged cheese |
| | Add eggs/fish/ chicken to the above only twice a week | Add eggs/fish/ chicken to the above only twice a week | Add eggs/fish/ chicken to the above only twice a week |

| Meal 4: Evening meal, 3 p.m.–5 p.m. | Option A: Roasted chana and jaggery/ Chana jor garam/Bhel/ Sattu sherbet/ *Buttermilk/ Thandai/Gond kateera sherbet/* Murabba/ Roasted or boiled jackfruit seeds/Fruit and aged cheese/ Roasted poha chivda | Option A: Aliv laddu/Roasted chana and jaggery/Chana jor garam/Horse gram soup/ Bhel/Roasted or boiled jackfruit seeds/Fruit and aged cheese/ Murabba/ Roasted poha chivda/*Kulthi laddu* | Option A: Aliv laddu/Roasted chana and jaggery/Rajgira laddu/Horse gram soup/Gajar kanji/Bhel/ Ponkh bhel/ Besan gond laddu/Fruit and aged cheese/ Chikki/Roasted poha chivda/ Shakarkandi chaat/*Kulthi laddu* |
|---|---|---|---|
|  | Option B: Any meal from Option B breakfast | Option B: Any meal from Option B breakfast | Option B: Any meal from Option B breakfast |
| Daruhald and chitrak tea 30 minutes before dinner | | | |
| Meal 5: Dinner, by 7 p.m. latest | Khichri with gujrati kadhi/ Ukad with tamatar saar/ Bhakri and saag | Khichri with gujrati kadhi/ Ukad with tamatar saar/ Bhakri and sabzi | Khichri with gujrati kadhi/ Ukad with tamatar saar/ Bhakri and sabzi |
| Trikatu after dinner | | | |
| Meal 6: After bedtime, if hungry | *Any one summer tea from Table 31 below* | *Any one monsoon tea from Table 31 below* | *Any one winter tea from Table 31 below* |
| Triphala at bedtime | | | |

| Meal timings | East region | | |
|---|---|---|---|
| | **Summer** | **Monsoon** | **Winter** |
| Meal 1: On rising | *Any one summer tea from Table 31 below* | *Any one monsoon tea from Table 31 below* | *Any one winter tea from Table 31 below* |
| Daruhald and chitrak tea 30 minutes before breakfast | | | |
| Meal 2: Breakfast, by 9 a.m. latest | Option A: Millet flakes with dahi/*Makhana smoothie*/*Jau ki ghaat*/Chira with dahi and gur/ Assamese jalpan | Option A: Millet flakes with dahi/*Makhana smoothie*/Chira with dahi and gur/*Jau ki ghaat*/ Assamese jalpan | Option A: *Makhana smoothie*/Millet *porridge* |
| | Option B: Millet upma/ Chilka roti with chutney/Ghugni and kurmura/ Bihari dal pitha | Option B: Foxtail millet upma/ Chilka roti with chutney/Ghugni and kurmura/ Soru chokli pitha/ Bihari dal pitha | Option B: Foxtail millet upma/ Chilka roti with chutney/Ghugni and kurmura/ Soru chokli pitha/ Bihari dal pitha |
| Trikatu after breakfast | | | |
| Meal 3: Lunch, 11 a.m.–1 p.m. | Panta or pakhala bhat with fish/ meat, onions and bhaja/Rice and fish/Kolkata biryani/Millet roti, dal, rice, sabzi/ Whole wheat sourdough bread, eggs, veggies, white butter, pickled olives and aged cheese | Bhat, dal, aloo posto/Rice and fish/Rice, dal, bhaja/Kolkata biryani/Millet rice, dal, curry and chutney/ Whole wheat sourdough bread, eggs, veggies, white butter, pickled olives and aged cheese | Bhat, dal, aloo posto/Rice and fish/Rice, dal, bhaja/Kolkata biryani/Millet roti, millet rice, dal, sabzi/Whole wheat sourdough bread, eggs, veggies, white butter, pickled olives and aged cheese |
| | Consume eggs/ fish/chicken only twice/week | Consume eggs/ fish/chicken only twice/week | Consume eggs/ fish/chicken only twice/week |

| Meal 4: Evening meal, 3 p.m.–5 p.m. | Option A: Roasted chana and jaggery/ Chana jor garam/ Jhal moori/ Sattu sherbet/ *Buttermilk/Gond kateera sherbet/* Murabba/ Roasted or boiled jackfruit seeds/Mishti doi with nuts and dried fruits/Roasted makhana/Fruit and aged cheese | Option A: Sattu laddu/Roasted chana and jaggery/Chana jor garam/Horse gram soup/Jhal moori/Roasted or boiled jackfruit seeds/ Mishti doi with nuts and dried fruits/Roasted makhana/Fruit and aged cheese/ *Kulthi laddu* | Option A: Sattu laddu/Roasted chana and jaggery/Chana jor garam/Horse gram soup/ Gajar kanji/ Jhal moori/ Mishti doi with nuts and dried fruits/Roasted makhana/Fruit and aged cheese/ Sweet potato chaat/*Kulthi laddu* |
|---|---|---|---|
| | Option B: Any meal from Option B breakfast | Option B: Any meal from Option B breakfast | Option B: Any meal from Option B breakfast |
| Daruhald and chitrak tea 30 minutes before dinner | | | |
| Meal 5: Dinner, by 7 p.m. latest | Khichri/Rice and kadhi/Rice and curry/Millet roti and sabzi/ *Millet khichri* | *Millet khichri/* Rice dal/Millet roti and bhaji/ Odia ambula rai and pulao | Khichri/*Millet khichri/*Millet roti and bhaji/Odia ambula rai and pulao |
| Trikatu after dinner | | | |
| Meal 6: After bedtime, if hungry | *Any one summer tea from Table 31 below* | *Any one monsoon tea from Table 31 below* | *Any one winter tea from Table 31 below* |
| Triphala at bedtime | | | |

# Phase 3 Meal Plans

*Mix up the following meal options with meals listed in phase 1 and phase 2.*

| Meal timings | North region | | |
|---|---|---|---|
| | **Summer** | **Monsoon** | **Winter** |
| Meal 1: On rising | *Any one summer tea from Table 31 below* or warm milk with or without jaggery | *Any one monsoon tea from Table 31 below* or warm milk with or without jaggery | *Any one winter tea from Table 31 below* or warm milk with or without jaggery |
| Meal 2: Breakfast, by 9 a.m. latest | Option A: Daliya porridge/Millet flakes in milk, nuts and dried fruits/Millet pops with milk and nuts/Barley porridge<br><br>Option B: Wheat Suji chilla/Suji upma/Barley upma/Sevaiya upma | Option A: Daliya porridge/Millet flakes in milk, nuts and dried fruits/Amaranth pops with milk, nuts and fruits/ Barley porridge<br><br>Option B: Suji chilla/Suji upma/Barley upma/Sevaiya upma | Option A: Daliya porridge/Millet flakes in milk, nuts and dried fruits/Amaranth pops with milk, nuts and fruits<br><br>Option B: Suji chilla/Suji upma/Daliya upma/Sevaiya upma |

| Meal 3: Lunch, 11 a.m.–1 p.m. | Stuffed (with aloo/any other vegetable) paratha with dahi, achaar/ Besan ki roti, raita and lunji/ Sprouted wheat bread with white butter, egg or paneer bhurji<br><br>Add eggs/fish/ meat to the above only twice a week. Red meat only once a week. | Stuffed (with aloo/any other vegetable) paratha with dahi, achaar/ Missi roti, raita and lunji/ Sprouted wheat bread with white butter, egg or paneer bhurji<br><br>Add eggs/fish/ meat to the above only twice a week. Red meat only once a week. | Stuffed (with sweet potato/ hara choliya) paratha with dahi, achaar/ Mutton biryani/ Lapsi with kadhi/Sprouted wheat bread with white butter, egg or paneer bhurji<br><br>Add eggs/fish/ meat to the above only twice a week. Red meat only once a week. |
|---|---|---|---|
| Meal 4: Evening meal, 3 p.m.–5 p.m. | Option A: Fruit milkshake/Lassi with rabdi/ Makhane ki kheer/Barley water<br><br>Option B: Any meal from Option B breakfast | Option A: Sonth and methi laddu/ Makhane ki kheer<br><br>Option B: Any meal from Option B breakfast | Option A: Sonth and methi laddu/ Makhane ki kheer<br><br>Option B: Any meal from Option B breakfast |
| Meal 5: Dinner, by 7 p.m. latest | Barley roti and dahi/Daliya porridge/Barley khichri | Daliya porridge/ Whole wheat phulka, dal/ Barley roti and sabzi | Daliya porridge/ Whole wheat phulka, dal |
| Meal 6: After bedtime, if hungry | *Any one summer tea from Table 31 or any one milk preparation from Table 32* | *Any one monsoon tea from Table 31 or any one milk preparation from Table 32* | *Any one winter tea from Table 31 or any one milk preparation from Table 32* |

| Meal timings | South region | | |
|---|---|---|---|
| | **Summer** | **Monsoon** | **Winter** |
| Meal 1: On rising | *Any one summer tea from Table 31 below* or warm milk with or without jaggery | *Any one monsoon tea from Table 31 below* or warm milk with or without jaggery | *Any one winter tea from Table 31 below* or warm milk with or without jaggery |
| Meal 2: Breakfast, by 9 a.m. latest | Option A: Broken wheat huggi/Millet flakes in milk, nuts and dried fruits/Millet pops with milk and nuts/Barley porridge<br><br>Option B: Suji upma/Barley upma | Option A: Broken wheat huggi/Amaranth pops with milk, nuts and fruits/ Wheat kanji<br><br>Option B: Suji upma/Barley upma | Option A: Broken wheat huggi/Amaranth pops with milk, nuts and fruits/ Wheat kanji<br><br>Option B: Suji upma/Barley upma |
| Meal 3: Lunch, 11 a.m.–1 p.m. | Wheat parotta with curry/ Parotta and paneer curry/ Sprouted wheat bread with white butter, egg or paneer, veggies and mushrooms<br><br>Add eggs/fish/ meat to the above only twice a week. Red meat only once a week. | Wheat parotta with curry/ Khichri kheema and khatta/ Sprouted wheat bread with white butter, egg or paneer, veggies and mushrooms<br><br>Add eggs/fish/ meat to the above only twice a week. Red meat only once a week. | Wheat parotta with curry/ Khichri kheema and khatta/ Sprouted wheat bread with white butter, egg or paneer, veggies and mushrooms<br><br>Add eggs/fish/ meat to the above only twice a week. Red meat only once a week. |

| Meal 4: Evening meal, 3 p.m.–5 p.m. | Option A: Payasam/Fresh Fruit milkshake/ Masala paal | Option A: Payasam/Fresh Fruit milkshake/ Masala paal | Option A: Payasam/Fresh Fruit milkshake/ Masala paal |
|---|---|---|---|
| | Option B: Any meal from Option B breakfast | Option B: Any meal from Option B breakfast | Option B: Any meal from Option B breakfast |
| Meal 5: Dinner, by 7 p.m. latest | Barley khichri/ Barley kanji/ Wheat puttu and curry | Barley khichri/ Barley kanji/ Wheat puttu and curry | Wheat puttu and curry/Wheat kanji |
| Meal 6: After bedtime, if hungry | *Any one summer tea from Table 31 or any one milk preparation from Table 32* | *Any one monsoon tea from Table 31 or any one milk preparation from Table 32* | *Any one winter tea from Table 31 or any one milk preparation from Table 32* |

| Meal timings | West region | | |
|---|---|---|---|
| | **Summer** | **Monsoon** | **Winter** |
| Meal 1: On rising | *Any one summer tea from Table 31 below* or warm milk with or without jaggery | *Any one monsoon tea from Table 31 below* or warm milk with or without jaggery | *Any one winter tea from Table 31 below* or warm milk with or without jaggery |
| Meal 2: Breakfast, by 9 a.m. latest | Option A: Daliya porridge/Millet flakes in milk, nuts and dried fruits/Millet pops with milk and nuts/Barley porridge | Option A: Daliya porridge/Millet flakes in milk, nuts and dried fruits/Amaranth pops with milk, nuts and fruits/ Barley porridge | Option A: Daliya porridge/Millet flakes in milk, nuts and dried fruits/Amaranth pops with milk, nuts and fruits/ Wheat raab with gond, nuts |
| | Option B: Wheat Suji chilla/Suji upma/Barley upma/Sevaiya upma | Option B: Wheat Suji chilla/Suji upma/Barley upma/Sevaiya upma | Option B: Sweet potato tikki/ Sevaiya upma |

| Meal 3: Lunch, 11 a.m.–1 p.m. | Puran poli, katachi amti or milk/Thalipeeth with loni, buttermilk, pickle/Thepla with dahi, chunda/Sprouted wheat bread with white butter, egg or paneer bhurji, veggies and mushrooms | Thalipeeth with butter, pickle/ Thepla with dahi, chunda/Pav bhaji/Sprouted wheat bread with white butter, egg or paneer bhurji, veggies and mushrooms | Til gur ki roti with achaar/Sweet potato paratha with dahi, achaar/ Methi na dhebra with achaar, dahi, sabzi and chutney/Sprouted wheat bread with white butter, egg or paneer bhurji, veggies and mushrooms |
|---|---|---|---|
| | Add eggs/fish/ meat to the above only twice a week. Red meat only once a week. | Add eggs/fish/ meat to the above only twice a week. Red meat only once a week. | Add eggs/fish/ meat to the above only twice a week. Red meat only once a week. |
| Meal 4: Evening meal, 3 p.m.–5 p.m. | Option A: Khakra with ghee and pickle/ Fruit milkshake | Option A: Sonth and methi laddu/ Aliv kheer/ Khakra with ghee and pickle | Option A: Sonth and methi laddu/ Aliv kheer/ Khakra with ghee and pickle |
| | Option B: Any meal from Option B breakfast | Option B: Any meal from Option B breakfast | Option B: Any meal from Option B breakfast |
| Meal 5: Dinner, by 7 p.m. latest | Dal dhokli with buttermilk/Varan phal with papad, achaar/Fada ni khichri/Barley khichri | Dal dhokli with buttermilk/Varan phal with papad, achaar/Fada ni khichri/Barley khichri | Dal dhokli with rice/Varan phal with papad, achaar/Fada ni khichri/Barley khichri |
| Meal 6: After bedtime, if hungry | *Any one summer tea from Table 31 or any one milk preparation from Table 32* | *Any one monsoon tea from Table 31 or any one milk preparation from Table 32* | *Any one winter tea from Table 31 or any one milk preparation from Table 32* |

| Meal timings | East region | | |
|---|---|---|---|
| | **Summer** | **Monsoon** | **Winter** |
| Meal 1: On rising | *Any one summer tea from Table 31 below* or warm milk with or without jaggery | *Any one monsoon tea from Table 31 below* or warm milk with or without jaggery | *Any one winter tea from Table 31 below* or warm milk with or without jaggery |
| Meal 2: Breakfast, by 9 a.m. latest | Option A: Chira and nuts in milk/ Moori in milk/ Khoi and nuts in milk | Option A: Amaranth pops with milk, nuts and fruits/Moori in milk/Khoi and nuts in milk | Option A: Amaranth pops with milk, nuts and fruits/Moori in milk/Khoi and nuts in milk |
| | Option B: Suji upma/Barley upma | Option B: Suji upma/Barley upma | Option B: Suji upma/Barley upma |
| Meal 3: Lunch, 11 a.m.–1 p.m. | Pyaz paratha with sabzi, dahi, achaar/Luchi and aloo/Litti chokha/Sattu ka paratha with dahi, achaar and sabzi/Sprouted wheat bread with white butter, egg or paneer, veggies and mushrooms | Postdana kaa paratha with saag, achaar/ Luchi and aloo/ Sattu ka paratha with dahi, achaar and sabzi/Rice and lamb curry | Litti chokha/ Sweet potato paratha with dahi, achaar/ Sattu ka paratha with lehsun chutney and sabzi/Rice and lamb curry |
| | Add eggs/fish/ meat to the above only twice a week. Red meat only once a week. | Add eggs/fish/ meat to the above only twice a week. Red meat only once a week. | Add eggs/fish/ meat to the above only twice a week. Red meat only once a week. |

| Meal 4: Evening meal, 3 p.m.–5 p.m. | Option A: Nariyal laddu/ Fresh fruit milkshake | Option A: Nariyal laddu/ Fresh fruit milkshake | Option A: Nariyal laddu/ Fresh fruit milkshake |
|---|---|---|---|
| | Option B: Any meal from Option B breakfast | Option B: Any meal from Option B breakfast | Option B: Any meal from Option B breakfast |
| Meal 5: Dinner, by 7 p.m. latest | Barley porridge/ Daliya porridge | Mutton khichri/ Daliya porridge | Mutton khichri/ Daliya porridge |
| Meal 6: After bedtime, if hungry | *Any one summer tea from Table 31 or any one milk preparation from Table 32* | *Any one monsoon tea from Table 31 or any one milk preparation from Table 32* | *Any one winter tea from Table 31 or any one milk preparation from Table 32* |

## Hangover Remedy Plan (For Phase 3)

| Meal timings | Meal plan* |
|---|---|
| Meal One: On rising | Black-seeded raisins that have been soaked overnight. Also, drink up the water in which they were soaked. |
| Meal Two: Breakfast | Coconut smoothie/Rice kanji/Porridge |
| Meal Three: Mid-morning | Coconut water/Sugarcane juice/Kokum sherbet/ Neera |
| Meal Four: Lunch | Rice or roti, yellow moong dal and sabzi |
| Meal Five: Mid-afternoon | Pomegranate/Banana milkshake |
| Meal Six: Early dinner | Khichri with ghee and homemade pickle |

*Keep sipping water throughout the day.*

## FAQs

1.  What are the non-negotiable aspects that I should keep in mind while planning my meals?
    - Start your day with a warm drink.
    - Eat only when hungry.
    - Lunch must be the biggest meal, between 11 a.m. and 1 p.m.
    - Breakfast and dinner must be lighter meals.

2.  Can I increase or decrease the total number of meals in a day?

Yes, feel free to do so. As I said, the most important aspect is eating only when you are hungry. If due to certain circumstances, like say, some unexpected stress, feeling under the weather, etc., you do not feel hungry, then you do not *have to* eat just because the plan says so. Likewise, if you get hungry at a time not mentioned in the plan, then you do not *have to* starve or restrain yourself from eating.

3.  Does my breakfast necessarily have to be liquid or semi-liquid meals? What if I don't find it satiating enough?

The choice of breakfast should be such that it allows you to get hungry for a hearty lunch by noon. It doesn't necessarily have to be a smoothie or porridge. But if you are feeling full by lunch-time (11 a.m.–1 p.m.) or not hungry enough, then it is a sure indication that you need to reduce your breakfast. More often than not, a smoothie or thin porridge, kanji or khichri works the best.

4.   Can I have fruit or vegetable juices as breakfast?

No. Stick to smoothie, porridge, kanji or khichri.

5.   I belong to south India but live in the north. Which plan
     should I follow?

Stick to a 50–50 rule. For 50 per cent of the time, follow your
traditional meals, and for the remaining 50 per cent, choose
meal options that are native to the place you are living in—in
this case, the north.

6.   I am a Gujarati living in Nairobi. What should I do?

Stick to a 60–40 rule. For 60 per cent of the time, follow your
traditional meals, and for the remaining 40 per cent, choose
non-Indian meal options that are native to the place you are
living in—in this case, Nairobi.

7.   Can I eat out at a restaurant?

Considering that phase 1 is a detox phase, it helps to avoid
restaurants as much as possible. However, if you are travelling
or unable to avoid going out to a restaurant, then ensure that
you restrain yourself from having foods mentioned in the
'forget' list of phase 1. A few meals that you can order are rice,
yellow dal and veggies, soups, pulao with veggies, rice and
sambhar, poha, rasam-rice, congee, etc.
      In phase 2, eating out at your favourite restaurant once
a week is completely fine. Only ensure you stay away from
foods in the 'forget' list of phase 2.

8.   What if I goof up and eat foods from the 'forget' list?

Whether you are in phase 1 or 2, if you do end up eating any
food from the 'forget' list, it's completely OK and you don't
have to start the phase all over again. Of course, the more
you stick to the plan, the more benefits you will see. Having
said that, do not stress about one-off goof ups; just do the
best you can.

9.   What if I do not want to restrict any food and not follow
     the 3 phases?

Let me assure you that following the three-phased TBBD
is rewarding in a way that no other programme can be.
However, if you are not ready for it at present, then you can
skip the phases and instead, plan your meals following the
Three Rs of TBBD, the seven TBBD Lifetime Guidelines
and the seven TBBD Meal-Planning Guidelines. Doing
this will not give you benefits similar to the three-phased
programme but will certainly make you feel (and weigh)
lighter and better.

10.  I live outside India. Dairy recommendations for me?

   •   Ghee: Look for clarified butter in health food stores.
   •   Butter: Look for cultured, white, organic unsalted
       butter in health food stores.
   •   Curd or yoghurt: Look for unsweetened ones labelled
       'contains active cultures'. The best thing is to set the
       curd or yoghurt at home. Using an electric yoghurt

maker, thermal casserole dish, or a pre-heated warm oven (make sure the heat is off) are reliable methods for cold countries.

- Cheese: Look for artisanal cheese.
- Milk: Look for free-grazing, grass-fed cow milk, which should be full fat, and hormone and antibiotic free. Raw milk regulation varies around the world. Buy raw milk if its sales are legal in your state or country, otherwise go for pasteurized milk.

11. What is the best time to have chaat, deep-fried or dessert treat? How often? Which phase?

Frequency: Once a week

Phase: Phases 2 and 3 (ensure that you restrict foods from the 'forget' list)
Best time: 11 a.m.–4 p.m.
You can have these foods as a wholesome meal for lunch—for example, chole bhature, shrikhand puri, halwa puri sabzi, dal baati churma, etc. You can also have them as an evening snack—for example, gulgula, samosa, vada, murukku, pakode, etc.

12. What is the best time to have non-veg foods?

Lunch is the best time. Have it along with grains and cereals, like chicken curry and roti, fish curry with rice, etc. If you want to have in the evening or for dinner, then have it in the form of a soup, congee or khichri.

13. Do I need to cut down on oil or ghee on a daily basis?

No, not at all! Meals that contain fat make you feel fuller for longer than fat-free or low-fat meals. Use desi ghee or cold pressed (filtered), nut and seed-based oils (coconut, sesame, mustard, groundnut) to cook your meals. How much? That would depend on the recipe. Different recipes require differing amounts of oil or ghee. It is best to not tamper with traditional recipes, so use them as is.

14. What if I work out in the evening?

*Pre-workout meal:* Banana (or any other fruit) 15 to 30 minutes before you start to work out. If you have had lunch 120 minutes before or your evening meal 60 minutes before you start to work out, then there is no need for an extra pre-workout meal.

*Post-workout meal:* You may straightaway eat your dinner or have the post-workout protein smoothie.

15. I work night shifts. What about me?

First and foremost, follow the night shift guidelines mentioned in Chapter 8. Food-wise, start your day exactly in the same way, only shift the timings accordingly. Have the more substantial meal during the early part of the shift and eat lighter during the last few hours.

16. What if I am unable to eat my dinner around sunset? Do I still need to keep 12 hours' fast between the last meal of my day and the first of the next day?

The culture of not eating until 9–9.30 p.m. is so deeply entrenched in us that dinner at sunset sounds almost abnormal, but going by the law of nature, it is the most normal thing to do. So first, give your best and work towards having an early dinner. On days you are unable to do so, you can have a meal around 6–7 p.m. if you are hungry (choose from the breakfast options) and then a smaller dinner later.

The 12 hours' fast between the last meal of the day and the first of the next day is the ideal thing to do, but on the days you are eating late, you don't *have to* maintain the 12 hours' fast. Next morning, start your day as usual with the warm drink and eat your next meal as per your hunger.

17. What is your take on sugar?

It is absolutely fine to add some form of sugar to your herbal tea, coffee, smoothies, porridges, laddus, halwas, etc. The forms that I approve of are:

- Honey (shahad): Look for unprocessed, unfiltered, non-pasteurized, raw honey. Also, honey should never be heated and used in cooking. Simply add it to foods, beverages, teas that are lukewarm and not piping hot. For cooking purposes, you may choose either jaggery or unrefined sugar.

- Jaggery (gur): You can use either cane jaggery or palm jaggery. Jaggery is warming in nature compared to sugar, but that doesn't mean you should have it only in the winter months. The southern and eastern region of India have an indigenous tradition of using palm jaggery through the year.
- Unrefined sugar (shakkar): Look for either mishri or khaand or khadi shakkar. These are easily available online and in organic stores.

It is important to alter between different forms of sugar so that you don't end up having excess of any one kind. The weekly routine I usually ask my clients to follow is: Of the seven days in a week, have honey for four days, jaggery for two days and unrefined sugar for one day.

18. A few of my traditional foods are not included in the meal plans in the book. Can I add them to my meals?

Yes, you must! The only foods that you need to restrict are given in the 'forget' lists. Barring those, you are free to choose any ingredient and cook up a meal. Though I have made an honest attempt, for a country where food and food habits change every 100 km, preparing meal plans that include all the diverse, traditional and seasonal foods of all regions of India is not a possible feat to achieve.

# Seasonal Food Guide

## Table 28: Vegetables

| Summer | Monsoon | Winter |
|---|---|---|
| Gavthi kakri (Snake cucumber) | Phodshi (Safed mulsi) | Hara lahsoon (Green garlic) |
| Madras kakdi (Madras Cucumber) | Pyaz (Onion) | Piyaaz kali (Spring onion flowers) |
| Khira (Cucumber) | Kantola (Spine gourd) | Laal and kaali gajar (Red and black carrot) |
| Ambadi (Gongura) | Taakla (Coffee weed) | Wild hemp buds and flowers |
| Lauki (Bottle gourd) | Gud gud alambe (Thunder mushrooms) | Kacha kela (Raw green banana) |
| Gawaar (Cluster beans) | Laal maath (Amaranth leaves) | Shakarkandi (Sweet potato) |
| Papita (Raw papaya) | Arbi (Colocasia leaves) | All varieties of kand/ratalu (Yams) |
| Kathal (Raw jackfruit) | Dukkar kand (Air potato) | Petha kaddu (Ashgourd) |
| Baingan (Brinjal) | Karela (Bitter gourd) | Khaprichi bhaji/Punarnava |
| Keri (Raw mango) | Bhindi (Ladies' finger) | Hara pyaaz (Spring onion) |
| Karela (Bitter gourd) | Ambushi (Indian sorrel) | Aloo (Potato) |
| Turiya (Ridge gourd) | Mayalu (Indian spinach/Malabar nightshade) | Kohlrabi/Knolkhol (Turnip cabbage) |
| Tinda (Indian squash) | Kanphuti (Balloon vine/Heart peas) | Mooli (Radish) |
| Parval (Pointed gourd) | Nali (Water spinach) | Matar (Green pea) |
| Bhindi (Lady finger) | Aghada leaves (Prickly chaff flower) | Phoolgobi (Cauliflower) |
| Kaddoo (Pumpkin) Squash | Gokhru (Small caltrops) | Paatagobi (Cabbage) |
| Pyaz (Onion) | Jungli suran (Dragon stalk yam) | Sarson (Mustard leaves) |
| Shenga phali (Drumstick) | Moras bhaji (Roselle) | Suva (Dill) |
| Faras bean (French bean) | Desi bhutta (Corn cob) | Surti papdi (Flat beans) |
| Tamatar (Tomato) | Moringa leaves (Sahjan patte) | Chawli leaves (Amaranth leaves) |
| Kacha kela (Raw green banana) | Shenga phali (Drumstick) | |
| | Kacha kela (Raw green banana) | |

|  |  | Harbhara/choliya (Green chana) Kamal kakdi (Lotus stems) Turnip (Shalgam) Beetroot (Chukandar) Bathua leaves (Lamb's quarter) Taro root (Arbi) Palak (Spinach) Methi (Fenugreek) Hurda/Ponkh (Tender sorghum) |

## Table 29: Fruits

| Summer | Monsoon | Winter |
|---|---|---|
| Aam (Mango) Tarbooj (Water melon) Kharbooj (Musk melon) Tadgola (Ice apple) Safed jamun (Rose apple) Bibbe (Raw cashew) Kokum (Garcinia indica) Rai amla (Star gooseberry) Bimbli (Tree cucumbers)★ Ber (Indian jujube)★ Rasbhari (Cape gooseberry)★ Litchi (Lychee) Katahal (Jackfruit) | Jamun (Indian blackberry) Anar (Pomegranate) Kela (Banana) Anaras (Pineapple) Chakotra (Pomelo) Ramphal (Bullocks heart) Green sharbati lemons Kamrakh (Star fruit) Sitafal (Custard apple)★★ Nashpati (Pear)★★ Katahal (Jackfruit) | Kamrakh (Star fruit) Anar (Pomegranate) Strawberry Angoor (Grapes) Amrud (Guava) Papita (Papaya) Sapota (Chiku) Anaras (Pineapple) Santra (Orange) Kela (Banana) Mosambi (Sweet lime) Amla (Indian gooseberry) Fresh anjeer (Figs) Sitaphal (Custard apple) Kavat/Kotha Ganna (Sugarcane) Saeb (Apple) |

| | | |
|---|---|---|
| Jamun (Indian blackberry)<br>Shahtoot (Mulberry)<br>Anar (Pomegranate)<br>Kamrakh (Star fruit)<br>Falsa (Indian sherbet berries)<br>Karonda (Cranberry)<br>Jungli jalebi (Camachile)<br>Churna (Cotton fruit)<br>Kaju phal (Cashew apple)<br>Ambarella (Indian hog plum)<br>Bael fruit (Wood apple)<br>Santra (Orange)<br>Kela (Banana)<br>Angoor (Grapes)<br>Ramphal (Bullocks heart)<br>Imli (Tamarind)<br>Papita (Papaya)<br>Aadoo (Peach)<br>Aloobukhara (Plum)<br>Khubani (Apricot) | | |

* February–March, ** August–October

## Table 30: Fish

| Summer | Monsoon | Winter |
|--------|---------|--------|
| Black pomfret | Largescale tonguesole | Obtuse barracuda |
| Bullet tuna | Lizardfish | Black pomfret |
| Striped eel catfish | Mackerel | Bullet tuna |
| Cobia | Emperor | Blacktip sea catfish |
| Pike eel | Prawn | Smalltooth emperor |
| Eel | Bigeye snapper | Goldband snapper |
| Yellowstripe goatfish | Deepwater ribbonfish | Gray eel catfish |
| Indian halibut | Fringescale sardine | Torpedo scad |
| Lizardfish | Sardine | Common dolphinfish |
| Oil sardine | Silverbellies | Pike eel |
| Emperor | Skipjack tuna | Silver pomfret |
| Pink-ear emperor | Notched threadfin | Indian goatfish |
| Pomfret | Threadfin bream | Cinnabar goatfish |
| Prawn | Spotty-faced anchovy | Spinycheek grouper |
| Squid | White snapper | Malabar grouper |
| Threadfin | Whitecheek monocle | Lizardfish |
| Tuna | bream | Spangled emperor |
|  | Whitefish |  |

*To know their regional names and more fish varieties, visit www.inseasonfish.com*

## Recipes

Herbal Drinks

These drinks are for all three phases: phases 1, 2 and 3. They will help reset your body clock and kick-start your day. They may also be had post dinner or at bedtime, if desired.

## Table 31: Herbal Drinks for All Three Phases of TBBD

|  | Summer | Monsoon | Winter |
|---|---|---|---|
| 1. | **Fennel tea**<br><br>Keep a handful of fennel seeds soaked in 200 ml of hot water overnight. Next morning, strain the solution and warm it a bit. Mix a pinch of black salt and mishri in it and drink.<br><br>*Works as an anti-inflammatory, cooling, digestive, detoxifier.* | **Turmeric tea**<br><br>In 1.5 cups of water, add 1/4 tsp dried ginger powder, a pinch of black pepper powder, 1/4 tsp turmeric powder, 1/4 tsp ghee and jaggery to taste. Boil for 10 minutes. Strain and drink.<br><br>*Works as a decongestant, strengthens immunity, helps fight seasonal allergies. Have it only once a day, twice a week.* | **Ginger pepper tea**<br><br>In 1.5 cups of water, add 1/4 tsp dried ginger powder, a pinch of black pepper, a pinch of coriander powder, a pinch of cumin powder and jaggery to taste. Boil for 5–10 minutes. Strain and drink.<br><br>*Helps clear the sinuses and keep the body warm. Have it only once a day, twice a week.* |
| 2. | **Mint tea**<br><br>Add around 6–7 mint leaves to 1 cup of hot water. Let it steep for 10 minutes. Strain and drink hot.<br><br>*Use this if you are prone to acne or heat rashes in summer season.* |  |  |

| 3. | Summer cool tea | | |
|----|-----------------|---|---|
| | In 1.5 cups of water, add 2 cloves (crushed), 1–2 cardamom (crushed), 1/4 tsp coriander seeds, 1/4 tsp cumin seeds. Boil for 5–10 minutes. Add mishri to taste. Strain and drink. | | |
| | *Works against bloating, acidity, nausea, loss of appetite—symptoms that are common in summers.* | | |
| 4. | **Amla tea** | | |
| | In 4 cups water, add 1 tsp dried amla powder and 1 tsp dried ginger powder. Simmer till only 1 cup remains. Add a pinch of rock salt, honey to taste and drink. | | |
| | *Helps strengthen immunity and detoxify the liver, and aids weight loss.* | | |
| 5. | **Ginger lemon honey tea** | | |
| | Steep 1 tsp grated ginger in 1 cup hot water for 10–15 minutes, keeping the cup covered with a lid or saucer. Stir in 1 tsp honey and a few drops of lemon just before drinking. | | |
| | *Excellent remedy for coughs, colds; acts as a digestive and metabolism enhancer.* | | |

| | |
|---|---|
| 6. | **Neem tea** <br><br> Boil 4–5 neem leaves and 1/2 inch ginger (crushed) in 1.5 cups water for 5–10 minutes. Strain. Add honey to taste. <br><br> *Works as a blood purifier, helps detoxify. Use in phase 1 and phase 3 (only once a day, twice a week).* |
| 7. | **Cinnamon tea** <br><br> Add 1–2 crushed cloves, 1 cardamom, and 1/4 tsp of cinnamon to 1 cup of water. Boil for a few minutes and drink. <br><br> *Works as anti-inflammatory, helps fight free radicals, and promotes health and well-being. You may have it once a day every day for six months, then take a break for a month, and then repeat.* |

## Night Caps

These drinks can help you get into a healthy sleep routine.

## Table 32: Recipes for Night Caps

| **Bedtime herbal tea** | **Licorice and fennel tea** | Both licorice and fennel exert calming effects on the body and mind. |
|---|---|---|
| Can be used in phases 1, 2 and 3 <br><br> Good for all seasons | Boil a licorice stick (2 inches) and 2 tsp fennel seeds in 1.5 cups water for 10 minutes. Strain and drink at bedtime for better sleep. | *Note:* You can take this tea for 6 months every day, then take a break of 1 month and then repeat. |

| Bedtime milk preparations | Spiced milk | This blend works wonders for anxiety-related sleeplessness. |
|---|---|---|
| Substituting milk with nut milk in these recipes may not deliver the same therapeutic benefits. | Add a pinch of nutmeg and cinnamon powder, 3–4 strands of saffron to a cup of warm milk, and drink it before bedtime for deep sleep. |  |
| Use in phase 3. | **Fennel milk** Boil 5 gm fennel seeds in 50 ml water till only 20 ml remains. Add the 20 ml to 150–200 ml warm milk and drink for deep sleep. | Fennel works as a relaxant and has been traditionally used for insomnia. |
| Good for all seasons. |  |  |
|  | **Gond katira milk** Add soaked gond katira (1 tsp soaked in a bowl of water for a minimum of 5–6 hours) and a pinch of dried ginger powder to lukewarm milk and drink at bedtime. | This helps relieve constipation and fatigue. It is destressing, and promotes deep sleep. |
|  | **Turmeric milk** Heat 1 tsp ghee, add 1 tsp turmeric powder, a generous pinch of pepper powder and a pinch of dry ginger powder. Pour this mixture in hot milk and drink. | Have it every day only if you are feeling under the weather. For general immunity, you should have it only twice a week. |

# Meal Recipes

Kanji/Khichri/Porridge

## 1. Uluva Kanji (Rice Fenugreek Porridge)

This sweet porridge with rice, coconut and fenugreek as its main ingredients is traditionally eaten in Kerala during monsoons to help cope with the season's ailments.

To be consumed in phases 2 and 3 (only once a week).

## Method

- Soak 2 tbsp fenugreek and 1.5 tsp cumin seeds overnight. In the morning, discard the water.
- In a pressure cooker, add 1 cup broken rice, 1 cup shredded coconut, the soaked fenugreek and cumin seeds and 5 cups of water. Add a pinch of salt.
- Cook for 2 whistles or until it's done.
- Open the cooker and add 3/4 cup jaggery syrup. If you do not want it sweet, avoid the jaggery and put more salt as required.
- While serving, pour a tablespoon (or as much desired) of ghee into it. Serve hot.

*Optional: You can soak aliv seeds (garden cress seeds) in water or coconut water for 2–3 hours. Once it swells up, you can mix it in the porridge.*

## 2. Kutki (Little Millet) Kanji

You can substitute little millet with other millet rice like foxtail, barnyard and proso in this recipe. You can also use pearl millet or sorghum, but in that case, first grind them lightly in a mixie and then use this broken variety in the recipe.

To be consumed in phases 1, 2 and 3.

### Method

- Wash and soak 2 tbsp little millet in water for 20 minutes. Once done, drain the water and keep the millet aside.
- Roast 2 tbsp green moong dal and grind coarsely in a mixer.
- Heat 1 tsp oil in a pressure cooker. Add 2 cloves, 1/4 cinnamon stick, a few curry leaves and 1 tsp mustard seeds. Add 1 finely chopped onion and 1–2 green chilies.
- Next, add 1/4 tbsp ginger-garlic paste, 1/4 cup chopped carrot, 1/4 tsp turmeric powder and 3–4 cups of water (or chicken broth) and mix well.
- Add in the soaked millet and ground green gram. Add a pinch of pepper powder and 1/2 tsp coriander powder, with salt to taste. Allow to boil for a minute.
- Cook in a pressure cooker for 2–3 whistles. Once done, sprinkle lemon juice. Serve.

*Note:* Depending on your preference and the phase you are in, you may add 1/2 cup milk or coconut milk at the end as it will enhance the taste. You may add other veggies like peas, beans, etc. and shredded chicken to the kanji.

### 3.  Kangni (Foxtail Millet) Khichri

You can substitute foxtail millet with other millet rice like little millet, barnyard and proso in this recipe. You can also use pearl millet or sorghum, but in that case, first dry-grind them lightly in a mixie, then dry roast them in a kadhai. Use this broken, roasted variety in the recipe.

To be consumed in phases 1, 2 and 3.

### Method

- Wash 1 cup foxtail millet rice and 1/3 cup green moong dal. Soak in water for 15 minutes. Once done, drain the water and keep the millet and dal aside.
- Heat 2 tbsp oil or ghee and add 1/4 tsp mustard seeds. When it splutters, add 2 tsp finely-chopped ginger, 2 sprigs of curry leaves, 1 cup mixed chopped veggies (onions, pumpkin, beans, etc.) and salt to taste.
- Add 3 cups of water and allow the mixture to boil.
- Now add the millet rice and dal and cook till done.
- Sprinkle with 2 tbsp chopped coriander leaves, mix and serve.

### 4.  Jowar (Sorghum) Porridge

I do not prefer using sorghum flour directly in this recipe since it results in a raw taste and smell to the porridge. Dry roasting the millet first and then grinding it coarsely gives a better consistency, texture and flavour to the kanji. You can try this recipe with pearl millet too.

To be consumed in phases 1, 2 and 3.

**Method**

- Dry roast 1 cup sorghum millet on low flame and grind it coarsely.
- Boil 1 litre of water and gradually sprinkle the ground coarse flour while stirring continuously to avoid lumps.
- Add salt and cook on slow fire till well-cooked.
- For the tempering, heat ghee in a pan. Add mustard seeds, hing, curry leaves and chopped green chilies, and let them crackle for a few seconds.
- Pour the tempering over the kanji/porridge.

*Note:* While cooking the flour, you can also add grated veggies that have been sautéed separately.

## 5. Rajgira (Amaranth) Porridge

With its high protein content, amaranth is one grain that gives a tough competition to quinoa. If you are looking for a quick breakfast that will keep you full for a long time, go for this one!

To be consumed in phases 1, 2 and 3.

**Method**

- Add 1/2 cup rajgira (amaranth) seeds and 1 small stick of cinnamon to 3/4 cup of water.
- Cook on a medium flame for 7–8 minutes while stirring occasionally.
- Add 1 cup almond milk and cook for a further 2 minutes.

- Switch off the flame and discard the cinnamon stick. Add honey to taste.
- Top the porridge with chopped fruit (any one fruit) like apple, banana (small variety), etc.
- Serve immediately as it may get lumpy after a while.

## Indian Traditional Breakfast Smoothies

These smoothies or drinks from different regions of India have been traditionally consumed as breakfast to stay cool and hydrated during summer months. I suggest that you look for more such recipes instead of digging out fancy smoothie recipes online.

### 1. Jau Ki Ghaat (Barley Drink)

The overnight fermentation helps break down the gluten in barley, making this authentic Rajasthani preparation a great gluten-free, synbiotic meal that's rich in both prebiotics and live microbes.

To be consumed in phases 2 and 3.

### Method

- Grind 3 tbsp hulled or pearl barley to a coarse powder. Add 1 cup chaas or buttermilk to it.
- Boil 1 cup water. Add 1/2 cup finely chopped onions and salt to it.
- Add the barley–buttermilk mixture to the hot water and keep stirring (otherwise it will curdle) till it starts boiling.

- Let it boil for another 5–6 minutes before turning off the heat.
- Let the mixture sit and ferment overnight.
- In the morning, add 1/2 cup fresh curd to the mixture. Depending on whether you like it thick or thin, adjust the consistency using water. Sprinkle roasted jeera powder and red chilli powder and drink up.

## 2.  Bajre ki Khatti Rabdi (Pearl Millet Drink)

Yet another recipe from the treasures of Rajasthani cuisine, this healthy, easy and fuss-free millet gruel is teeming with live, friendly microbes. Due to the overnight fermentation, the bajra that is otherwise heating gets transformed. Therefore, this age-old recipe has been traditionally used to beat the harsh heat of the deserts of Rajasthan.

To be consumed in phases 2 and 3.

## Method

- In a clay pot (or any pan), combine 1 cup curd, 1 cup water, 1/2 cup bajra flour, salt, 1/4 tsp cumin and carom seeds, and whisk well.
- Cook this mixture for around 10 minutes on a low flame while stirring it as it cooks.
- Turn off the heat and let the mixture sit overnight.
- In the morning, whisk 1 cup curd with water. Mix it well with the fermented rabdi.
- Sprinkle cumin powder and drink up.

## 3. Ellu Juice (Sesame Smoothie)

Ellu is a popular summer drink in and around the coastal areas of Mangalore and Udipi. The cooling properties of the coconut help neutralize the heating effects of the sesame seeds in the recipe, resulting in a drink that helps beat the heat. Beat that?

To be consumed in phases 2 and 3 (only once a week).

### Method

- In a mixie jar, take 1 cup fresh grated coconut, 1/2 cup roasted white sesame seeds and 3–4 cardamom pods, and grind with some amount of water.
- Filter the ground mixture with the help of a kitchen strainer and extract the milk.
- Take the residue from the strainer and grind again in the mixie with some more water. Repeat this 2–3 times.
- Discard the roughage. Add jaggery to the collected smoothie as per taste and serve chilled.

## Other Breakfast Smoothies

### 1. Coconut Smoothie

Nayanthara fell in love with this drink the first time I introduced it in her meal plan. This is one of her go-to breakfast/evening meal options.

To be consumed in phases 1, 2 and 3.

## Method

- Add 2 cups coconut water, 1 cup tender coconut, 1/2 cup coconut milk and sugar as per taste in a blender jar. Blend well until smooth and no lumps remain.
- Add a pinch each of cinnamon and cardamom powder, ice cubes (if you like) and pour in a glass.

## 2. Post-Workout Protein Smoothie

That Rakul Preet loves to work out is known to all. Now you can also know about her favourite drink. A blend of easy-to-digest whey isolate, fruit, seeds and spices, this drink is easily her most favourite and makes for a great post-workout breakfast or evening meal.

*Note:* It can be had on non-workout days and by non-exercisers too!

To be consumed in phases 1, 2 and 3.

## Method

- Mix 2/3 cup unsweetened fresh almond milk, 2/3 cup water, 1 scoop whey isolate powder, 1 tbsp whole flaxseeds and 1–2 banana (the smaller variety), and blend them together.
- Sprinkle a pinch of cinnamon and cardamom powder. Add honey if required.

*Notes:*

- Once you come to phase 2, you can use curd and water instead of nut milk, if you desire.

- Once you come to phase 3, you can substitute nut milk with dairy milk.
- If the smaller variety of banana is not available, then use any other fruit.

## 3. Makhana (Lotus Seed) Smoothie

Lotus nuts have the highest resistant starch (RS) content amongst all nuts, way higher than cashews, peanuts, etc. Super rich in prebiotic content, this smoothie is what you need if you want to have something light yet filling.

To be consumed in phases 2 and 3.

## Method

- In a mixer, add 1 cup roasted makhana, 2 tbsp roasted peanuts and 2 tbsp almonds and grind them along with 1 glass milk (use nut milk in phase 2).
- Add honey to taste and mix well. Garnish with soaked raisins and mixed seeds.

## Snacks

### 1. Samvat Chawal (Barnyard Millet) Pancake/Neer Dosa/Lace Dosa

Neer dosas are thin, soft dosas that do not require any fermentation, unlike regular dosas. Though this recipe uses barnyard millet, you can use other millet rice varieties too.

To be consumed in phases 1, 2 and 3.

**Method**

- Wash and soak 1 cup barnyard millet for at least 6–8 hours. You can soak it overnight too.
- Drain the water and make a very thin, watery batter by grinding the millet into a smooth paste along with 1/4 cup grated coconut, water (around 1.25–1.5 cups) and salt.
- Pour the batter on a hot pan with the help of a ladle, making sure the gaps are filled in with the batter itself. You don't have to spread it like a regular dosa.
- Use oil around the edges and cook for a few minutes.
- Serve hot with peanut or coconut chutney and/ or sambar.

### 2. Kulthi (Horse Gram) Laddu

The ghee in this recipe helps reduce the heating effects of kulthi. Thus the laddu can be had throughout the year, except for a few of the peak summer months.

To be consumed in phases 2 and 3.

**Method**

- Dry roast 1 cup horse gram on a low flame till the colour changes slightly and it gives off a nice aroma. Allow it to cool and then grind into a flour.
- Sieve the flour. Add to it 1 cup grated jaggery, 1 tsp broken cashews and 1 tsp raisins that has been roasted in ghee, 2 pinch cardamom powder, a pinch of dry ginger powder and half a pinch of salt. Mix well.

- Take a small amount of this mixture, mix it with some ghee and roll it into a laddu using your hands. Repeat the same process to make more laddus.

## 3. Ragi (Finger Millet) Payasam/Kheer

The ghee and moong dal in this recipe helps reduce the heating effects of ragi. Thus the payasam can be had throughout the year, except for a few of the peak summer months.

To be consumed in phases 1, 2 and 3.

## Method

- Roast 1/2 cup ragi flour over a slow fire. Dissolve the roasted flour in a little water and keep aside.
- Cook 5 tbsp rice (using broken rice will be preferable) and keep aside.
- Take water in a pan and cook 1/4 cup split green gram. When done, add the cooked rice.
- Next, add the dissolved ragi flour and mix well.
- When the mixture boils, add 1 cup jaggery and 50 ml ghee.
- Add 1 tsp each of grated coconut, roasted cashews and raisins; 2 pinches of dry ginger powder and 1/2 tsp of cardamom powder.
- Mix well and serve.

## 4.    Indian Sourdough Bread—Bhatura

Someone has rightly said, 'You can take a person out of "Dillee" but you cannot take "Dillee" out of the person.' Like

a true-blue Delhite, Taapsee loves to feast on chole bhature.
And now you can too!

The recipe for your very own gluten-free, Indian
sourdough bread, bhatura, is here. Remember, the long
fermentation process is important to render the bread gluten-
free and make it more nutritious.

To be consumed in phases 2 and 3 (once a week).

## Method

- In a bowl, take 3/4 cup fresh dahi (ensure it isn't sour),
  3/4 cup maida, 2.5 cups gehu (whole wheat) atta and 1/2
  tbsp sugar.
- Mix all the ingredients well. You may or may not require
  water to knead it into a dough.
- Cover the bowl with a cloth or lid and set it aside in a
  warm place overnight or for 7–8 hours to allow it to
  naturally ferment.
- Next morning, add 1 tsp salt and 1 tbsp ghee to the
  fermented mixture. Add warm water if required (not hot
  water).
- Gather the dough into a compact ball. Use a damp cloth
  to cover it. Again, set it aside in a warm place for 2 hours.
- Knead the dough again. Shape into 15–20 balls. Roll into
  bhaturas and deep fry in ghee.
- Serve it hot with chole, pickled ginger and onions.

# Traditional Summer Drinks

## 1. Panakam

Panakam is a traditional summer drink prepared mostly during Sri Rama Navami and given in temples in south India. This not only tastes but smells divine!

To be consumed primarily in phase 1, but can be carried forward to phases 2 and 3 as well.

## Method

- Add 1 cup grated jaggery to 4 cups (1 litre) of water (preferably matka water) and mix until it dissolves.
- Add 3 (crushed) cardamoms, crushed 7–8 black peppercorns and 1/2 tsp dry ginger powder and mix.
- Now squeeze the juice from half a lemon and add it to the jaggery water. Strain the liquid. Pour into glasses and serve.

## 2. Gond Kateera Sherbet

Gond Kateera is different from the gond with which laddus are made. While the former is cooling, the latter is heating. Perfect for all summer woes, gond kateera is easily available online.

To be consumed in phases 2 and 3.

## Method

- Soak 1 tsp of gond kateera in a bowl of water for 6–7 hours. The gum will swell up and look like crushed ice or transparent jelly.
- Add 4 tsp powdered sugar, 1/4 tsp roasted jeera powder, 1/4 tsp black salt, lemon juice from 1 big lemon and the soaked gond kateera to 1 glass water (preferably matka water).
- Stir till the sugar dissolves and serve.

## 3.  Buttermilk

Traditional buttermilk is the liquid left behind after churning makhan (butter) out of curd or malai (cream). Presented here is the quick version of buttermilk. Both the versions are rich in live, beneficial microbes. Depending on the requirements, I suggest adding seeds, spices and herbs to the buttermilk.

To be consumed in phases 2 and 3.

## Method

- Use a wooden churner and whisk 1/2 cup curd with 1.5 cups water. This is buttermilk.
- Take equal quantity of flaxseed, cumin seeds and fenugreek seeds and grind into a fine powder. Taking 1 tsp of this mixture and adding it to your buttermilk for a few weeks everyday will help burn fat and lower down cholesterol.

**OR**

- Add 1/2 cup sattu in 1.5 cups of thin buttermilk. Mix in chopped coriander, green chilli, a pinch of roasted cumin powder and black salt. This can reduce post-lunch sugar cravings and the infamous afternoon slump.

## 4. Thandai

Thandai is a traditional drink popular in UP and Rajasthan and made especially during the Holi festival. It has a cooling effect on the body, hence the name Thandai. You may not know it, but the classic version is made with water and not milk, so depending on the phase you are in, you can choose your base accordingly.

To be consumed in phases 2 and 3.

## Method

- In 1 cup of warm water, soak for 1–2 hours the following mix: 3 tbsp almonds, 2 tbsp unsalted pistachios, 2 tbsp white poppy seeds (khus khus), 1/4 cup melon seeds, 2 tbsp dried rose petals, 1 tbsp fennel seeds, 1/2 tsp whole black pepper.
- Grind this soaked mixture very finely (along with the water in which it was soaked) in a jar together with 1/2 cup sugar, a pinch of saffron and cardamom powder (use 3–4 green cardamoms).
- This is your thandai paste that can be kept in the refrigerator for a week.

- To prepare the thandai, take about 4 tbsp of thandai paste in a glass. Top it up with cold water (or chilled milk, once you come to phase 3). Add a pinch of haldi powder for colour. Mix well.
- Garnish with rose petals, chopped almonds and serve.

*Note:* Instead of dried rose petals, you can use 2 tbsp gulkand. In that case, the amount of sugar will have to be adjusted accordingly.

## Indian Soups

### 1. Amla Ginger Soup

A unique combination of amla and ginger, this recipe is full of anti-inflammatory, immunity strengthening and detox benefits.

To be consumed primarily in phase 1 but can be carried forward to phases 2 and 3 as well.

### Method

- Start by pressure cooking 3 amlas and fresh ginger (an inch long) in around 1 cup of water. Add salt to it.
- Once done, separate the boiled amla and ginger. Keep the stock aside.
- Discard the amla seeds and make a paste of boiled amla and ginger.
- Next, make a dry coarse paste with 1–2 green chillies, 4 sprigs of curry leaves, 1.5 tsp of whole peppercorns and 1.5 tsp of cumin seeds.

- Heat 1 tsp of ghee, add a pinch of hing, 1/2 tsp haldi powder and the ground coarse paste.
- Next, add the amla–ginger paste along with the stock. Add another 2–3 cups of water.
- Let it simmer for 15 minutes.
- Either drink it as is or strain the soup before consuming if you prefer a clear soup.

## 2. Turmeric Soup

Turmeric (anti-oxidant, anti-inflammatory) has been intelligently combined with garlic, onions and ginger (antimicrobial) in this recipe, making it a must-have soup during monsoons and winters, or simply because you are feeling under the weather.

To be consumed primarily in phase 1 but can be carried forward to phases 2 and 3 as well.

## Method

- Heat 1 tbsp of ghee in a pan. Sauté 1 onion (diced) till it gets translucent.
- Add 1 tbsp minced garlic, fresh grated turmeric (a 2-inch piece), 1.5 tbsp grated ginger and sauté them for 2 minutes.
- Add 3 carrots (diced) and sauté again.
- Next, add 4 cups vegetable stock and let it simmer for 20 minutes.
- With the help of a blender or the back of a spoon, give the soup a good blend and check if the carrots are cooked.
- Squeeze in some lemon and serve hot.

### 3.  Moringa (Drumstick) Soup

Drumsticks are a very good source of iron and can help detox the system. Moringa leaves along with lentils are also made into a soup that is equally therapeutic.

To be consumed primarily in phase 1 but can be carried forward to phases 2 and 3 as well.

### Method

- Cut drumsticks into long pieces and slice it into halves.
- Take a pan and cook the drumsticks in water till done.
- Strain and keep the stock aside.
- Remove the flesh from the cooked drumsticks and discard the skin.
- Heat 1 tsp of ghee, add 1/4 cup chopped onions, 2 cloves chopped garlic and the drumstick flesh and mix well.
- Blend the mixture in a blender.
- In a pan, add the blended puree and the reserved stock.
- Add 1 tsp cumin powder, salt and pepper powder to taste.
- Bring the soup to a boil, while removing the scum off. Let it simmer for some time.
- Add 3 tbsp chopped coriander leaves just before serving.

## Indian Chutneys

### 1.  Amla Chutney with Curry Patta

Curry leaves help in eliminating bad bacteria and correcting dysbiosis, and have detoxifying effects.

To be consumed primarily in phase 1 but can be carried forward to phases 2 and 3 as well.

**Method**

- Chop 6 fresh amlas, discard its seeds.
- Take the chopped amlas, 6–8 green chillies, 16–20 sprigs of curry leaves, 6–8 garlic cloves and 10–12 peppercorns and grind them together.
- Add salt to taste and empty in a glass bowl. The chutney stays good for 3–4 weeks if kept in the fridge.

*Bonus tip: Boil moong dal and make a plain soup. Add this chutney to the soup. It will make for a spicy, flavourful and quick lentil soup.*

## 2. Neem Flower Chutney

This is a traditional detox and deworming formula. It is consumed in Tamil Nadu along with the main meals. The bitterness of the neem flower is reduced by the addition of tamarind, chilly and jaggery to the recipe.

To be consumed in phase 1.

**Method**

- Roast 2 tsp dried neem flowers on a low flame for a few seconds (dried neem flowers are available online) in 1/2 tsp ghee.
- In a mixie jar, add 2 red chillies and pinch of hing powder (that have been roasted together in oil previously), a

small marble-sized tamarind (that has been soaked in lukewarm water), 4 tsp grated coconut, 1 tsp jaggery, 4 black peppercorns and roasted neem flowers, and grind to a smooth paste.

- Add salt to taste.

*Note:* The chutney lasts for up to a week if kept in the fridge.

# Acknowledgements

This book would not exist if it weren't for a few people in my life. In no specific order, I would like to express my deepest gratitude to the following people.

Most of this book was written at a time when our country went into a complete lockdown owing to the pandemic. Domestic helps were on leave, and videos of people doing *jhaadu-katka* at home were going viral on social media. In the absence of my domestic workforce, it was only because of my mom, Smt. Sashi Ganeriwal (Rasiwasia), that I could invest the entire lockdown time in writing this book without worrying about the day-to-day running of the house. My heartfelt thanks for her selfless love and care.

My daughter Devika for being super independent, flexible and patient (it helps me work effectively and guilt-free), for breaking the monotony of writing with her jokes (much-needed breaks I would say), for pretending to understand my writing every time I insisted she should listen to me read aloud from my manuscript (daughters are loving, I know). Her unconditional love makes motherhood a joyous journey.

Taapsee was one of the first few people with whom I had shared the idea of writing my debut book. I thank her not only for writing a heartfelt foreword for this book but also for being the person whom I can rely on for genuine advice, feedback and suggestions. When it comes to her diet and health, I do lead her, but in a few places, she is the one leading me, and it's gratifying that we interchange these roles effortlessly.

Dr Ravi Mooss, for our long, never-ending discussions on food, lifestyle and holistic health. I also thank all the doctors, scientists, professors, researchers and teachers from Sivananda and Iyengar Yoga community—their teachings, scientific findings and discoveries have helped me develop my practice and ultimately write this book.

Ancient teachings are living traditions maintained by the practice of *guru–shishya parampara*. It is imperative to study under a competent teacher who can correctly translate the teachings for you, and I am grateful that I have found one. I pay obeisance to my *Vedanta* teacher Shri Ravi Easwaran. Raviji has studied *Vedanta* and the *Upanishads* under Swami Paramarthanandaji.

For being the first person to read the manuscript, for acquiring this book and for also turning it into what it looks like today, I thank my editor Shreya Punj. My book couldn't have been in better hands.

To all my clients from the day I started working until now, thanks for putting your faith in me and choosing me to partner with you in your health journey.

My team for shielding me from too much work, for taking over most of the work at the office so that I could complete writing this book.

No matter how much effort goes into creating it, without an audience, there can be no film or theatre. Likewise, no matter how hard an author works, there can be no book without its readers. My sincere thanks to all my readers for giving your love, and most importantly, your time to this book.

# References

## CHAPTER 1

India State-Level Disease Burden Initiative Suicide Collaborators. 'Gender differentials and state variations in suicide deaths in India: The Global Burden of Disease Study 1990–2016'. *The Lancet Public Health* 3(10), 1 October 2018, E478–E489.

Yang, B., Wei, J., Ju, P., et al. 'Effects of regulating intestinal microbiota on anxiety symptoms: A systematic review'. *General Psychiatry*, 2019. Available at https://gpsych.bmj.com/content/32/2/e100056.

## CHAPTER 2

American Gastroenterological Association. 'IBS and bloating: When gut microbiota gets out of balance.' *ScienceDaily*, 10 March 2014.

Bailey, L.C., Forrest, C.B., Zhang, P., Richards, T.M., Livshits, A., and DeRusso, P.A. 'Association of antibiotics in infancy with early childhood obesity'. *JAMA Pediatr* 168(11), 2014, 1063–1069.

Mann, T., Tomiyama, A.J., Westling, E., Lew, A.M., Samuels, B., and Chatman, J. 'Medicare's search for effective obesity treatments: diets are not the answer'. *Am Psychol* 62(3), 2007, 220–233.

Okoro, C.A., Strine, T.W., Eke, P.I., Dhingra, S.S., and Balluz, L.S. 'The association between depression and anxiety and use of oral health services and tooth loss'. *Community Dentistry and Oral Epidemiology* 40, 2012, 134–144.

Sender, R., Fuchs, S., and Milo, R. 'Revised estimates for the number of human and bacteria cells in the body'. *PLoS Biol* 14(8), 2016. Available at https://journals.plos.org/plosbiology/article?id=10.1371/journal.pbio.1002533.

Thaiss, C., Itav, S., Rothschild, D., et al. 'Persistent microbiome alterations modulate the rate of post-dieting weight regain'. *Nature* 540, 2016, 544–551.

## CHAPTER 3

Christian, Lisa M., Galley, Jeffrey D., Hade, Erinn M., Schoppe-Sullivan, Sarah, Dush, Claire Kamp, and Bailey, Michael T. 'Gut microbiome composition is associated with temperament during early childhood'. *Brain, Behavior and Immunity* 45, 2015, 118. doi: 10.1016/j.bbi.2014.10.018.

Clarke, Gerard, Stilling, Roman M., Kennedy, Paul J., Stanton, Catherine, Cryan, John F., and Dinan, Timothy G. 'Minireview: Gut microbiota: The neglected endocrine organ'. *Molecular Endocrinology* 28(8), 1 August 2014, 1221–1238.

Gou, Wanglong, Fu, Yuanqing, Yue, Liang, Chen, Gengdong, Cai, Xue, Shuai, Menglei, Xu, Fengzhe, Yi, Xiao, Chen, Hao, Zhu, Yi, Xiao, Mian-li, Jiang, Zengliang, Miao, Zelei, Xiao, Congmei, Shen, Bo, Xiaomai, Wu, Zhao, Haihong, Ling, Wenhua, Wang, Jun, and Zheng, Ju-Sheng. 'Gut microbiota may underlie the predisposition of healthy individuals to COVID-19', 2020. doi: 10.1101/2020.04.22.20076091.

Jacka, F.N., O'Neil, A., Opie, R., et al. 'A randomised controlled trial of dietary improvement for adults with major depression (the 'SMILES' trial)'. *BMC Med* 15(23), 2017. Available at https://doi.org/10.1186/s12916-017-0791-y.

Jouet, Pauline, Coffin, Benoit, and Sabaté, Jean-Marc. 'Small intestinal bacterial overgrowth in patients with morbid obesity'. *Digestive Diseases and Sciences* 56(2), 2011, 615, author reply 615–616. doi: 10.1007/s10620-010-1356-5.

Kiecolt-Glaser, Janice K., Derry, Heather M., and Fagundes, Christopher P. 'Inflammation: Depression fans the flames and feasts on the heat'. *American Journal of Psychiatry* 172(11), 2015, 1075–1091.

Lombardi, Vincent C., De Meirleir, Kenny L., Subramanian, Krishnamurthy, Nourani, Sam M., Dagda, Ruben K., Delaney, Shannon L., and Palotás, András. 'Nutritional modulation of the intestinal microbiota; future opportunities for the prevention and treatment of neuroimmune and neuroinflammatory disease'. *The Journal of Nutritional Biochemistry* 61, 2018, 1–16, ISSN 0955-2863.

Madrid, A.M., Poniachik, J., Quera, R., and Defilippi, C. 'Small intestinal clustered contractions and bacterial overgrowth: a frequent finding in obese patients'. *Digestive Diseases and Sciences* 56(1), 2011, 155–160.

Maes, Michael, Kubera, Marta, and Leunis, Jean-Claude. 'The gut–brain barrier in major depression: intestinal mucosal dysfunction with an increased translocation of LPS from gram negative enterobacteria (leaky gut) plays a role in the inflammatory pathophysiology of depression'. *Neuro Endocrinol Lett* 29(1), 2008, 117–124.

Phillips, C.M. 'Dietary inflammatory index and mental health: A cross-sectional analysis of the relationship with depressive symptoms, anxiety and well-being in adults'. *Clinical nutrition* 37(5), 2018, 1485–1491. doi: 10.1016/j.clnu.2017.08.029.

Qin, Yufeng, and Wade, Paul A. 'Crosstalk between the microbiome and epigenome: messages from bugs'. *Journal of biochemistry* 163(2), 2018, 105–112.

Tayefi, M. 'Depression and anxiety both associate with serum level of hs-CRP: A gender-stratified analysis in a population-based study'. *Psychoneuroendocrinology* 81, 2017, 63–69. doi: 10.1016/j.psyneuen.2017.02.035.

Xu, K., Cai, H., Shen, Y., et al. 'Management of corona virus disease-19 (COVID-19): The Zhejiang experience' [in Chinese]. *Zhejiang Da Xue Xue Bao Yi Xue Bao* 49(1), 2020.

Yano, Jessica M., et al. 'Indigeneous bacteria from the gut microbiota regulate host serotonin biosynthesis'. *Cell*, 13 April 2015. doi: 10.1016/j.cell. 2015.02.047.

## Chapter 4

Chaix, Amandine, Zarrinpar, Amir, Miu, Phuong, and Panda, Satchidananda. 'Time-restricted feeding is a preventative and therapeutic intervention against diverse nutritional challenges'. *Cell Metabolism* 20(6), 2014, 991–1005, ISSN: 1550-4131.

Forbes, J.D., Azad, M.B., Vehling, L., et al. 'Association of exposure to formula in the hospital and subsequent infant feeding practices with gut microbiota and risk of overweight in the first year of life'. *JAMA Pediatr* 172(7), 2018. doi: e181161. doi: 10.1001/jamapediatrics.2018.1161.

Hall, K.D., et al. 'Ultra-processed diets cause excess calorie intake and weight gain: an inpatient randomized controlled trial of *ad libitum* food intake'. *Cell Metabolism* 30, 2019, 67–77.

Jakubowicz, D., Barnea, M., Wainstein, J., and Froy, O. 'High caloric intake at breakfast vs. dinner differentially influences weight loss of overweight and obese women'. *Obesity* 21, 2013, 2504–2512. doi: 10.1002/oby.20460.

Jakubowicz, Daniela, Wainstein, Julio, Landau, Zohar, Raz, Itamar, Ahren, Bo, Chapnik, Nava, Ganz, Tali, Menaged, Miriam, Barnea, Maayan, Bar-Dayan, Yosefa, and Froy, Oren. 'Influences of breakfast on clock gene expression and postprandial glycemia in healthy individuals and individuals with diabetes: a randomized clinical trial'. *Diabetes Care* 40(11), November 2017, 1573–1579. doi: 10.2337/dc16-2753.

Panda, Satchidananda, Sato, Trey K., Castrucci, Ana Maria, Rollag, Mark D., DeGrip, Willem J., Hogenesch, John B., Provencio, Ignacio, and Kay, Steve A. 'Melanopsin (*Opn4*) requirement for normal light-induced circadian phase shifting'. *Science*, 13 December 2002, 2213–2216.

Pot, G.K., Hardy, R., and Stephen, A.M. 'Irregularity of energy intake at meals: prospective associations with the metabolic syndrome in adults of the 1946 British birth cohort'. *The British Journal of Nutrition* 115(2), 2016, 315–323. doi: 10.1017/S0007114515004407.

University of Bath. 'Eating breakfast burns more carbs during exercise and accelerates metabolism for next meal.' *ScienceDaily*, 15 August 2018.

Vollmers, Christopher, Gill, Shubhroz, DiTacchio, Luciano, Pulivarthy, Sandhya R., D. Le, Hiep, and Panda, Satchidananda. 'Time of feeding and the intrinsic circadian clock drive rhythms in hepatic gene expression'. *Proceedings of the National Academy of Sciences* 106(50), 2009, 21453–21458. doi: 10.1073/pnas.0909591106.

## Chapter 5

Bonassa, Ana Cláudia Munhoz, and Carpinelli, Angelo Rafael. 'Intermittent fasting for three months decreases pancreatic islet mass and increases insulin resistance in Wistar rats'. Presented at the 20th European Congress of Endocrinology, Barcelona, Spain, 19–22 May 2018.

Brinkworth, G.D., Buckley, J.D., Noakes, M., Clifton, P.M., and Wilson, C.J. 'Long-term effects of a very low-carbohydrate diet and a low-fat diet on mood and cognitive function'. *Arch Intern Med* 169(20), 2009, 1873–1880. doi:10.1001/archinternmed.2009.329.

Cleveland Clinic. 'New link between heart disease and red meat: New understanding of cardiovascular health benefits of vegan, vegetarian diets'. *ScienceDaily*, 7 April 2013. Available at www.sciencedaily.com/releases/2013/04/130407133320.htm.

Ley, Sylvia H., Sun, Qi, Willett, Walter C., Eliassen, A. Heather, Wu, Kana, Pan, An, Grodstein, Fran, and Hu, Frank, B. 'Associations between red meat intake and biomarkers of inflammation and glucose metabolism in women'. *The American Journal of Clinical Nutrition* 99(2), February 2014, 352–360. Available at https://doi.org/10.3945/ajcn.113.075663.

Lu, Q.Y., Summanen, P.H., Lee, R.P., Huang, J., Henning, S.M., Heber, D., Finegold, S.M., and Li. Z. 'Prebiotic potential and chemical composition of seven culinary spice extracts'. *J Food Sci* 82(8), August 2017, 1807–1813.

Molloy, J., Allen, K., Collier, F., Tang, M.L., Ward, A.C., and Vuillermin, P. 'The potential link between gut microbiota and IgE-mediated food allergy in early life'. *International Journal of Environmental Research and Public Health* 10(12), 2013, 7235–7256. Available at https://doi.org/10.3390/ijerph10127235.

Montonen, J., Boeing, H., Fritsche, A., Schleicher, E., Joost, H.G., Schulze, M.B., Steffen, A., and Pischon, T. 'Consumption of red meat and whole-grain bread in relation to biomarkers of obesity, inflammation, glucose metabolism and oxidative stress.' *European Journal of Nutrition* 52(1), 2013, 337–345. Available at https://doi.org/10.1007/s00394-012-0340-6.

Sheta, Mehul M., Kikani, Kunjan M., Kavathia, Parth, Thakkar, Jainy, and Rangnani, Twinkle. 'Study of antimicrobial activity of Triphala and its individual components'. *International Journal of Herbal Medicine* 4(5), 2016, 41–43.

Sivakumar, V., and Sivakumar, S. 'Effect of an indigenous herbal compound preparation "Trikatu" on the lipid profiles of atherogenic diet and standard diet fed Rattus norvegicus'. *Phytother. Res.* 18, 2004, 976–981. doi: 10.1002/ptr.1586.

Wongsawan, K., Chaisri, W., Tangtrongsup, S., and Mektrirat, R. 'Bactericidal effect of clove oil against multidrug-resistant *Streptococcus suis* isolated from human patients and slaughtered pigs'. *Pathogens* 9(14), 2020.

## Chapter 6

Agarwal, Kailash, and Bhasin, S. 'Feasibility studies to control acute diarrhoea in children by feeding fermented milk preparations actimel and Indian dahi'. *European Journal of Clinical Nutrition* 56(Suppl 4), 2002, S56–59. doi: 10.1038/sj.ejcn.1601664.

Bhanwar, S., Bamnia, M., Ghosh, M., and Ganguli, A. 'Use of Lactococcus lactis to enrich sourdough bread with γ-aminobutyric acid'. *Int J Food Sci Nutr* 64(1), February 2013, 77–81. doi: 10.3109/09637486.2012.700919. Epub 6 July 2012. PMID: 22765269.

Cani, P., Joly, E., Horsmans, Y., et al. 'Oligofructose promotes satiety in healthy human: a pilot study'. *Eur J Clin Nutr* 60, 2006, 567–572.

Chen, M., et al. 'Dairy consumption and risk of type 2 diabetes: 3 cohorts of US adults and an updated meta-analysis'. *BMC Medicine* 12(1), 2014, 215.

Couch, Grace W., 'Effect of sourdough fermentation parameters on bread properties'. *All Theses*, 2581, 2016.

Cutler, David M., Glaeser, Edward L., and Shapiro, Jesse M. 'Why have americans become more obese?'. *Journal of Economic Perspectives* 17(3), 2003, 93–118.

David, L., Maurice, C., Carmody, R., et al. 'Diet rapidly and reproducibly alters the human gut microbiome'. *Nature* 505, 2014, 559–563.

Dewulf, E.M., Cani, P.D., Neyrinck, A.M., Possemiers, S., Van Holle, A., Muccioli, G.G., Deldicque, L., Bindels, L.B., Pachikian, B.D., Sohet, F.M., Mignolet, E., Francaux, M., Larondelle, Y., and Delzenne, N.M. 'Inulin-type fructans with prebiotic properties counteract GPR43 overexpression and PPARγ-related adipogenesis in the white adipose tissue of high-fat diet-fed mice'. *J Nutr Biochem* 22(8), August 2011, 712–722.

Gratz, S.W., Hazim, S., Richardson, A.J., et al. 'Dietary carbohydrate rather than protein intake drives colonic microbial fermentation during weight loss'. *Eur J Nutr* 58, 2019, 1147–1158.

Hertzler, Steve, and Clancy, Shannon. 'Kefir improves lactose digestion and tolerance in adults with lactose maldigestion'. *Journal of the American Dietetic Association* 103, 2003, 582–587. doi: 10.1053/jada.2003.50111.

Hill, C., Guarner, F., Reid, G., et al. 'The international scientific association for probiotics and prebiotics consensus statement on the scope and appropriate use of the term probiotic'. *Nat Rev Gastroenterol Hepatol* 11, 2014, 506–514.

Jones, N. 'Friendly bacteria cheer up anxious mice'. *Nature,* 2011.

Kapp, Julie M., and Sumner, Walton. 'Kombucha: a systematic review of the empirical evidence of human health benefit'. *Annals of Epidemiology* 30, 2019, 66–70, ISSN 1047-2797.

Lappi, Jenni, Selinheimo, Emilia, Schwab, Ursula, Katina, Kati, Lehtinen, Pekka, Mykkänen, Hannu, Kolehmainen, Marjukka, and Poutanen, Kaisa. 'Sourdough fermentation of wholemeal wheat bread increases solubility of arabinoxylan and protein and decreases postprandial glucose and insulin responses'. *Journal of Cereal Science* 51(1), 2010, 152–158.

Le Roy, Caroline I., Wells, Philippa M., Si, Jiyeon, Raes, Jeroen, Bell, Jordana T., and Spector, Tim D. 'Red wine consumption associated with increased gut microbiota α-diversity in 3 independent cohorts'. *Gastroenterology*, 2019. doi: 10.1053/j. gastro.2019.08.024.

Levine, M.E., Suarez, J.A., Brandhorst, S., Balasubramanian, P., Cheng, C.W., Madia, F., Fontana, L., Mirisola, M.G., Guevara-Aguirre, J., Wan, J., Passarino, G., Kennedy, B.K., Wei, M., Cohen, P., Crimmins, E.M., and Longo, V.D. 'Low protein intake is associated with a major reduction in IGF-1, cancer, and overall mortality in the 65 and younger but not older population'. *Cell Metab* 19(3), 4 March 2014, 407–417. doi: 10.1016/j.cmet.2014.02.006.

Mazidi, Mohsen, Katsiki, Niki, Mikhailidis, Dimitri P., Sattar, Naveed, and Banach, Maciej. 'Low-carbohydrate diets and all-cause and cause-specific mortality: a population-based cohort study and pooling prospective studies'. *European Heart Journal* 39(Supplement), 2018, 1112–1113.

Nigudkar, M.R. 'Estimation of resistant starch content of selected routinely consumed Indian food preparations'. *Curr Res Nutr Food Sci* 2(2), 2014.

Piqué, N., Berlanga, M., and Miñana-Galbis, D. 'Health benefits of heat-killed (tyndallized) probiotics: an overview'. *Int J Mol Sci* 20(10), 2019, 2534. doi:10.3390/ijms20102534.

Queipo-Ortuño, M.I., Boto-Ordóñez, M., Murri, M., Gomez-Zumaquero, J.M., Clemente-Postigo, M., Estruch, R., Cardona Diaz, F., Andrés-Lacueva, C., and Tinahones, F.J. 'Influence of red wine polyphenols and ethanol on the gut microbiota ecology and biochemical biomarkers'. *Am J Clin Nutr* 95(6), June 2012, 1323–1334. doi: 10.3945/ajcn.111.027847.

Rao, R., and Samak, G. 'Role of glutamine in protection of intestinal epithelial tight junctions'. *J Epithel Biol Pharmacol* 5(Suppl 1-M7), 2012, 47–54. doi:10.2174/1875044301205010047.

Rizzello, C.G., De Angelis, M., Di Cagno, R., Camarca, A., Silano, M., Losito, I., De Vincenzi, M., De Bari, M.D., Palmisano, F., Maurano, F., Gianfrani, C., and Gobbetti, M. 'Highly efficient gluten degradation by lactobacilli and fungal proteases during food processing: new perspectives for celiac disease'. *Applied and Environmental Microbiology* 73(14), 2007, 4499–4507. Available at https://doi.org/10.1128/AEM.00260-07.

Steffi, Sonia, Fiastuti, Witjaksono, and Rahmawati, Ridwan. 'Effect of cooling of cooked white rice on resistant starch content and glycemic response'. *Asia Pac J Clin Nutr*, 24(4), 2015, 620–625. doi: 10.6133/apjcn.2015.24.4.13.

Sturniolo, G.C., Fries, W., Mazzon, E., Di, Leo V, Barollo, M., and D'inca, R. 'Effect of zinc supplementation on intestinal permeability in experimental colitis'. *J Lab Clin Med* 139(5), May 2002, 311–315. doi: 10.1067/mlc.2002.123624.

Tapsell, L.C. 'Fermented dairy food and CVD risk'. *British Journal of Nutrition*, 113(S2), 2015, S131–S135.

University of California, Los Angeles (UCLA), Health Sciences. 'Changing gut bacteria through diet affects brain function'. *ScienceDaily*, 28 May 2013.

**CHAPTER 7**

Kuijer, R.G., and Boyce, J.A. 'Chocolate cake. Guilt or celebration? Associations with healthy eating attitudes, perceived behavioural control, intentions and weight-loss'. *Appetite* 74, March 2014, 48–54. doi: 10.1016/j.appet.2013.11.013.

Oliveira, Diana, Wilbey, Andrew, Grandison, Alistair, and Roseiro, Luisa. 'Milk oligosaccharides: A review'. *International Journal of Dairy Technology* 68(3), 2015. Available at https://doi.org/10.1111/1471-0307.12209.

Tremblay, A., and Gilbert, J.A. 'Human obesity: is insufficient calcium/dairy intake part of the problem?' *J Am Coll Nutr* 30(5 Suppl 1), October 2011, 449S–453S. doi: 10.1080/07315724.2011.10719989. PMID: 22081691.

## CHAPTER 8

Arendt, Josephine. 'Shift work: coping with the biological clock'. *Occupational Medicine* 60(1), January 2010, 10–20. Available at https://doi.org/10.1093/occmed/kqp162.

Leproult, R., Holmbäck, U., and Van Cauter, E. 'Circadian misalignment augments markers of insulin resistance and inflammation, independently of sleep loss'. *Diabetes* 63(6), 2014: 1860–1869. doi:10.2337/db13-1546

O'Reardon, J.P., Cristancho, P., and Peshek, A.D. 'Vagus nerve stimulation (VNS) and treatment of depression: to the brainstem and beyond'. *Psychiatry* (Edgmont) 3(5), 2006: 54–63.

Smith, R.P., Easson C., Lyle, S.M., Kapoor, R., Donnelly, C.P., Davidson, E.J., et al. 'Gut microbiome diversity is associated with sleep physiology in humans'. *PLoS ONE* 14(10), 2019.

Yuan, H., and Silberstein, S.D. 'Vagus nerve and vagus nerve stimulation, a comprehensive review: Part I'. *Headache* 56(1), January 2016, 71–78. doi: 10.1111/head.12647.